slanted

# Content

# A Symphony of Glyphs

# Introduction by Matthieu Salvaggio

There's an analogy I have always liked: if a logo is a company's face, a font is its voice. Think about it, outside of the designer-client relationship prism and consider this core idea: "A font is a voice." Well, one can only be in wonder of today's tremendous excitement in the type design community. We see countless new fonts on a daily basis: new shapes, forms, ... and with variable fonts kicking it in more than ever, there are so many ways to have these static glyphs turn into beautiful—ever growing—organic shapes.

What is the timbre of those voices echoing into the design world? One can be stunned by the vastness of the maelstrom, but one would still have to consider how rich, however evolving this design field is.

We have the chance today, to witness an awakening of the type design industry where it's never been this easy to access the knowledge needed to design fonts, where it's never been this easy to work with font design software, with a caring community eager to share its knowledge. We are so blessed today to put our own voices on words, to have designers from all around the world learn about type design with ease, to share in the wealth of knowledge of font design.

We do what we do because we are compelled by this craving to design shapes, to speak out, to be loud in this world, to leave something behind. We are capturing on screens what others once carved into stones. In the long tradition of human history, we are humble providers of glyphs for others to use to tell stories and share knowledge. Still, our letters speak, their voice is heard.

The *Yearbook of Type* is but a modest representation of these voices. This collection contains over two hundred typefaces, each of which represents a unique voice, with its own particular sound. It's a showcase of amazing notes displaying this year's music. These are no mere objects to design with: each font speaks, each is music to our eyes, each whispers a story. Here, we shall find the dedicated work of over a hundred enthusiasts, designers, and aficionados alike. All are students of fonts, singing together in a beautiful choir. Everything must end, but what will remain in the ether is the echo of their voices, coming together to form the sound of a generation.

Matthieu Salvaggio is a type designer, art director, founder of the international independent type foundry Blaze Type, co-founder of The Box type foundry with Léon Hugues, and foundry partner of Type Network. His typefaces have become powerhouses in the high-end and European design scenes.

# A Essays & Tutorials

# Crossing Your t-s and Dotting Your i-s

## by Lies Wolf

## A Typographical Journey of Changing the World, One Print-Run at a Time

We are so used to the presence of type in our modern landscape that we tend to forget there was a time when letters were just funny little drawings to all but the reading three percent. I'm talking right around the European Middle Ages—a long period. When Gutenberg established the printing press with moveable type in the 15th century, he set the stage for a printed world—a typographical world.

It is this world that I want to draw your attention to. I would take a wager and say every schoolchild can name at least one font. Designers probably hundreds. Most people can read. We know the word "cliché" and like to make a good first impression. We mind our *q*-s and our *p*-s without knowing that it's because they are easily mixed up while typesetting. We cut and paste, we're out of sorts, and we've all seen a logo. This text explores some of the many ways in which typography has changed modern conversations, leaving its mark not just on paper but on our collective minds.[1]

Before we ever printed a single word on a Gutenberg Press, we were already writing for about 3,000 years. What we consider modern typography is closely linked to the reproduction of these written words. Taking a handwritten note and being able to reproduce it however often we would like, making it available to however many people—that's what changed the game. To reproduce words, we need a system—rules, shapes, and patterns that allow us to recognize what might have once been somebody's horrible handwriting. That is what typography does for us to this day. Yes, even *Comic Sans*. It's the ability to accurately and quickly reproduce and understand texts, which has allowed us to share information in the way that we do. Literacy has become one of the mainstays of our information civilization.

The fact that most of us can decode writing nowadays (alright, you could also just say read) is very much related to the improvements in printing technology. Books and printed matter became widely available in the centuries following the Gutenberg Press, significantly contributing to the spread of literacy and education in Europe. It democratized information in a way that still benefits us today.

Typography is often considered in terms of aesthetics, but rarely in the purpose that it first served: The ability to reproduce texts precisely, legibly, cheaply, and largely without errors. The first fonts mimicked the handwriting of the clergy, sensible since it was the job of a scribe to reproduce texts for many centuries. However, if a printing press makes 100 copies of the Gutenberg bible, each will say exactly the same thing. If five monks write five copies of the bible, we'll have five different versions. Maybe one of them has a fun idea for a new parable or better wording as well.[2] Printing, and in turn, modern typography, is more of an exact science.[3] Forget to cross a *t* in your Bible copy? You'll reap the consequences from the Big G. A good set of lead type and a printing press will solve that for you.

Of course, content matters as well. Had Luther not translated the bible that Gutenberg would later print, very few people would have been able to read the Latin texts inside, no matter how widely available they were. On the other hand, said translation might have sat in Luther's study forever, had it not been reproduced. Knowledge is power and print spreads the word. Thanks, typography!

Modern typography didn't just change how we access information; it also changed the way we speak. It is no wonder that idioms like "a dab hand" are often related to the work of typesetting, referring to the patience and skill required. But what does that have to do with dotting *i*-s and crossing *t*-s? Before we automated most printing processes and invented desktop publishing, typesetting and everything associated with it was a tedious process. The title of this text refers to this detail-loving aspect of typography. When you've dotted your *i*-s and crossed your *t*-s you've really checked everything. What a wonderful typographical saying! Words and phrases from typography have made their way into many of our most common proverbs. What do we have to do to find them? Look closely at the details.

When Gutenberg established his invention, the printing process was improved[4] but by no means fast. Later attempts to speed things up tried casting syllables or entire words whole. Those pieces were called logotypes—from Ancient Greek "lógos," meaning "word." However, it was nearly impossible to keep track of the hundreds of compartments needed in a typical case. While this way of typesetting didn't catch on, it still became common to cast words that were frequently used in one piece: Newspaper section headlines, which had to be used every day, for example, or the name of the publication itself. They were the very first logos ever made. Nowadays, they are so ubiquitous

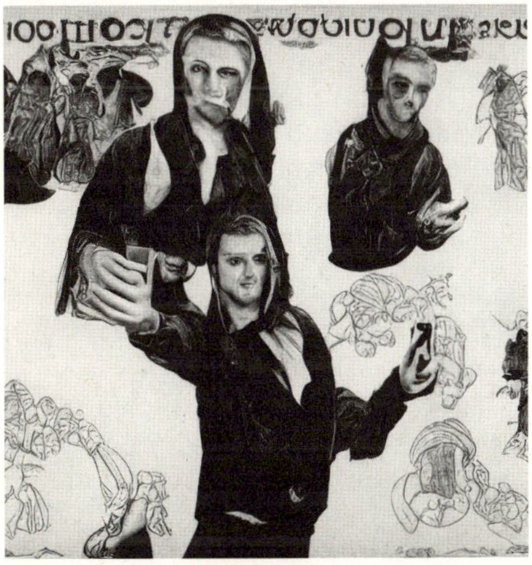

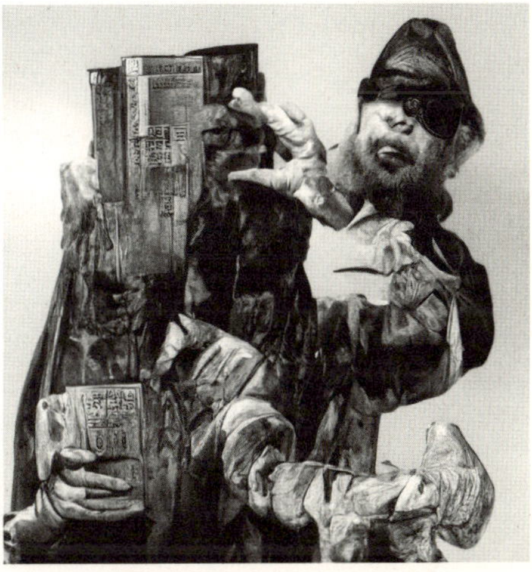

The past imagined by the future. Text-to-image artwork, collaboration of the author and GAN artist Ümüt Yildiz *(instagram.com/uemuetyildiz).*

that we've reversed the process in a way and turned them back into images. Words become funny little drawings once more. We print them on shoes and shirts and make patterns of them.

In the infancy of moveable type, adding an image to a letterpress form required printing blocks that behaved just like metal letters. Creating them was a time-consuming process. Luckily, there was a workaround: Instead of creating single-use printing blocks with images, generic images were made, and print shops could use them for multiple prints and several clients. The pros called these printing blocks clichés, and it caught on. People outside the printing world gradually started using the word cliché for all that is not original, overused, generic, or ... Stereotypical.

Yes, "stereotype" is also a word from typography. I've mentioned it before—creating letterpress forms with text and printing blocks is a finicky process. Even worse, if a reprint was needed, it was essentially necessary to start from scratch, recreating the typesetting and the entire layout. It was possible to store the original letterpress forms to be used later, but that meant that all the letters and printing blocks used were not available for other prints. There were only so many e's to go around so this was rarely an option. This is where the stereotype came in.

A material like paper-mâché was pressed on the letterpress form and created a precise negative impression of the entire layout. And from that, a new single form could be made. Using this technique had another benefit: the new cast didn't necessarily have to be reused flat like the original letterpress form. It could also be cast in a cylindrical shape for the much faster rotary printing presses with cylindrical printing forms. And just like the word cliché, the word stereotype began being used outside the printing world—in a more metaphorical sense, referring to generalized and replicated ideas or images.

It makes sense that ideas of replication were connected to printing from the beginning. It was one of the first mass-produced products in a world that was still filled with unique items. What we find important finds its way into our vocabulary, as we've seen. Sometimes it's also a matter of what technology came first. Now we just type on our laptops, but the words we use come from the earliest typographical days.

[1] It's by no means a complete compilation, but definitely something to hand to the relative that keeps asking why typography is so important.

[2] The sheer amount of forged or changed documents from medieval times says it all.

[3] Obviously, there were already some layouting rules or best practices that even the monks adhered to, but there wasn't an agreed-upon canon on how to do things. This emerged when things had to become standardized for print reproduction. The rules we apply to our modern layouts in modern typesetting are heavily influenced by the mechanical constraints of the printing presses and the way lead type is set.

[4] From handwriting or carved blocks.

[5] Just an idea ;)

# Syllaba—A Typeface with a Story

## by So-Hyun Bae

In the early 2000s, my brother created my first email address for me so that I could send emails to our father who was living in Korea while we were living in France. I was allowed only a limited time on the computer and my typing skills in both French and Korean were very poor. All the more, I couldn't concentrate on writing the emails because I was having more fun typing weird characters to watch them get composed, *jamo* by *jamo,* as they got compressed or extended, stacked or broken apart. Typing Hangeul felt like watching little animations. Eventually, I would run out of time and my emails ended up being short messages like "We miss you." or "Mom said to drink more water." My fascination for typed Hangeul persisted into adulthood and I wondered whether it would be possible to recreate this typing experience with the Latin alphabet.

During my studies at the Haute école des arts du Rhin in Strasbourg, I came across a copy of *Slanted Babylon* (2013), a special issue focused on multi-script type design in which I encountered the notion of "typographic matchmaking." Naturally, I was drawn to this idea—somehow naively and idealistically—and began asking myself what could result from a Latin and Hangeul matchmaking.

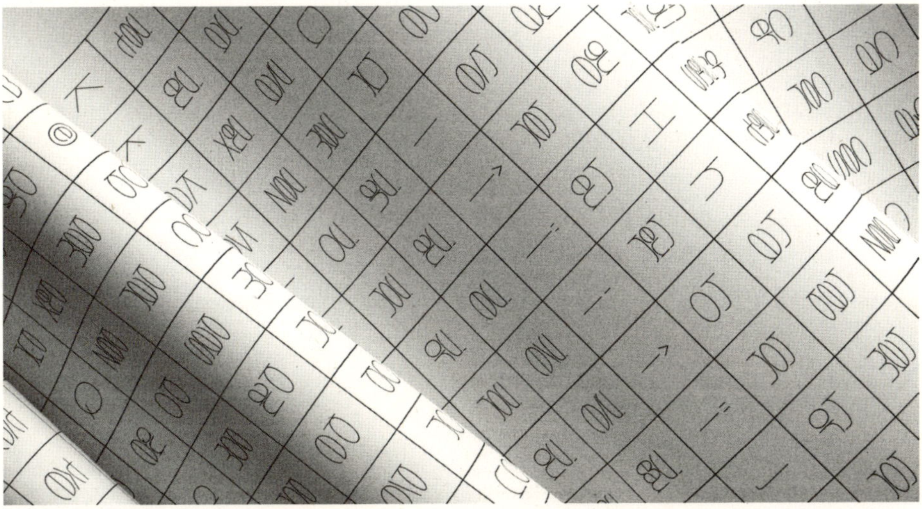

Hangeul, or the Korean alphabet, is a phonetic writing system that includes 24 basic letters called *jamo* with 14 consonants called *jaeum* and ten vowels called *moeum.* These *jamo* are combined together into syllabic blocks—each representing one syllable that includes at least one *jaeum* and one *moeum.* With its different *jamo* and ways of composition, Hangeul can be composed of up to to 11,172 characters with densities varying from one character to another. When it comes to text, this variety of density creates a very irregular texture, making the harmonization with Latin texts almost impossible. Hangeul-Latin matchmaking usually occurs at the scale of letterforms and focuses on finding an optical balance in weights by fine-tuning the thickness of the strokes. However, what triggered my interest and curiosity the most was the *text*-ure. I wanted to try out a radical color-matching of both scripts by breaking the smoothness of Latin texts so that texts in both scripts have uneven textures. At first, this idea felt superficial, almost too parody-like. But somehow this all came to make sense to me. Yes, what I am working with are texts in the Latin alphabet, but what I am *really* dealing with is French. French words are made out of syllables, so why shouldn't a French syllabary make sense? As a person who grew up speaking Korean, it's true that languages were wired in that way, seeing all words cut into syllables. It also seemed like a way to offer a different reading experience of French, challenging the readers to read words in blocks from top to bottom and then pass on to the next syllable.

So, how to apply this logic of Hangeul to the Latin alphabet? And more specifically to the French language? (I have to emphasize that this font I developed is specifically adapted for the French language. Indeed, many European languages share the Latin alphabet, but they all have their own distinct syllables.) First, I began by listing the 36 phonemes of the French language to put together an "extended alphabet," without forgetting that in French there can be several different spellings for the same phoneme. For example, the phoneme /o/ can be written as: "o," "au," "aud," "ault," "aux," "eau," "eaux," and so on. Other than simple phonemes such as /ʃ/, /ɲ/, and /f/ ("ch," "gn," "ph"), I also included "extended alphabet" composed phonemes such as /bʁ/, /kʁ/, /fʁ/ ("br," "cr," "chr," "phr").

There are mainly six ways to compose Hangeul: three for *open* syllables, or syllables that end with a vowel, and another three for *closed* syllables, those that end with a consonant. *Batchim* or the final consonant of a closed syllable is always placed at the bottom of each character. Following a similar logic, I began drawing the French syllables either based on a structure in two "stories," for syllables that are in pairs consonant(C)-vowel(V) or V-C, or in three "stories" for "sandwiched" syllables in C-V-C, or C-V-silent letters.

Statistically speaking, if 11,172 is the number of characters that can be composed out of 24 Hangeul jamo and its different ways of composition, I leave it to the readers to imagine the number of French syllables that can exist ...

During my master's—with an art student's lightning motivation to graduate—I managed to draw about 700 glyphs, which was already enough to start composing texts, enabling me to carry out several graphic experiments.

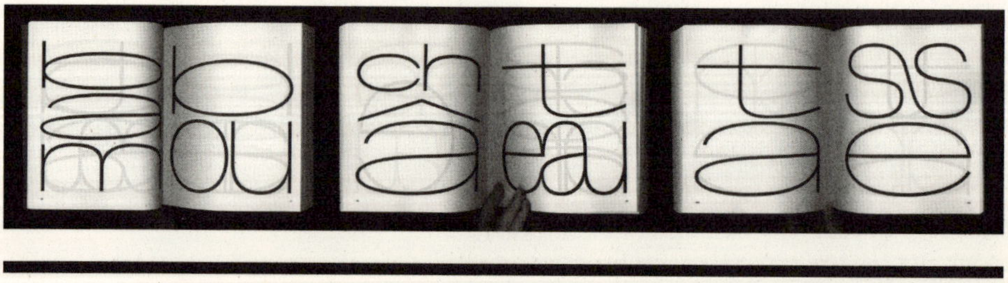

But as a Korean speaker, I could not detach myself from its Hangeul reference. Partially frustrated and curious about how a person without the knowledge of Korean would react and use this typeface, I launched a call for projects, asking a larger audience to experiment with my typeface to create whatever inspired them. Various contributions came in, from writers, poets, designers, or people outside of the creative field, replying back with calligrams, concrete poetries, and textural tapestries. Hangeul was gone. This typeface was henceforth French. Although I ambitioned to draw its Hangeul pair, this eventually felt unnecessary.

Later on, I named this typeface *Syllaba,* after the same Latin term that originates from the Greek "syllavi" which means "that which is taken together." In this case, French and Hangeul are "syllavi."

In a sense, *Syllaba* is an autobiographical typeface, telling the story of my family, of myself. I was born in Korea but I grew up mostly in France. Despite the fact that we were living in France, our parents made sure that we spoke Korean at home and that we cherish Korean values. I recently found out that there is a term to designate such generation as my brother's or mine: the 1.5 generation. This refers to a "first-generation immigrant who immigrated to the new country before or during their early teens. They earn the label the "1.5 generation" because while they spend their formative years engaging in assimilation and socialization in the new country, they often still maintain native language, cultural traits and even national identities from their country of origin." *Syllaba* illustrates this kind of generation, that straddles France and Korea, that, while "engaging in assimilation and socialization in the new country," is also a generation that seeks ways to reconcile cultural values acquired from both countries—a cultural "matchmaking" of some sort. Perhaps *Syllaba* is a reconciliation in letterforms?

Type design turned out to be one of my means to convey such a personal narrative—by creating *Syllaba,* I talk about identity and tell a story. Additionally, *Syllaba* is about French. For me, it's important to say that *Syllaba* is a French font more than a Latin font, although this was done by mixing both Latin and Hangeul scripts. The focus is rather on the language than the writing system, even the term "language design" could be appropriate. Questioning the boundaries between scripts and languages pushed me to draw *Syllaba* with its unconventional letterforms but to realize especially the vast potential this query can lead to in type design.

[1,2] Jamo are the basic components of the Korean alphabet called Hangeul.

[3] Typographic matchmaking is the practice of designing or pairing typefaces of different scripts to obtain a harmonized ensemble.

[4] What I mean by "superficial" and "parody-like" is to express my fear to repeat another *Frankenstein Arabic*—Pater, Ruben. *The Politics of Design,* BIS Publishers, 2016, p. 32.), a pastiche of Hangeul with Latin letterforms.

[5] Silent letters are very common in French which makes it often difficult to predict the pronunciations of words. Due to this and many other spelling quirks, French is considered to be one of the languages with the most opaque orthographies. Fitting all these silent letters in each syllabic block was often a challenge.

[6] Immigrant generations. Wikipedia, Wikimedia Foundation, last edited on July 4th, 2022, *en.wikipedia.org/wiki/Immigrant_generations*

# Monolith

by Karen Ann Donnachie
& Andy Simionato

## What could digital typefaces become once they can contain an unlimited number of characters? On the Unicode standard and the transforming role of typefaces in a post-literate society.

In Stanley Kubrick's science-fiction film *2001: A Space Odyssey* (1968), a mysterious monolith of unknown origin appears at various points in history. Each time humans contact the monolith they appear to make evolutionary and technological advances, from acquiring the ability to use simple tools to exploring the outer reaches of the galaxy.

Prior to the widespread use of computers, the number of characters, punctuation and symbols in a writing system were limited by the ability of the sage, scribe or artisan to reproduce them. Through the invention of movable typography these typefaces became more efficient and standardized. In virtual space, however, the number of glyphs in a font are now only limited by the storage and computational capacity of the device and software on which it is displayed. Today, the Unicode consortium supports fonts for a growing number of languages, with any single font now able to contain over 144,697 glyphs/graphemes (or individual characters and symbols).[1]

If a contemporary standard Qwerty-format keyboard offers access to typing around 100 characters, it would take 1,400 of these keyboards to cover all the characters available in a typeface which used all its available glyphs. If these characters appeared on an imaginary single keyboard, it would be over 400 m long. If a human attempted to type every Unicode character just once typing at 400 characters per minute, it would take them over six hours to complete the task.

It is very unlikely that the Unicode consortium was imagining a keyboard hundreds of metres long when expanding the number of possible glyphs in a typeface. However, we started to think about a typeface which uses the full

Unicode character set and we asked: What would it look like? How would we experience such a typeface? Would it even be possible to make a typeface with 144,697 glyphs?

These initial considerations brought us to rethink a typeface where the glyphs can be viewed as a sequence of images, or "characters per second." We quickly realized that an analogous time-based medium which is also "read" as a sequence of images is cinema.

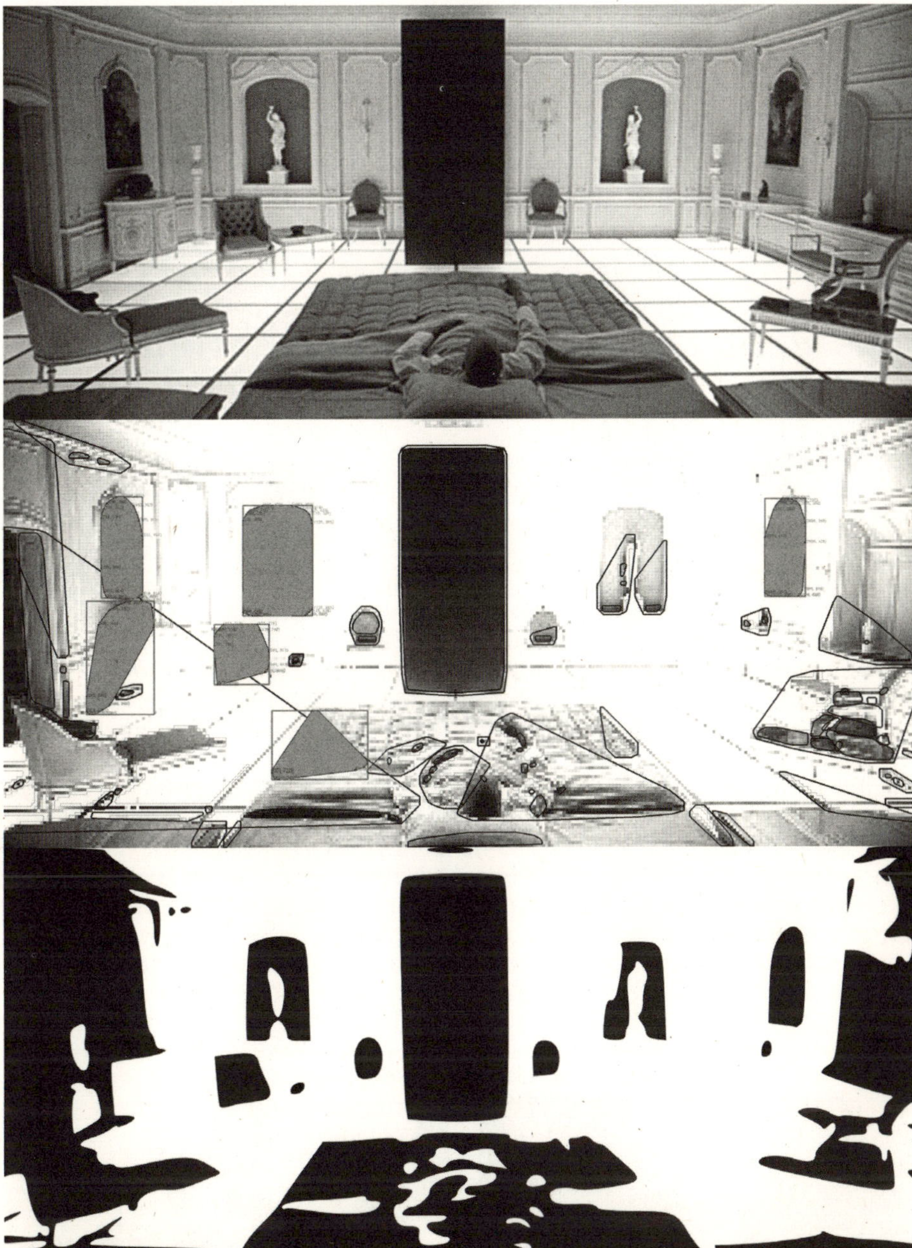

Still-image from *2001: A Space Odyssey* (1968), Stanley Kubrick and the corresponding glyph in the typeface *Monolith*.

We set out to test the seemingly ever-expanding boundaries of contemporary digital typefaces by attempting to transform sequences of cinematic frames into typographic glyphs. Through this process we explored the transforming role of typography in what is sometimes considered a post-literate era inspired by critical writings in new technologies, textual artworks such as Paul Chan's *Alternumerics* (2000) which in turn form part of the absurdist traditions in the visual arts and literature.

Through these algorithmically made typefaces, which together we have titled *Monolith* after the project's major work, we can possibly experience a kind of "universal" font containing hundreds of thousands of glyphs, and we begin to question what new potential such a font may hold for humans. Underlying the work is perhaps the most intriguing and fantastic question of all: if a font can potentially contain hundreds of thousands, if not millions, of glyphs, are we approaching something like the Monolith in Kubrick's film? A unifying system of symbols which functions like a font of knowledge capable of triggering the evolution of humans? But before we get too far ahead, we should describe how this system functions.

**Process**

These typefaces are produced through a custom-coded python-based algorithm which uses computer vision and machine learning to automatically convert video files into vector outlines which are then automatically added as glyphs into the Unicode HEX character space in order to finally generate an original Open Type font.

In order to "view," debug and test the process, we created bespoke auxiliary JavaScript web-apps that would allow for the automated linear viewing of the Unicode characters, at a speed analogous to animation (between 24 and 30 frames per second).

With this process we have successfully generated original OpenType fonts from several public domain and commercial films, beginning with the *Sortie de L'Usine* (1895) by the Lumiére Brothers, understood as the first work of cinema, displaying workers entering and exiting a factory. The duration of this short piece of early cinema is 46 seconds and was filmed at 16 frames per second, which results in 800 frames, or 800 characters of a typeface.

Although these short films were useful as a "proof of concept," we wanted to see how much a typeface could "hold" and so we began testing the algorithm on movies of longer duration, including *The Water Magician* (1933) by Kenji Mizoguchi, Vittorio de Sica's *Ladri di Biciclette* (1948), and *King Harishchandra* (1913) by Dhundiraj Govind Phalke. Finally, we turned the algorithm to the feature length film *2001: A Space Odyssey* (1968) by Stanley Kubrick, and from which this project takes its name.

The algorithm required around 25 hours to convert each frame of the science-fiction film into vectorial data of 1,000 nodes or less, before adding it in sequence to the typeface as a glyph. Ultimately, every frame of the film

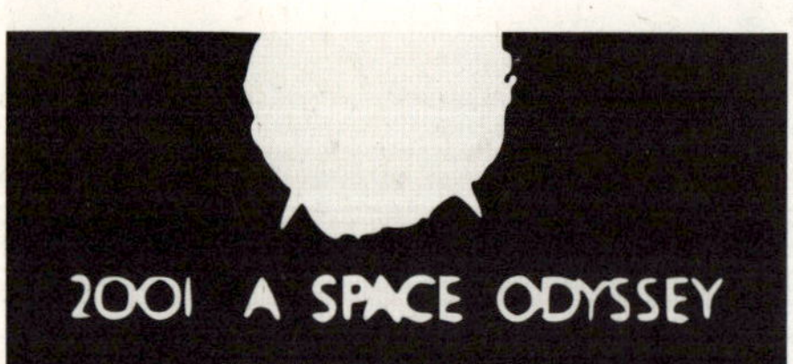


→ Character: ዥ, Unicode: U+12E5

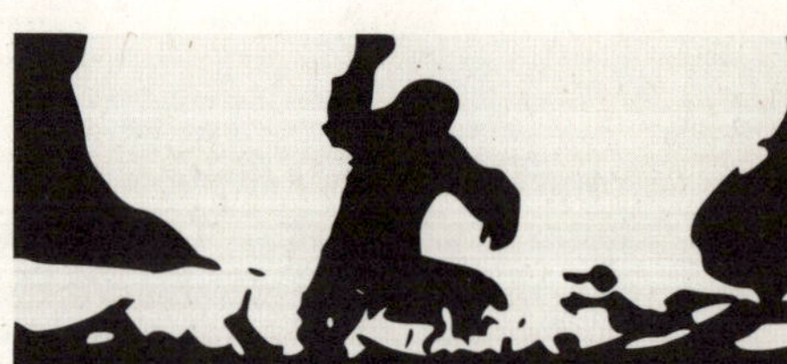

→ Character 鬒, Unicode: U+FAA2.

occupied one of the available glyph spaces in the typeface, which amounted to over 400 MB of font data when encoded as an OpenType font.

Through the project *Monolith* we use computational typography to explore the limits of contemporary digital writing systems, in order to reflect on what may lie beyond language as we approach what we have called elsewhere, "the infinite knowable." The "infinite knowable" is a notion that we described as a body of knowledge that is both computable (that is, knowledge which can be calculated and stored by computers) yet lies beyond any single human's comprehension.

So in conclusion did we answer our initial questions?

Yes, it is possible to make a typeface which uses every one of its 144,600+ possible glyphs. Although its practical uses are clearly limited to theoretical or artistic discourses, we can begin to visualize what such a "universal" typeface may look like, as well as experimenting ways to experience such a typeface by viewing it in "characters by second," like film or animation. But we were, as was expected, unable to answer the most fantastical question of this inquiry, and so leave it here answered: could such a universal typeface, containing every possible character and symbol, also function like a font of evolutionary knowledge, or does it remain impenetrable and meaningless, like the Monolith?

1 "Unicode has the explicit aim of transcending the limitations of traditional character encodings." Unicode 14.0 contains a total of 144,697 characters.–*Unicode* in Wikipedia. Accessed May 1st, 2022. *en.wikipedia.org/wiki/unicode*

2 For argument's sake we reductively infer a 'Pre-literate age' to be that which precedes the onset of moveable type and the mass-production of the book from the 16th century, while the 'Post-Literate age' is one in which our literary works have been dematerialised through the mass-digitisation of the book such as through the Google Books project (among others), and long-form reading is disrupted by other patterns of information retrieval.

3 Aaron Levy & Jean-Michel Rabaté write "Unlike conventional fonts like *Arial, Helvetica,* or *Comic Sans,* Chan's fonts are comprised of phrases and sentence fragments instead of letters and other alphanumeric characters, so that what is typed on the keyboard is not what shows up on the screen, or what is printed on paper. Alternumerics turn traditional letters into foreign symbols that disrupt and create new forms of meaning, exploring the relationship between what is typed, what is translated—and fundamentally—what is communicated." – Levy, Aaron, and Jean-Michel Rabaté, 2015. *Alternumerics* in *Slought Resources* (Philadelphia: Slought org), accessed on January 1st, 2022. *slought.org/resources/alternumerics*

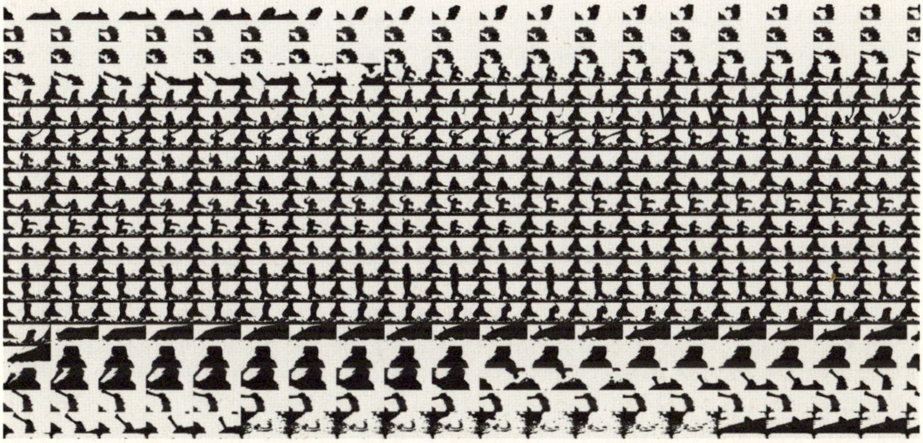

Glyph sequence from the corresponding scene of Stanley Kubrick's *2001: A Space Odyssey* (1968).

# Behind the Letters— Type Foundries in Focus:

# Interview with Jeremy Tankard

## Established type designer Jeremy Tankard gives us an insight into his work with Jeremy Tankard Typography and his take on the type design industry.

**Please introduce yourself and your type foundry briefly.**
I'm a graduate of Central Saint Martins and the Royal College of Art. Following five years in corporate design I established Jeremy Tankard Typography to develop a library of original typeface designs, and to work with companies to realize their typographic ambitions. I'm based in the university city of Cambridge just north of London and although it's just myself, I work in two studio spaces—the primary studio is where all the computers and books are. This is the main office and production space. The other studio is a garden studio which I try and keep as a quiet space away from distractions. I do a lot of photography here as well as draw and develop initial ideas.

**You have been designing typefaces since 1998. What has changed in your work, process, and mentality since then?**
My first foray into typeface design was a college brief during my Foundation Year at Lincoln College of Art and Design in 1987. Derived from the brush-stroke art of Roy Lichtenstein, it was painted in Indian ink on CS10 board. Four years later I began work on *Disturbance* and *Bliss.* These were both eventually released; *Disturbance* in 1993 and *Bliss* in 1996. My growing interest in the history and potential of type led me to leave my job in corporate design and focus purely on the design of type, this was 1998.

It was a hugely exciting time. Technology opened up the production and manufacture of fonts, allowing designers to leapfrog the traditional closed approach to designing type. The changes in technology have also brought increased typographic ability. Once a font was generally produced in quite a limited range of characters and languages. Support for Central and East European languages had to be a different font, as did advanced typographic characters such as Small Capitals, Fractions, Swashes, and so on. This all changed with the OpenType font format. A font was no longer limited to just over 200 characters—every single font could now contain 1,000s of glyphs.

This fundamental development now opened up a pandora's box of opportunities; a designer is only limited by their own imagination.

My working process has developed a pattern over the years, yet I still find myself changing how I do things with each new typeface. Each type is different and tries to push what a type can do in certain ways. Because of this, I usually find myself adopting different processes to develop it. This may be simply slowing down and taking time to ink in some drawings to see them in a pre-digital form, or it could be using programming to manipulate an idea. I like to spend a lot of time on the early stages, exploring ideas through drawing. I've always kept sketchbooks, and they are now dedicated to the development of each typeface. The books are dated throughout and show all stages from initial ideas through to production and marketing—they've become the typeface diaries. Alongside the sketchbooks, each typeface has a ring binder for the core stages of development.

As a result of having designed type across shifts in technology, applications, and fashion, I'm more determined to design what I want instead of bending to the whims of a certain time. Creative thinking and approaches are more rewarding, especially in consideration of the time spent on the design of a type. For me, a typeface is a lot more than a collection of glyphs. I like to dig deeper into what underpins its design and explore diverse avenues around its inspiration. Without the support of wider thinking, a typeface can be hollow. A typeface needs integrity and conviction. I wrote about this in *Principles of Type,* published as part of the *Claymore* specimen. It's easy to make a font, but not so easy to design a typeface.

**Your custom and commercial typefaces are all very individual and original. How do you approach the design of a new typeface? What drives you in the direction you are going?**

Both client and personal work have different origins, though I try and bring the client work into the way I approach a personal project. If a client says that they want their version of an existing typeface I would generally walk away. I don't work on other peoples' Intellectual Property. However, if there is scope to expand an idea and explore where else it can be pushed, then it's worth doing. I see little point in repeating what has already been done, and generally think that if I'm spending a chunk of time (from six months to a year) on a design, I want the whole project to be fulfilling and challenging.

When it comes to my own typeface designs, an idea presents itself either directly through reading about type or obliquely from all manner of outside influences. The latter is usually far more exciting. I have a strong belief that

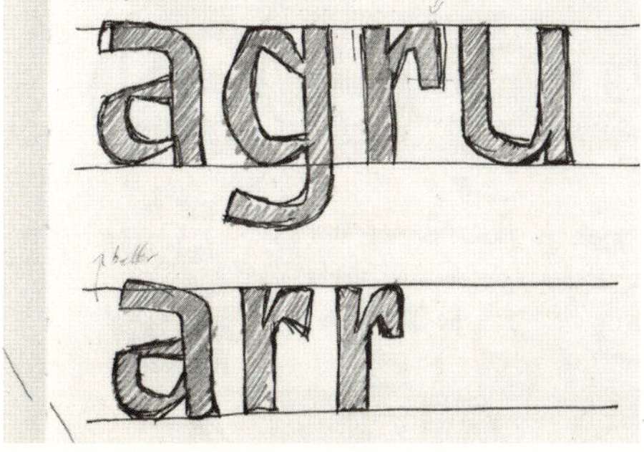


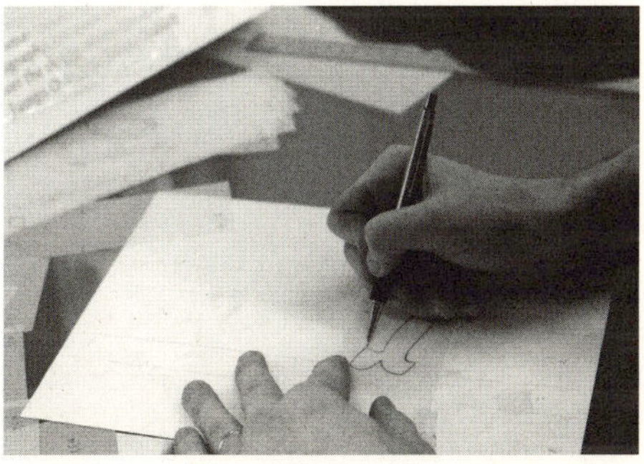

← Working development sketches for Jeremy Tankard's typeface *Brucker.*
→ Trace drawings for *De Worde* are used to more easily review combinations before digitizing.

there always has to be more, and a better way to do something, so I question everything at all stages. This keeps me doggedly pursuing the end goal and keeping all elements in flux until the final build. Although I'm quite traditional in the way I work, I'm also a product of our digital times. I certainly wouldn't be designing type if it wasn't for the computer, and the flexibility that the computer brings to the process allows me to work the way I do.

**What was the inspiration and goal for your typeface *Rockhopper* and its striking details?**
Rockhopper is the culmination of two ideas. I've always had an awkward relationship with the rounded sans style. One part of the project was to tackle that Achilles' heel and look at the historical development of the rounded Sans; how technology has shaped it over time, and how current technology can be used to its advantage now. The other part looked at how the letter shape is softened by interrupting its outline. This got me thinking of a way to change and obscure the shape through additional elements. The swashes grew from an old idea I had several years back which looked at developing a range of attachments that could be stuck on any letter to add a level of decoration. I just ran with this thought and pushed it from one or two swashes to "overkill"—which obliterates the underlying text, but remarkably doesn't necessarily render it illegible.

We are at a point where type can be far more than purely "essentially utilitarian and only accidentally aesthetic" (to quote Stanley Morison from *First principles of typography*). Type and our modern culture require (and expect) a more visual level of communication. Type no longer needs to quietly sit back but can take central stage in a design and have a strong visual voice. As a challenge, it's interesting to look at how a typeface can move between both of these levels of expression and ultimately find new ways to be.

**You have a generous repertoire of high quality and elaborate type specimens as well as a unique "Explorer" section for your typefaces on your website. Why is this kind of presentation of typefaces so important to you, where does your passion for that stem from?**
I think my desire to make specimens stems from my college years when I first started looking intently at the history of type. The twentieth century was full of typography, typographic development, and experimentation. Supporting this were several journals, many books, articles, and marketing materials. The same is true today, but the big difference is the lack of celebrating a typeface through marketing material. I find that sad. I'm a strong advocate of the physical specimen. Yes, it costs money to do, but that's a small price to

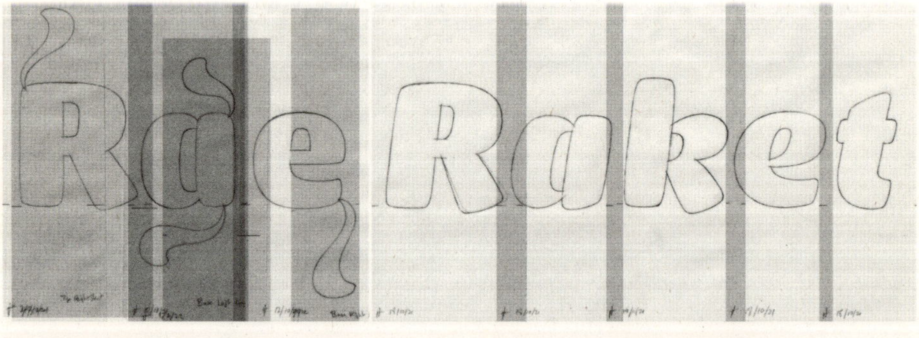

Trace drawings for *Rockhopper* with swashes that can easily be moved around to test.

pay considering the commitment and time it takes to make a typeface. It can be a simple showing or a more expressive and personal statement. There's a depth to a physical specimen that isn't there in a digital one—it touches more of the senses.

In a world that expects more than print I also produce digital material. The Gallery uses the computer to generate typographic images. Purely aesthetic; these exist just to be visual and draw attention to the juxtaposition of shape, detail, and color—all placed within a square.

Another form of the digital specimen is the "Explorer." Think of it as a large tank, in which different expressions of typography are floating about. These shift as you move around, some slow, some fast. Clicking on one of the cross symbols will show information relating to its specific piece of typography such as the font weight, style, and features used.

Complementing all the marketing is the educational and inspirational work which is provided through *studiotype.com*—a second site developed in 2017. The site not only shows the bespoke typefaces but also tells the stories behind my original type designs in an informal sketchbook manner. A vast amount of information contributes to the design of a typeface, and I strongly believe it's worth explaining various aspects of each design. I think it is important to show that some ideas are grounded in history, whilst others are oblique and unfathomable.

**How do you see the future of type design and what goals have you set for yourself?**

We have almost unlimited access to so much typographic knowledge—the problem is selecting which bits to absorb at any given time. There's huge potential for type, especially as there are ever more opportunities where type can appear and be used. As language is constantly evolving so does type. The categories and specific traits of Text and Display typefaces often reflect the ideas of convention and avant-garde. It would be good to see how type designers and type users can develop these concepts. Through cleverly tweaking and twisting preconceptions and perceptions new styles will emerge.

For myself, I continue to question and look for more. Type has endless possibilities and in each of the typeface sketchbooks, I note down potential ideas for future projects. These crop up as a reaction to a current stage of work or something I've read or noticed. They stay at the back of my mind and ferment, sometimes dying off but other times they're the spark that's needed for a future design. There's always more to do and new ways to do it. I increasingly worry less about making type that meets the expectations of others and instead try to show how much more type can be.

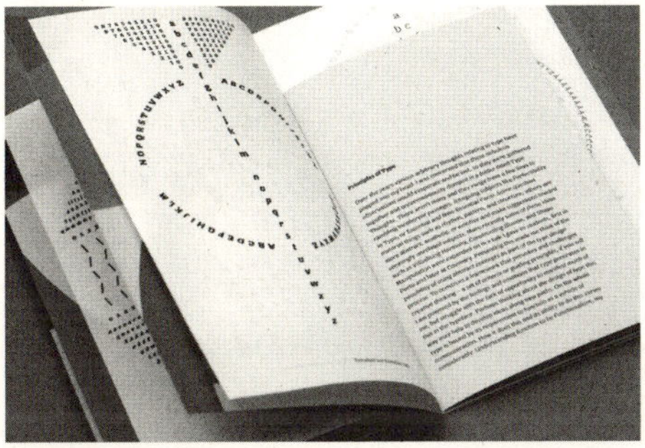

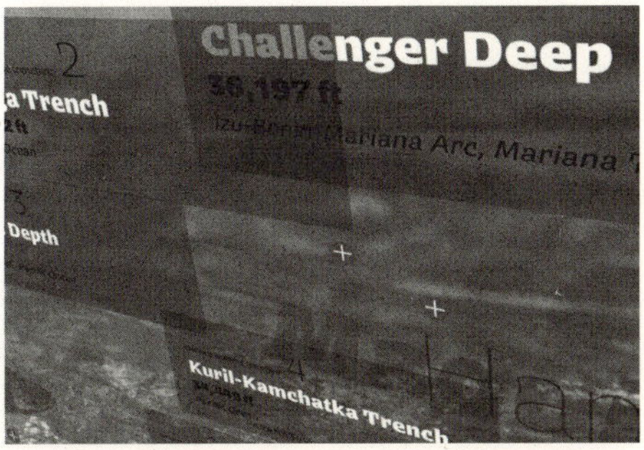


← Printed type specimen for the *Claymore* typeface.
→ The *Claymore Explorer* is a digital type specimen at *typography.net.*

# Several Thoughts on Writing Taught In Schools

## by Martin Tiefenthaler

## Children learning to write, have the right to a highly functional and equally elegant type—and better handwriting leads to more enjoyment of learning.

**1—Methods Dispute**

In the discussion around teaching writing in schools, a) voices are raised that declare handwriting obsolete due to the influence of new technology, b) didactic approaches are advanced that cast doubt on the need for a second form of writing once capital letters have been learned, and c) even among advocates of a second, cursive form of writing, different didactic camps are opposed to one another on fundamentals.

Concerning the acquisition of writing in two steps, there is broad consensus, with a few exceptions, on the order: first to be taught is writing upright and unconnected block letters (in most cases, called *Grundschrift* or basic writing). This serves the purpose of learning the fundamental architecture of letters, and establishes a connection to those letters most commonly seen in daily life and thus represents an optimal aid in learning to read.

Following this, a joined-up cursive form of writing is taught, then called *Lateinische* or *(Schul-)Ausgangsschrift* (Model Latin Script or Model School Script), or *Vereinfachte Ausgangsschrift* (Simplified Model Script), whereby the various didactic approaches differ in the method used in joining up the letters. Generally, the struggle for theoretical supremacy centers on the question of whether school children should write with separate, partially-joined, or continuously joined-up writing.

In this, all proponents of the various approaches to teaching who air their views publicly can either assert their political position, and/or their own teaching experience, as well as put forward studies and experiments that are intended to prove and substantiate their points of view. Teaching practitioners then adhere to regulations and guidelines that differ in terms of when and where they were introduced, or modify them as they see fit according to their personal experiences in the classroom.

The one camp (historically older) insists on a continuously joined-up script; the other (younger) camp advocates partial linking up of letters, or even lettering that is not joined up at all. Indeed, some of these approaches go so far as to suggest that those learning to write, while being supported in the didactic sense, should develop joined-up cursive lettering on their own.

Both didactic convictions show similar demands in terms of motoric skills and there is no reason to assume that one kind of writing places greater or fewer demands on children than the other—provided they are taught caringly and thoroughly. Basic line orientation, stroke position, contact points of strokes, retracing the writing movement, correct indication of the stroke, ending the stroke correctly, mastery of proportions: all these elements remain in principle the same with regard to the demands they place on learners.

As can clearly be seen in the handwriting of those who write a lot, are highly literate, and enjoy an affinity for writing, there is no fully joined-up handwriting style. Besides the mandatory interruptions after diacritic signs such as the dots on *i's*, double dots on umlauts and accents, there are also chirographically useful ones that prevent overly long cover strokes, sprawling and/or awkward loops and connecting curves with turning points.

Writing for school must therefore provide a model that conceives of and suggests to those inexperienced in writing an optimal method of joining up between all the letters. In the transition from the upright, unconnected writing to the ideally faster, joined-up style, children can then experience for themselves where they wish to join up and where not. And should the child wish to join up the letters, then she or he has a clear, chirographically tested template and does not need to invent something, thereby saving circuitous routes or wrong turns. The energy thereby saved is then available for work on spelling and above all on content.

**2—Scientific Studies**

In the history of studying typography, it has become evident[1] that it is very difficult in the area of reading and writing—above all, in studies into legibility, speed of reading, acquisition of writing skills, and literacy and the like—to put together homogenous and comparable groups for the purposes of comparison and checks. If the test and check groups are homogenous, their number of cases is too small. If the number of cases is high enough, the groups become too varied and can be recorded statistically in a limited way only, and interpreted only vaguely. The creation and selection of study criteria is made more difficult as the cultural technologies of reading and writing are affected by many factors, making it hard to differentiate.

In the disputes concerning the "right" form of school writing, there is no didactic theory that is not also opposed. This, and the sometimes polemically conducted discussions, indicate that nobody should lay claim to "pure teachings." No conclusive proof will be found for the advantage of one or the other principle of teaching, nor for one or the other of the writing methods. This could be taken as proof that the way in which each particular form of writing is taught is the key point here.

It is striking that representatives of their respective theories are less clear in what they say about the forms—i.e. the strokes not only in their sequence, but in their architecture, too—of the letters to be taught. In their study questions, inadequate attention is given to examining which letter models are used, and in only a few cases is the question of the definitive letterforms preceded by a respective theory, and in most cases, though not all, followed by it. As writing is a physical process, however, consideration of the forms of each individual letter must be the foundation of all thoughts concerning didactics.

For example, the concept of the German Simplified Model Script, which connects most capital letters with a uniform down-stroke, is simplified and poorly conceived in terms of form. This becomes clear when treating the most frequent letter in all Romanic languages, the *e* (on average, 17% letter frequency).

Here, motor skills are imposed which do not result from a fluid writing movement, rather from unmanageable problems in digitization and in a simplification of the writing forms that is thereby forcibly brought about.

Too rarely were letter templates designed for school writing with sufficient quality and by renowned handwriting designers. Among the few historical designs and templates that contain some to many usable elements and approaches are those of Alfred Fairbank (Dryad Writing Cards, Beacon Writing; *A Handwriting Manual,* 1932[2]), Renate Tost and Elisabeth Kaestner (*Vereinfachte Schulausgangsschrift,* GDR 1968), Hans Eduard Meier (*Schweizer Schulschrift A, B, C,* 2002), and the German-Swiss (DCH) Basic Writing by Robert Bossart in collaboration with Sibylle Hurschler, which was developed from Meier's work and simplified in 2016. Other interesting attempts come from Petra Dočekalová, Just van Rossum (*FF Schulschrift* at Fontshop, 1991), Rosemary Sassoon (Sassoon Primary Series; *Handwriting of the Twentieth Century,* 2007), the handwriting teachers Nan Jay Barchowsky and Gunnlaugur Briem (*The Icelandic Method,* 1985) as well as Maria-Anna Schulze Brüning.

We also have Thomas Bettinger to thank for key suggestions for the creation of a new school handwriting approach; Bettinger, using sound arguments, criticized the state of Austrian school handwriting and the pedagogics of handwriting arising from that.

**3–The School Setting**

The way in which every child conceives of reading and writing is dependent upon fundamentally individual conditions (e.g. self-confidence, physical dexterity, and general manual skill ...), which depend upon prevailing circumstances specific to the learning (e.g. previous knowledge, intrinsic motivation to write and read ...), which depend upon family circumstances (e.g. communication and empathetic practice ...), which in turn are driven by socio-political parameters (e.g. the parents' educational level, socio-economic status ...).

In a randomly assembled class, which as a group will develop a specifically individual learning ambiance and class atmosphere, in which several friendships are made and some of these friends become influential peers with regard to learning behavior, this individual conception of writing then encounters a particular teacher. This educator possesses specific preconditions, such as pedagogical orientation, status within the teaching staff, and not least of all, professional training or further education in the teaching of writing, as well as their own relationship to that activity. Moreover, the educator is embedded within and influenced by such elements as the quality of the teaching- and learning material, the general orientation and atmosphere prevailing at the school concerned, and the type of school, with differing, subject-specific, and cross-disciplinary peculiarities and conditions relating to the instruction practiced there, such as the quality of the curriculum, the school's management, etc.

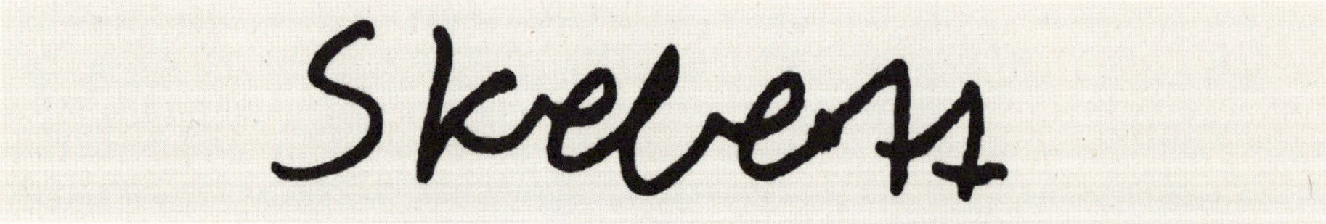

Simplification of form for technical reasons–as can be seen in the flawed, inorganic letter connection of the *e*–leads to unergonomic writing movements and difficulties with legibility. Illustration from: 2018, *Siegener Erklärung zur Schrift in der Schule,* Wolfgang Steinig, Katrin Eisfeld, Viola Oehme, and Maria-Anna Schulze Brüning.

Under these conditions, a form of school writing is needed that optimally supports all learning methods and circumstances. This can only be ensured by easy-to-follow, professionally crafted, and historically tried and tested letterforms and combinations. A good system of school writing cannot be prescribed; rather it is a suggestion, a recommendation that seeks to persuade practitioners to adopt the best possible support for methodological approaches.

### 4—Considerations of Form

**4.1** If simple movement sequences and clear forms are to be achieved, then an unconnected kind of writing should be available that is as close as possible to the letterforms with which children are confronted as readers in daily life. That should be followed by joined-up handwriting whose forms do not diverge too greatly from those of the unconnected writing. This includes slight "italicization" of the unconnected letters, as they are written by hand, too.

**4.2** Flourishes that serve no function should be left out, loops should not be larger than is necessary, and forms that are too round should be replaced by more dynamic, elliptical shapes. Loops need deliberately to be kept small so that they initially indicated the direction of the writing, and later could be converted into covering strokes. Initial capitals remain unconnected if a connecting stroke would change their form too greatly or require too long a path.

**4.3** There is no mandatory joining up of the letters, for truly fast writers never connect all the letters. However, the connections between the letters that have been tried and tested over the centuries should be available to children and it is then left up to them whether they wish to execute the connecting movements on paper or in the air. Letting them find the connections by themselves negates proven historical forms and wastes energies that are then lacking when it comes to concentrating on content.

For this reason, in good (mainly digital) templates, there are possibilities for breaking the flow: after capital and accented letters, after letters that could not be written fluently in one line (e.g. *t* or *k*), or with simple connections to the letters around them (e.g. *r, g, j, x,* and *y*).

Most of the digital school scripts currently available to teachers and publishers are inadequate: some are negligently digitized and the quality of the lines and curves of letters is not suitable to serve as a model for learning to write or for appreciating writing. The same applies to letter connections that are not mastered in terms of writing logic and/or the way they have been digitized. A school script pursues no other goal than to provide the basis for an individually shaped handwriting that develops from it. This basic principle, and the criteria previously mentioned for the most accessible school handwriting format possible were key in the development of *Prima Regular* and *Prima Italic* (p. 352/353).

1 "For typographers, legibility research is a controversial field because the validity of some of the research is difficult to ascertain: test material is often not shown, and testing is undertaken in laboratory conditions rather than 'real life' settings." – Walker, Sue & Black, Alison & Bessemans, Ann & Bormans, Kevin & Renckens, Maarten & Barratt, Mark (2018), Designing digital texts for beginner readers: performance, practice and process. In: Barzillai, Mirit & Thomson, Jenny & Schroeder, Sascha & Den Broek, Paul van (Editors) (2018), *Learning to read in a digital world. Studies in written language and literacy* (17); John Benjamins/Amsterdam, p. 34.

2 Fairbank on the school writing common at the time: "It has two shortcomings: there is nothing about it that gives a hint of development into a running hand and it has circular instead of elliptical movements." – Fairbank, Alfred (1932/1976), *A Handwriting Manual*; Watson-Guptill Publications/New York, p. 26.

# Build Your Own Pixel Font

## by Rainer Erich Scheichelbauer

## Enough reading about, and looking at, other people's fonts. Let's have some fun and make our own!

Download the free 30-day trial of Glyphs 3 from *glyphsapp.com/buy,* move it to your Applications folder, and double-click the app icon to open the application. Confirm the trial dialog, and choose File > New (Cmd-N) to make a new, empty font.

For a pixel font, we need two ingredients: a grid and a pixel. For the grid, open File > Font Info (Cmd-I) and switch to the "Other" tab of the window that

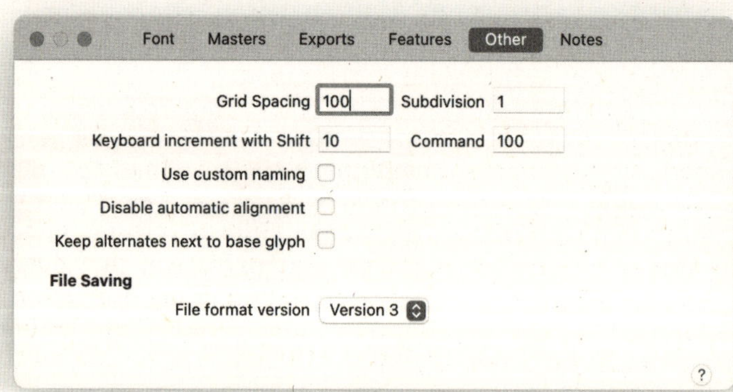


In the Font Info window, set the Grid Spacing value to the size of your pixels. For starters, a hundred units is a good idea.

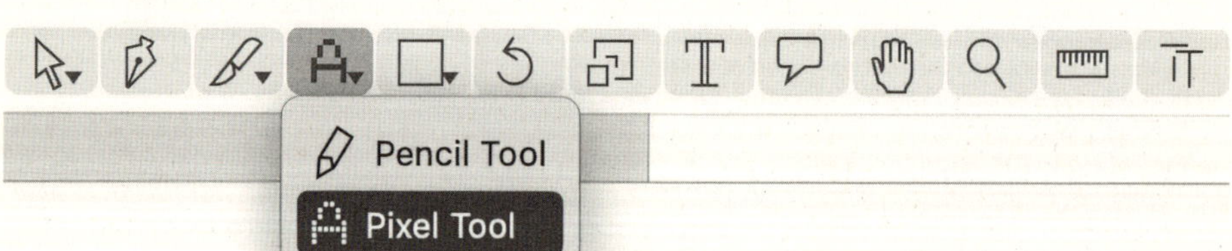


The Pixel Tool is tucked away in the depths of the toolbar. Access it by clicking and holding the Pencil Tool.

popped up. Change the Grid Spacing setting to 100 and press Enter to confirm. Close the Font Info again and return to the main window. Can we skip to the good part now? Yes, we can: double-click any of the letters, switch to the Pixel Tool, which hides behind the Pencil in the toolbar (click and hold the Pencil icon), and click in the grid. Oops, the app reminds us that we forgot to add a pixel glyph to the font. Oh well, click on the Add button, and we have one.

Now, with the Pixel Tool, you can click and drag through the grid to add pixel components. Click and drag across existing pixel components to remove them again. With the Text tool (T), you can type additional letters. To return to editing a letter, simply double-click it.

Tip: every time you are done with a letter, set its left sidebearing to zero and its right sidebearing to 100, the width of a pixel. You can do that in the gray info box (Cmd-Shift-I) at the bottom. Then double-click the next letter and put your Pixel tool to good use there. Make sure you keep your caps between the baseline (second from below) and the cap height (second from top).

Now the fun begins, because once you have a couple of letters, you can change the shape of the pixel: double-click one of the pixel components, and the original pixel glyph appears. If you change this one, all the components will change in all the letters you have drawn so far. Cool. Edit your pixel shape with the Select Tool (V) or draw a different shape with the Draw Tool (P). You may want to adjust the Grid Spacing or Subdivision in File > Font Info > Other for more flexibility. Make sure you have a sample word typed out while you change your pixel, just because it is more fun to see how much power a small change has.

Getting the hang of it? See what else you can do, and how you can put your font to use in your print and web designs: *glyphsapp.com/learn/pixelfont*

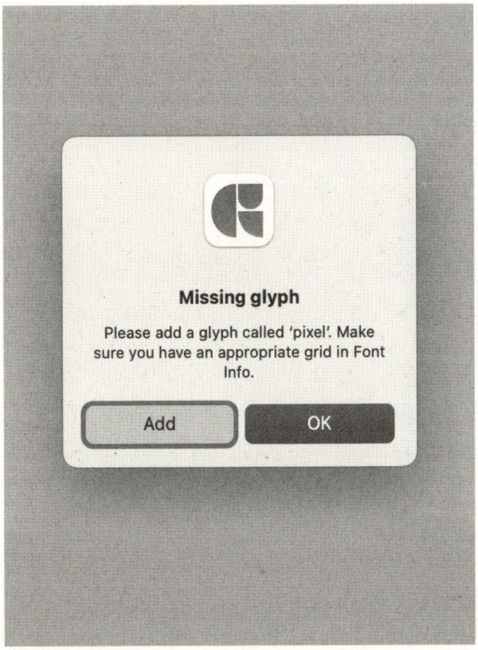


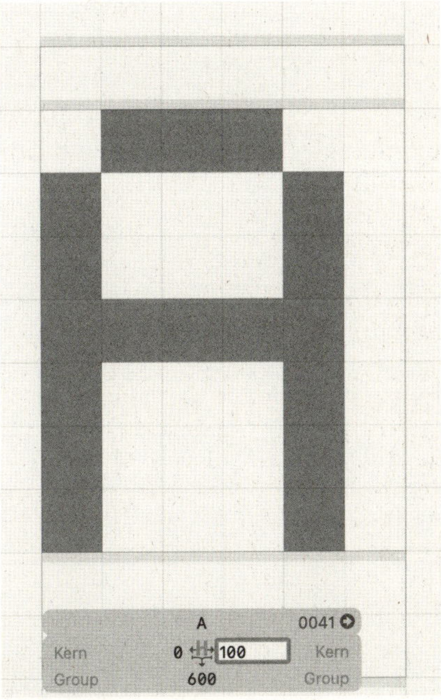


→ After you built a letter, it is a good idea to set the sidebearings to consistent values, e.g., zero on the left, and the size of a grid cell on the right.

← Forgot to create the pixel glyph? No worries, the Pixel Tool will add one for you in the grid size.

See all typefaces online at *yearbookoftype.com,* sorted by categories and linked to the foundries' websites. Enter the code: *YOT6MOVIES*

The specimens on the left pages were designed on the theme of movies and series. The trailers of the movies and series can be found here in a playlist:

DIRETTO DA
*Roberto Rossellini*

# {1945} ROMA *città aperta*

@ Marcello Pagliero * Aldo Fabrizi & Anna Magnani

Abstract

Abstract is a contemporary and eclectic serif typeface, inspired by today's life and created in times of the pandemic. This family includes a true italic variant—that has its own personality—Alternates, Lining, and Oldstyle Figures, Numerators, Denominators, and Cyrillic support.

**Design:** 2020, Luciano Vergara → p. 484, Rodrigo Fuenzalida → p. 475

**Foundry:** Los Andes Type, Chile, latinotype.com → p. 490

**Language support:** Latin Extended, Cyrillic

**OpenType features:** Proportional Oldstyle, Proportional Lining, Standard Ligatures, Ordinals, Fractions, Numerator, Denominator, Stylistic Alternates, Stylistic Sets, Localized Forms, Case Sensitive Forms

**Test version available:** No

**Web font format available:** Yes

abcdefghijklmnopqrstuvwxyzæfiåçéñöûß
ABCDEFGHIJKLMNOPQRSTUVWXYZÆÇØß
1234567890@.,!?')]§*“”»«/–½©€$£¥&

абвгдеёжзийклмнопрстуфхцчшщъыьэюя
АБВГДЕЁЖЗИЙКЛМНОПРСТУФХЦЧШЩЪЫЬЭЮЯ
1234567890@.,!?')]§*“”»«/–½©€$£¥&

Abstract is a typeface of seven weights plus *Italics*: Thin, *Thin Italic*, Light, *Light Italic*, Regular, *Italic*, Medium, *Medium Italic*, **Semi Bold**, ***Semi Bold Italic***, **Bold**, ***Bold Italic***, **Black**, ***and Black Italic***


→ P. 454, 459

I wish
I knew
how to
quit → @ you!

Jake
GYL
LENN
haal

↘ BROKEBACK
MOUNTAIN
(2001)

1980

Acherus Grotesque is inspired by *Brandon Grotesque* and *Gotham* fonts. It is mostly designed for headlines and posters.

**Design:** 2020, Ufuk Aracıoğlu → p. 472

**Foundry:** Horizon Type Foundry, Turkey, horizontype.com → p. 489

**Language support:** Latin Extended, Cyrillic, Greek

**OpenType features:** Proportional Oldstyle, Proportional Lining, Tabular Oldstyle, Proportional Lining, Standard Ligatures, Discretionary Ligatures, Fractions, Numerator, Denominator, Stylistic Alternates, Stylistic Sets, Superscript, Subscript

**Test version available:** Yes

**Web font format available:** Yes

→ P. 448, 459

abcdefghijklmnopqrstuvwxyzæfjåçéñöûß
ABCDEFGHIJKLMNOPQRSTUVWXYZÆÇØ
1234567890@.,!?')]§*“”»«/–½©€$£¥&↔

абвгдеёжзийклмнопрстуфхцчшщъыьэюя
АБВГДЕЁЖЗИЙКЛМНОПРСТУФХЦЧШЩЪЫЬЭЮЯ
1234567890@.,!?')]§*“”»«/–½©€$£¥&↗

Acherus Grotesque is a typeface of ten weights plus *Italics:* Thin, *Thin Italic,* Extra Light, *Extra Light Italic,* Light, *Light Italic,* Book, *Book Italic,* Regular, *Italic,* **Medium, *Medium Italic,* Semi Bold, *Semi Bold Italic,* Bold, *Bold Italic,* Extra Bold, *Extra Bold Italic,* Black, *and Black Italic***

MARCH 9TH, 1979
GUATEMALA CITY, *GUATEMALA*

# Óscar
# Isaac
# Hernández
# Estrada

**Adapter PE**

Adapter PE is a universal sans serif typeface with contemporary aesthetics—a straightforward typeface that is easy to use for a wide range of design genres. Two size-specific variants, Text and Display, come together in a type system that packs a wide range of weights and even the duplexed Italics into a single, lightweight variable font. The extended *Adapter PE World* collection currently supports Arabic, Cyrillic, Greek, Hebrew, and Latin scripts and it is determined to grow.

**Design:** 2019, William Montrose → p. 480, Sláva Jevčinová → p. 477

**Foundry:** Rosetta Type Foundry, Czech Republic, rosettatype.com → p. 491

**Language support:** Latin Extended, Cyrillic, Greek

**OpenType features:** Tabular Lining, Proportional Lining, All Caps, Superscript, Subscript, Ordinals, Fractions, Numerator, Denominator, Ornaments, Arrows, Stylistic Alternates, Stylistic Sets, Slashed Zero, Localized Forms, Case Sensitive Forms, Font Variations

**Test version available:** Yes

**Web font format available:** Yes

abcdefghijklmnopqrstuvwxyzæåçéñöûß
ABCDEFGHIJKLMNOPQRSTUVWXYZÆÇØẞ
12345678900@.,!?')]§*“”»«/–½©€$£¥&⇢❄

αβγδεζηθικλμνξοπρσςτυφχψωάέήίόώϊϋΰ
ΑΒΓΔΕΖΗΘΙΚΛΜΝΞΟΠΡΣΤΥΦΧΨΩΆΈΉΊΌΏΪΫ
12345678900@.,!?')]§*“”»«/–½©€$£¥&⇠❦

Adapter PE is a family of two styles: Display and Text. Text in seven weights plus *Italics:* Text Extra Light, *Text Extra Light Italic,* Text Light, *Text Light Italic,* Text Regular, *Text Italic,* Text Medium, *Text Medium Italic,* **Text Semi Bold,** ***Text Semi Bold Italic,*** **Text Bold,** ***Text Bold Italic,*** **Extra Bold, and** ***Extra Bold Italic.*** Display in nine weights plus *Italics:* Display Thin, *Display Thin Italic,* Display Extra Light, *Display Extra Light Italic,* Display Light, *Display Light Italic,* Display Regular, *Display Italic,* Display Medium, *Display Medium Italic,* **Display Semi Bold,** ***Display Semi Bold Italic,*** **Display Bold,** ***Display Bold Italic,*** **Display Extra Bold,** ***Display Extra Bold Italic,*** **Display Black,** ***and Display Black Italic***

→ P. 448, 459

{Some of the *greatest*
*Georgian films* through 110 years of
Georgian film-history}

ბროწეულის ფერი (1969)

იყო შაშვი მგალობელი (1970)

მანდარინები (2013)

**Adelle Sans Georgian**

As is typical with TypeTogether typefaces, the most demanding editorial design problems were taken into consideration when creating Adelle Sans Georgian, designed by Jan Charvát and Akaki Radmadze. The combination of lively character and unobtrusive appearance inherent to grotesque Sans Serifs make it an utterly versatile tool for every imaginable situation. Whether for branding, signage, editorial, or advertising, the keyword behind Adelle Sans Georgian's use is flexibility.

**Design:** 2021, Akaki Razmadze → p. 481, Jan Charvát → p. 473, Veronika Burian → p. 473, José Scaglione → p. 482

**Foundry:** TypeTogether, Czech Republic, type-together.com → p. 492

**Language support:** Latin, Georgian

**OpenType features:** Proportional Oldstyle, Tabular Lining, Proportional Lining, Tabular Oldstyle, Standard Ligatures, All Caps, Small Caps, Capitals to Small Caps, Superscript, Subscript, Ordinals, Contextual Alternates, Fractions, Alternative Fractions, Numerator, Denominator, Ornaments, Arrows, Stylistic Alternates, Stylistic Sets, Historical Forms, Slashed Zero, Localized Forms, Case Sensitive Forms

**Test version available:** Yes

**Web font format available:** Yes

abcdefghijklmnopqrstuvwxyzæfjåçéñöûß
ABCDEFGHIJKLMNOPQRSTUVWXYZÆÇØẞ
12345678900@.,!?')]§*""»«/–½©€$£¥&➡❤

აბგდევზთიკლმნოპჟრსტუფქღყშჩცძწჭხჯჰ
ჱჲჳჴჵჶჷჸჹჺᲐᲑᲒᲓᲔᲕᲖᲗᲘᲙᲚᲛᲜᲝᲞᲟᲠᲡᲢᲣᲤᲥ
ᲦᲧᲨᲩᲪᲫᲬᲭᲮᲯᲰᲱᲲᲳᲴᲵᲶᲷᲸᲹᲺ₾ჼ჻

Adelle Sans Georgian is a typeface of seven weights plus *Italics:* Thin, *Thin Italic,* Light, *Light Italic,* Regular, *Italic,* **Semi Bold,** ***Semi Bold Italic,*** **Bold,** ***Bold Italic,*** **Extra Bold,** ***Extra Bold Italic,*** **Heavy,** ***and Heavy Italic***

# אני מעדיפה להיות חכמה מאשר להיות כוכבת קולנוע.

NATALIE PORTMAN

**נטלי פורטמן**

# I'd rather be smart than a movie star.

Adelle Sans Hebrew is Liron Lavi Turkenich's translation of the Latin forms into the voice of more than nine million people. The combination of lively characters and unobtrusive appearance inherent to grotesque Sans Serifs make it an utterly versatile tool for every imaginable situation. Whether for branding, signage, editorial, or advertising, the keyword behind Adelle Sans Hebrew's use is flexibility.

**Design:** 2021, Liron Lavi Turkenich → p. 478, Veronika Burian → p. 473, José Scaglione → p. 482

**Foundry:** TypeTogether, Czech Republic, type-together.com → p. 492

**Language support:** Latin, Hebrew

**OpenType features:** Proportional Oldstyle, Tabular Lining, Proportional Lining, Tabular Oldstyle, Standard Ligatures, Discretionary Ligatures, All Caps, Small Caps, Capitals to Small Caps, Superscript Subscript, Ordinals, Contextual Alternates, Fractions, Alternative Fractions, Numerator, Denominator, Ornaments, Arrows, Stylistic Alternates, Stylistic Sets, Historical Forms, Slashed Zero, Localized Forms, Case Sensitive Forms, Mark Positioning

**Test version available:** Yes

**Web font format available:** Yes

abcdefghijklmnopqrstuvwxyzæfjåçéñöûß
ABCDEFGHIJKLMNOPQRSTUVWXYZÆÇØẞ
1234567890Ø@.,!?')]§*""»«/–½©€$£¥&

אבגדהוזחטיכךלמםנןסעפףצץקרשת
1234567890Ø₪ ־ ׳ ״ | @.,-:;!?')]§*"" «»/–€$&

Adelle Sans Hebrew is a typeface of seven weights: Thin, Light, Regular, **Semi Bold, Bold, Extra Bold, and Heavy**

→ P. 448

**YOU DON'T GET TO 500 MILLION FRIENDS**

ເຈົ້າບໍ່ສາມາດ-
ໄປຫາໝູ່ ໕໐໐
ລ້ານໄດ້ໂດຍບໍ່
ຕ້ອງສ້າງສັດຕູ
ໜ້ອຍໜຶ່ງ.

**WITHOUT MAKING A FEW ENEMIES**

Adelle Sans Lao

Adelle Sans Lao, designed by Suppakit Chalermlarp, was expected to handle the most demanding editorial design problems. This led to the modern and simplified design that combines the lively character and unobtrusive appearance inherent to grotesque sans serifs to make it an utterly versatile tool for every imaginable situation. Whether for branding, signage, editorial, or advertising, the keyword behind Adelle Sans Lao's use is flexibility.

**Design:** 2021, Suppakit Chalermlarp → p. 473, Veronika Burian → p. 473, José Scaglione → p. 482

**Foundry:** TypeTogether, Czech Republic, type-together.com → p. 492

**Language support:** Latin, Lao

**OpenType features:** Proportional Oldstyle, Tabular Lining, Proportional Lining, Tabular Oldstyle, Standard Ligatures, All Caps, Small Caps, Capitals to Small Caps, Superscript, Subscript, Ordinals, Contextual Alternates, Fractions, Alternative Fractions, Numerator, Denominator, Ornaments, Arrows, Stylistic Alternates, Stylistic Sets, Historical Forms, Slashed Zero, Localized Forms, Case Sensitive Forms, Mark Positioning

**Test version available:** Yes

**Web font format available:** Yes

→ P. 448

abcdefghijklmnopqrstuvwxyzæfjåçéñöûß
ABCDEFGHIJKLMNOPQRSTUVWXYZÆÇØẞ
12345678900@.,!?')]§*""»«/–½©€$£¥&

ກຂຄງຈສຊຍດຕຖທນບປຜຝພຟມຢຣລວຫ
ອຮຫຍຽະຳແແໂໄ ໆຯ₭ໜໝ
໐໑໒໓໔໕໖໗໘໙

Adelle Sans Lao is a typeface of seven weights: Thin, Light, Regular, **Semi Bold, Bold, Extra Bold, and Heavy**

John Thaw & Kevin Whately

# «Инспе́ктор Морс»
# Inspector MORSE

BY COLIN DEXTER

{1987–2000}

Θжff*ß

Adelphi PE

Adelphi PE is an approachable geometric Sans Serif influenced by the British modernist tradition. The contemporary, comprehensive, and durable type system comes with a pragmatic set of features including a wide array of weights and "duplex Italics." Variable extenders go from tall and flat in Adelphi PE Text to short and sharp in Adelphi PE Display, with default Adelphi PE standing midway between these two extremes.

**Design:** 2019, Nick Job → p. 477

**Foundry:** Rosetta Type Foundry, Czech Republic, rosettatype.com → p. 491

**Language support:** Latin Extended, Cyrillic, Greek

**OpenType features:** Tabular Lining, Proportional Lining, Standard Ligatures, All Caps, Small Caps, Capitals to Small Caps, Superscript, Subscript, Ordinals, Fractions, Alternative Fractions, Numerator, Denominator, Arrows, Stylistic Alternates, Stylistic Sets, Slashed Zero, Localized Forms, Case Sensitive Forms, Required Ligatures, Font Variations

**Test version available:** Yes

**Web font format available:** Yes

→ P. 448, 459

abcdefghijklmnopqrstuvwxyzæffåçéñöûß
ABCDEFGHIJKLMNOPQRSTUVWXYZÆÇØẞ
12345678900@.,!?')]§*""»«/–½©€$£¥&→

αβγδεζηθικλμνξοπρσςτυφχψωάέήίόώϊϋΰ
ΑΒΓΔΕΖΗΘΙΚΛΜΝΞΟΠΡΣΤΥΦΧΨΩΆΈΉΊΌΏΪΫ
12345678900@.,!?')]§*""»«/–½©€$£¥&↗

Adelphi PE is a family of three styles: Normal, Display, and Text, each in eight weights plus *Italics:* Thin, *Thin Italic,* Light, *Light Italic,* **Medium,** ***Medium Italic,*** **Extra Bold,** ***Extra Bold Italic,*** Display Extra Light, *Display Extra Light Italic,* Display Regular, *Display Italic,* **Display Bold,** ***Display Bold Italic,*** **Display Black,** ***Display Black Italic,*** Text Thin, *Text Thin Italic,* Text Light, *Text Light Italic,* **Text Medium,** ***Text Medium Italic,*** **Text Extra Bold,** ***and Text Extra Bold Italic***

TAKE
ME OUT
TO THE
BALL
GAME!

@1949&

ADS Display

ADS Display is a custom typeface for Artdeshine Official.

**Design:** 2022, Jiahui Tan → p. 483, Aditya Wiraatmaja → p. 484

**Foundry:** Fable Type Foundry, Singapore, fable.design/typefaces → p. 488

**Language support:** Latin

**OpenType features:** Stylistic Alternates

**Test version available:** No

**Web font format available:** No



abcdefghijklmnopqrstuvwxyz
ABCDEFGHIJKLMNOPQRSTUVWXYZ
1234567890@.,!?)]*/–©€$£¥&

ADS Display is a typeface of one Regular weight

→ P. 459, 469

0 1 2 3 4 5 6 7 8 9 ?

Space
Jam
!

x k K g

a b d

1996, 1h28min.

Aerobik

Aerobik is a display typeface with unique bouncing aesthetics made of outlines that do not match any existing typographic style. It refers as much to graffiti in some aspects as to the way motion and speed are represented in comic books. Conceived to be used with lower case or capital letters, it turns out to be surprisingly readable in both ways.

**Design:** 2020, Johan Mossé → p. 480, Quentin Berthelot → p. 481

**Foundry:** Lift Type, France, lift-type.fr → p. 490

**Language support:** Latin Extended

**OpenType features:** Standard Ligatures, Stylistic Alternates

**Test version available:** Yes

**Web font format available:** No

abcdefghijklmnopqrstuvwxyzæßjåçéñöž

ABCDEFGHIJKLMNOPQRSTUVWXYZÆÇØ

1234567890@.,!?')]*"”»«/-©€$£¥&

Aerobik is a typeface of one Regular weight

→ P. 459

# Ghazal Al Banat

**[1949]**

×

# AL-IRHAB WAL KABAB

# TERROR & KEBAB

{1993}

×

# Al-Mummia

**(1969)**

Afronaut & Yalla

Afronaut & Yalla—a family of two totally different styles, which were both inspired by vernacular Latin and Arabic typography from the Sahel region and Cairo. The vast array of strong Arabic headline type, geometric forms working in interesting ways, and contrasting with smooth, calligraphic details fed the design

**Design:** 2020, Mateusz Machalski → p. 479

**Foundry:** MACHALSKI.WTF, Poland, CAPITALICS.wtf → p. 490

**Language support:** Latin

**OpenType features:** Tabular Lining, Standard Ligatures, Discretionary Ligatures, All Caps, Superscript, Subscript, Ordinals, Numerator, Denominator, Arrows, Stylistic Alternates, Mark Positioning

**Test version available:** Yes

**Web font format available:** Yes

→ P. 459

abcdefghijklmnopqrstuvwxyzæffåçéñûß
ABCDEFGHIJKLMNOPQRSTUVWXYZÆÇØ
1234567890Ø@.,!?')]§*“”»«/–½©€$£¥&

Afronaut is a family of two styles: Normal and **Yalla**

→ **Gone with the Wind, 1939**

{ }

# Frankly, my dear, *I don't give a damn.*

HISTORICAL ROMANCE FILM

| | |
|---|---|
| **Scarlett O'Hara** | *(Vivien Leigh)* |
| **Ashley Wilkes** | *(Leslie Howard)* |
| **Melanie Hamilton** | *(Olivia de Havilland)* |
| **Rhett Butler** | *(Clark Gable)* |

Aktuell is a typographic performer: an efficient design featuring short ascenders and descenders, most suitable for composing compact text columns. Aktuell evokes a rather strict demeanor. To some, it may appear cold or rigid even, but its design is nothing but contemporary, reliable, and determined. Take a closer look at its screen typography—not books—and you will envision Aktuell excelling. Its evenness of color and legibility in space-conscious environments are hard to beat.

**Design:** 2020, Thomas Thiemich → p. 483

**Foundry:** TYPE BY, Belgium, typeby.com → p. 492

**Language support:** Latin Extended

**OpenType features:** Proportional Oldstyle, Tabular Lining, Proportional Lining, Tabular Oldstyle, Standard Ligatures, Discretionary Ligatures, All Caps, Superscript, Subscript, Ordinals, All Alternates, Contextual Alternates, Fractions, Numerator, Denominator, Arrows, Stylistic Alternates, Stylistic Sets, Historical Forms, Slashed Zero, Localized Forms, Case Sensitive Forms

**Test version available:** No

**Web font format available:** Yes

→ P. 454

abcdefghijklmnopqrstuvwxyzæfjåçéñöûß
ABCDEFGHIJKLMNOPQRSTUVWXYZÆÇØẞ
1234567890 0@.,!?')]§*""»«/–½©€$£¥&→

Aktuell is a typeface of five weights plus *Italics:* Blond, *Blond Italic,* Normal, *Normal Italic,* **Medium,** ***Medium Italic,*** **Semi Bold,** ***Semi Bold Italic,*** **Bold,** ***and Bold Italic***

***THIS IS THE WAY!***
THE MANDALORIAN
***suitable!***
versatile!
**determined!**
*angular!*
straightforward!

Albula Pro

Inspired by geometry and enhanced with unique form details, the shapes of Albula Pro are optically corrected to ensure an excellent reading experience and broad professional use. Albula Pro is an ideal choice to make your design and layout stand out. It performs perfectly in the headlines as well as for branding purposes. When designing Albula Pro, great importance was attached to legibility, so that a good reading experience is guaranteed regardless of the text length.

**Design:** 2021, Silvio Meier → p. 479

**Foundry:** Serpentype, Switzerland, serpentype.com → p. 491

**Language support:** Latin Extended

**OpenType features:** Proportional Oldstyle, Tabular Lining, Proportional Lining, Tabular Oldstyle, Standard Ligatures, Discretionary Ligatures, Superscript, Subscript, Fractions, Numerator, Denominator, Arrows, Stylistic Alternates, Stylistic Sets, Case Sensitive Forms

**Test version available:** Yes

**Web font format available:** Yes

→ P. 448

abcdefghijklmnopqrstuvwxyzæctåçéñöûß
ABCDEFGHIJKLMNOPQRSTUVWXYZÆÇØß
1234567890@.,!?')]§*""»«/-½©€$£¥&←

Albula Pro is a typeface of nine weights plus *Obliques*: Thin, *Thin Oblique*, Extra Light, *Extra Light Oblique*, Light, *Light Oblique*, Semi Light, *Semi Light Oblique*, Regular, *Oblique*, Medium, *Medium Oblique*, **Semi Bold**, ***Semi Bold Oblique***, **Bold**, ***Bold Oblique***, **Extra Bold**, ***and Extra Bold Oblique***

# Richie Finestra — Vinyl

"Less artists means less need to kiss the asses of those artists."

↘ premiered February 14th, 2016, concluded on April 17th, 2016.

♥ ¶

In 2010, Thomas Huot-Marchand and SPMillot were asked to develop the typographic identity of the Musée d'Orsay that had been based on Berthold Walbaum since its very beginnings. They proposed adding distant "cousins" in later typographic styles: a bold Grotesque and a thin Slab Serif. In 2020, Thomas Huot-Marchand decided to redesign them while developing an extended family. Album is a subtraction of *Walbaum:* with no serifs for Album Sans and with no contrast for Album Slab.

**Design:** 2021, Thomas Huot-Marchand → p. 477

**Foundry:** 205TF, France, 205.tf → p. 488

**Language support:** Latin Extended

**OpenType features:** Proportional Oldstyle, Tabular Lining, Proportional Lining, Tabular Oldstyle, Standard Ligatures, All Caps, Small Caps, Capitals to Small Caps, Superscript, Subscript, Ordinals, Contextual Alternates, Fractions, Numerator, Denominator, Ornaments, Arrows, Stylistic Sets, Slashed Zero, Localized Forms, Case Sensitive Forms

**Test version available:** Yes

**Web font format available:** Yes

abcdefghijklmnopqrstuvwxyzæfiåçéñöûß
ABCDEFGHIJKLMNOPQRSTUVWXYZÆÇß
1234567890Ø@.,!?')]§*""»«/–½©€$£¥&↗♥

Album is a family of two styles: Sans and Slab. Sans in eight weights plus *Italics:* Extra Light, *Extra Light Italic,* Light, *Light Italic,* Regular, *Italic,* **Book,** ***Book Italic,*** **Semi Bold,** ***Semi Bold Italic,*** **Bold,** ***Bold Italic,*** **Extra Bold,** ***Extra Bold Italic,*** **Black,** ***and Black Italic.*** Slab in three weights: Extra Light, Light, and Regular

→ P. 448, 458

c’est **NEO**

~1900

MEDITER-

RANEAN

– 1920

CLASSIC &

***DECO***

TR Aloma

TR Aloma is a type family intended for both text and display purposes. It is inspired on *Aloma* novel written by Catalan writer Mercè Rodoreda and published in Barcelona in 1938. The first ideas for the design were based on Deco magazine headlines and lettering and on the ideas behind Catalan Noucentisme movement. TR Aloma has a neoclassical flavor with classical Roman proportions that make it especially beautiful for headlines and short introductory texts.

**Design:** 2020, Andreu Balius → p. 472

**Foundry:** Typerepublic, Spain, typerepublic.com → p. 492

**Language support:** Latin Extended

**OpenType features:** Proportional Lining, Standard Ligatures, Discretionary Ligatures, Ordinals, Historical Forms, Slashed Zero, Localized Forms, Case Sensitive Forms, Required Ligatures

**Test version available:** Yes

**Web font format available:** Yes

→ P. 454, 459

abcdefghijklmnopqrstuvwxyzæfjåçéñöûß
ABCDEFGHIJKLMNOPQRSTUVWXYZÆÇØẞ
12345678900@.,!?’)]§*“”»«/–©€$£¥&

TR Aloma is a typeface of five weights plus *Italics:* Thin, *Thin Italic,* Light, *Light Italic,* Regular, *Italic,* **Semi Bold,** ***Semi Bold Italic,*** **Bold,** ***and Bold Italic***

αṋtȭ̰nɪ̭ɒ

# Mary Louise *"Meryl"* Streep

**BORN** June 22nd, 1949

Antonia

Antonia is an original type family of 46 fonts, seven weights, and four optical sizes. Born in the middle of the Alps, Antonia is as modern as it is down to earth. The multi-variant package includes text, display, and italic styles, looking crisp and perfect in all sizes and applications. Antonia is also available in a variable font format.

**Design:** 2019, Michael Hochleitner → p. 476, Franziska Weitgruber → p. 484

**Foundry:** Typejockeys, Austria, typejockeys.com → p. 492

**Language support:** Latin Extended, Teuthonista

**OpenType features:** Proportional Oldstyle, Tabular Lining, Proportional Lining, All Caps, Small Caps, Capitals to Small Caps, Superscript, Subscript, Ordinals, Contextual Alternates, Fractions, Numerator, Denominator, Arrows, Localized Forms, Optical size, Font Variations

**Test version available:** Yes

**Web font format available:** Yes

→ P. 454

abcdefghijklmnopqrstuvwxyzættåçéñöûß
ABCDEFGHIJKLMNOPQRSTUVWXYZÆÇØẞ
1234567890@.,!?')]§*“”»«/–½©€$£¥&↓❣

Antonia is a family of four styles: H1, H2, H3, and **Text.** H1 in seven weights plus *Italics:* H1 Light, *H1 Light Italic,* H1 Regular, *H1 Italic,* H1 Medium, ***H1 Medium Italic,*** **H1 Semi Bold,** ***H1 Semi Bold Italic,*** **H1 Bold,** ***H1 Bold Italic,*** **H1 Heavy,** ***H1 Heavy Italic,*** **H1 Black, *and H1 Black Italic.*** H2 and H3 in six weights plus *Italics:* H2 Light, *H2 Light Italic,* H2 Regular, *H2 Italic,* H2 Medium, *H2 Medium Italic,* **H2 Semi Bold,** ***H2 Semi Bold Italic,*** **H2 Bold,** ***H2 Bold Italic,*** **H2 Heavy,** ***H2 Heavy Italic,*** H3 Light, *H3 Light Italic,* H3 Regular, *H3 Italic,* H3 Medium, ***H3 Medium Italic,*** **H3 Semi Bold,** ***H3 Semi Bold Italic,*** **H3 Bold,** ***H3 Bold Italic,*** **H3 Heavy, *and H3 Heavy Italic.*** Text in four weights plus *Italics:* Text Regular, *Text Italic,* Text Medium, *Text Medium Italic,* **Text Semi Bold,** ***Text Semi Bold Italic,*** **Text Bold, *and Text Bold Italic***

デザイン思考で
世界を変える

サステナブルな暮らし

# 経済

# 地域

# 医療

みんなで作る社会

Digital Media & Technology

東経135度

**Aoto Gothic**

Aoto Gothic is a text sans serif typeface developed for use on screen. Its slightly modern style, simple and clean structure, and smaller letter face enable it to create a different expression from that of conventional modern Sans Serifs such as universal design types. The Latin alphabet of Aoto Gothic is based on *Sharoa Pro,* Italics are also provided.

**Design:** 2021, Masaru Kimura
→ p. 477

**Foundry:** Morisawa.Inc, Japan, morisawa.co.jp → p. 490

**Language support:** Latin, Japanese

**OpenType features:** Full Width, Half Width, Proportional Width, Traditional Forms, Vertical Writing, Vertical Alternates and Rotation

**Test version available:** No

**Web font format available:** Yes

→ P. 448

abcdefghijklmnopqrstuvwxyzæåçéñöûß
ABCDEFGHIJKLMNOPQRSTUVWXYZÆÇØ
12345678900@.,!?')]§*“”»«/–½©€$£¥&⇩☂

あいうえおかきくけこサシスセソタチツテト
永東愛国大見今糸力北心南西女分文父母子衣花
12345678900@.,!?')]§*“”»«/–½©€$£¥&⇔☃

Aoto Gothic is a typeface of seven weights: Extra Light, Light, Regular, Medium, Demi Bold, **Bold, and Extra Bold**

Big №1!

Mała

Great

Duża

Epic

Ah

→ P. 459, 467

Many calligraphic fonts follow precise and structured methods and Apice is no exception—although Apice is a totally different species when it comes to script typefaces. With a very rigid and structured design, Apice introduces itself as a single variable font that contains five pre-built optical sizes.

**Design:** 2022, Dino dos Santos → p. 482, Pedro Leal → p. 478

**Foundry:** DSType Foundry, Portugal, dstype.com → p. 488

**Language support:** Latin Extended

**OpenType features:** Proportional Oldstyle, Tabular Lining, Proportional Lining, Tabular Oldstyle, Standard Ligatures, Superscript, Subscript, Ordinals, Contextual Alternates, Fractions, Numerator, Denominator, Ornaments, Arrows, Stylistic Alternates, Stylistic Sets, Historical Forms, Slashed Zero, Localized Forms, Case Sensitive Forms, Terminal Form, Isolated Form, Optical size, Font Variations

**Test version available:** Yes

**Web font format available:** Yes

*a b c d e f g h i j k l m n o p q r s t u v w x y z æ ﬂ å ç é ñ ö û ß*

*A B C D E F G H I J K L M N O P Q R S T U V W X Y Z*

*1 2 3 4 5 6 7 8 9 0 0 @ . , ! ? ' ) ] § * " " » « / – ½ © € $ £ ¥ & ☆*

*Apice is a typeface of five weights: Small, Medium, Big, Colossal, and Epic*

William Wyler's
PRODUCTION OF
Sidney Kingsley's

# »DE« TEC TIVE STORY

&

Arsenica

The design of Arsenica takes its inspiration from Italian poster design from the beginning of the century, a time where typography, lettering, and illustration were closely interwoven. Dawning nationalist movements, rather than using the modernist language, Arsenica pushed on traditional old-style letterforms often imbued with Art Nouveau and Deco sensibility.

**Design:** 2021, Francesco Canovaro → p. 473

**Foundry:** Zetafonts, Italy, zetafonts.com → p. 492

**Language support:** Latin, Cyrillic

**OpenType features:** Proportional Oldstyle, Tabular Lining, Proportional Lining, Tabular Oldstyle, Standard Ligatures, Ordinals, Arrows, Stylistic Alternates, Stylistic Sets, Slashed Zero, Localized Forms, Mark Positioning, Optical size, Font Variations

**Test version available:** Yes

**Web font format available:** Yes

→ P. 454, 459

abcdefghijklmnopqrstuvwxyzæfjåçéñöûß
ABCDEFGHIJKLMNOPQRSTUVWXYZÆÇØß
1234567890Ø@.,!?')]§*""»«/–©€$£¥&↑

абвгдеёжзийклмнопрстуфхцчшщъыьэюя
АБВГДЕЁЖЗИЙКЛМНОПРСТУФХЦЧШЩЪЫЬЭЮЯ
1234567890Ø@.,!?')]§*""»«/–©€$£¥&

Arsenica is a family of four styles: Alt, Normal, Antiqua, and Text. Alt in seven weights: Alt Thin, Alt Light, Alt Regular, **Alt Medium, Alt Demi Bold, Alt Bold, and Alt Extra Bold.** Normal and Antiqua in seven weights plus *Italics:* Thin, *Thin Italic,* Light, *Light Italic,* Regular, *Italic,* Medium, ***Medium Italic,*** **Demi Bold, *Demi Bold Italic,* Bold, *Bold Italic,* Extra Bold, *Extra Bold Italic,*** Antiqua Thin, *Antiqua Thin Italic,* Antiqua Light, *Antiqua Light Italic,* Antiqua Regular, *Antiqua Italic,* Antiqua Medium, ***Antiqua Medium Italic,*** **Antiqua Demi Bold, *Antiqua Demi Bold Italic,* Antiqua Bold, *Antiqua Bold Italic,* Antiqua Extra Bold, *and Antiqua Extra Bold Italic.*** Text in four weights plus *Italics:* Light, *Light Italic,* Regular, *Italic,* **Bold, *and Bold Italic***

"I must go back to Asgard, but I give you my word.
*I will return for you.*"

# THOR
# DEAL?
# JANE:
# DEAL!

Dynamic and expressive, Asgard is a superfamily that manages to look brutal and refined at the same time. It gives a full range of options for typesetting, with the Normal and Fit widths providing basic display and text-sized alternatives, and the Wide width adding more display and titling options. The inclusion of backslanted italic styles gives Asgard an extra chance to add its voice to the typographic palette.

**Design:** 2021, Francesco Canovaro → p. 473

**Foundry:** Zetafonts, Italy, zetafonts.com → p. 492

**Language support:** Latin Extended, Cyrillic, Greek

**OpenType features:** Proportional Oldstyle, Tabular Lining, Proportional Lining, Tabular Oldstyle, Standard Ligatures, Discretionary Ligatures, Small Caps, Superscript, Subscript, Ordinals, Fractions, Numerator, Denominator, Stylistic Sets, Slashed Zero, Alternate Annotation, Case Sensitive Forms

**Test version available:** Yes

**Web font format available:** Yes

→ P. 448, 459

abcdefghijklmnopqrstuvwxyzæfiåçéñöûß
ABCDEFGHIJKLMNOPQRSTUVWXYZÆÇØẞ
12345678900@.,!?')]§*""»«/–½©€$£¥&↓

абвгдеёжзийклмнопрстуфхцчшщъыьэюя
АБВГДЕЁЖЗИИКЛМНОПРСТУФХЦЧШЩЪЫЬЭЮЯ
12345678900⓪@.,!?')]§*""»«/–½©€$£¥&↔

Asgard is a family of three widths: Normal, Fit, and Wide, each in eight weights plus *Italics and* Backslanteds: Thin, Thin Backslanted, *Thin Italic,* Extra Light, Extra Light Backslanted, *Extra Light Italic,* Light, Light Backslanted, *Fit Light Italic,* Fit Regular, Fit Backslanted, *Fit Italic,* **Fit Medium, Fit Medium Backslanted,** ***Fit Medium Italic,*** **Fit Bold, Wide Bold Backslanted,** ***Wide Bold Italic,*** **Wide Extra Bold, Wide Extra Bold Backslanted,** ***Wide Extra Bold Italic,*** **Wide Fat, Wide Fat Backslanted,** ***and Wide Fat Italic***

# Saturday Fiction

# 兰心大剧院

— 2019
Romance / War

# Crouching Tiger, Hidden Dragon

— 2000
Drama / Historical Fiction

# 卧虎藏龙

# Lust, Caution

# 色戒

— 2007
War / Drama

# The Last Emperor

— 1987
Biography / Drama

# 末代皇帝

# A City of Sadness

# 悲情城市

— 1989
Drama / War

Astronomer

Astronomer was initially commissioned for an exhibition about ancient Chinese astronomy. The inspiration comes from a star chart made in 1633 under the supervision of Xu Guangqi who was a scholar-bureaucrat, Catholic convert, agricultural scientist, astronomer, and mathematician in the Ming dynasty. It was an era of cultural hybridization—thus comes the concept of the font: hybridizing Chinese calligraphy and wood cut style with old-style Antiqua and metal type techniques, in a contemporary way.

**Design:** 2022, Zhiqian Li → p. 478

**Foundry:** 3type, China, 3type.cn → p. 488

**Language support:** Latin Extended, Chinese

**OpenType features:** Proportional Oldstyle, Tabular Lining, Proportional Lining, Tabular Oldstyle, Standard Ligatures, Discretionary Ligatures, All Caps, Small Caps, Capitals to Small Caps, Superscript, Subscript, Contextual Alternates, Contextual Ligatures, Fractions, Numerator, Denominator, Arrows, Stylistic Alternates, Stylistic Sets, Historical Forms

**Test version available:** Yes

**Web font format available:** Yes

→ P. 454

abcdefghijklmnopqrstuvwxyzæfjåçéñöûß
ABCDEFGHIJKLMNOPQRSTUVWXYZÆÇØ
12345678900@.,!?’)]§*“”»«/–©€$¥&

永迅兴一长米十土大古木甘夹皮来麦责真喜
中丫义希个令台父公谷山川向自立衣栾章赛
二冋日巨里昌马冒置豥要政摈炕犁纱畮黝耩

Astronomer is a typeface of one Regular weight

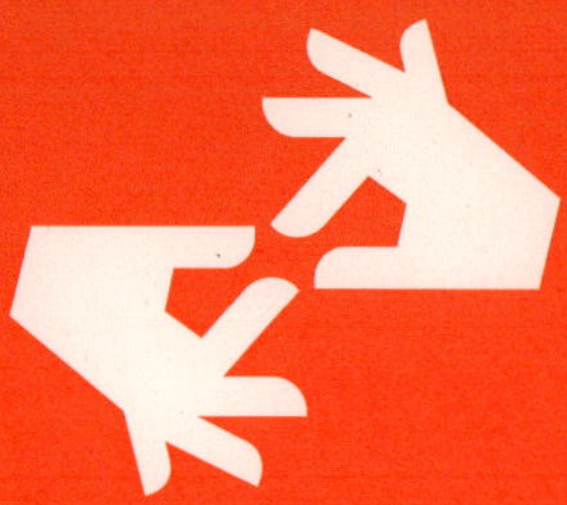

# 2005:

# Thank you

# FOR SMOKING!

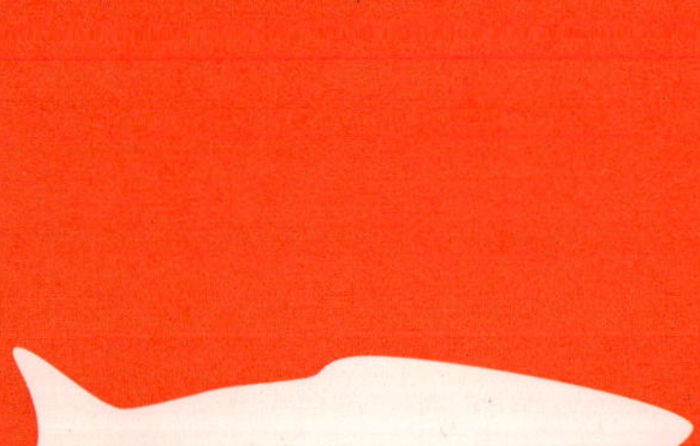

Working in the field of exhibition graphics, the designers of Atelier Brückner often faced the question as to whether a typeface is legible, accessible, offers a wide range of possibilities from display to running, and appropriate for an exhibition context and the different exhibition hierarchies. Consequently, they decided to create a variable sans serif grotesque typeface, dedicated to exhibition design and catering for all exhibition needs, from exhibition graphics and their hierarchies to digital Interactives.

**Design:** 2022, Sun Young Oh → p. 480, Rana Rmeily → p. 481

**Foundry:** Atelier Brueckner, Germany, atelier-brueckner.com → p. 488

**Language support:** Latin Extended

**OpenType features:** Standard Ligatures, Discretionary Ligatures, Ornaments, Arrows, Stylistic Alternates

**Test version available:** Yes

**Web font format available:** Yes

→ P. 448

abcdefghijklmnopqrstuvwxyzæfjåçéñöûß
ABCDEFGHIJKLMNOPQRSTUVWXYZÆÇØß
1234567890@.,!?')]§*"»«/–©€$£¥&↗

ATBT is a typeface of seven weights plus *Italics and Super Italics*: Thin, *Thin Italic, Thin Super Italic,* Light, *Light Italic, Light Super Italic,* Regular, *Italic, Super Italic,* **Medium, *Medium Italic, Medium Super Italic,*** **Bold, *Bold Italic, Bold Super Italic,*** **Heavy, *Heavy Italic, and Heavy Super Italic***

# STARDUST

TEGO LATA GWIAZDA SIĘ SFAŁSZOWAŁA. ROZPOCZYNA SIĘ POŚCIG.

# The Fairy Tale That Won’t Behave

**→ A faithful interpretation that captures the spirit of whimsy, action, and off-kilter humor of Neil Gaiman, Stardust juggles multiple genres and tones to create a fantastical experience.**

Avona Serif

Avona Serif began as an exploration into the essence of Carolingian calligraphy and was tamed into a serif typeface. It is constructed with wide, circular shapes, making it a unique choice for setting text in a landscape of more condensed forms. It was designed with the needs of game user interfaces in mind, particularly in the fantasy genre. It plays well with fantasy or medieval content, or can solidify a souvenir-esque 70's vibe.

**Design:** 2021, Alanna Munro → p. 480

**Foundry:** Alanna Munro Type Foundry, Canada, alannamunro.com → p. 488

**Language support:** Latin Extended

**OpenType features:** Proportional Oldstyle, Tabular Lining, Proportional Lining, Tabular Oldstyle, Standard Ligatures, Superscript, Subscript, Ordinals, Fractions, Arrows, Stylistic Sets, Localized Forms, Case Sensitive Forms, Mark Positioning

**Test version available:** Yes

**Web font format available:** Yes

→ P. 454

abcdefghijklmnopqrstuvwxyzæfjåçéñöûß
ABCDEFGHIJKLMNOPQRSTUVWXYZÆÇØß
1234567890@.,!?')]§*""»«/–½©€$£¥&↘

Avona Serif is a typeface of six weights: Light, Regular, Medium, **Semi Bold, Bold, and Black**

JOHANNA VON KOCZIAN

# AGATHA, LASS DAS MORDEN SEIN!

## LACHEN SIE HERZLICH MIT – ÜBER DIESEN »MORDSSPASS«

Babetta

Babetta was initially released in 2014 but got a major update in 2021, including Cyrillic language support. The inspiration for Babetta was an illuminated vintage shop sign of a famous bookstore in (East-)Berlin, called Karl-Marx-Buchhandlung. The aim was not to preserve the original lettering but to use it as a starting point for a typographical exploration. The slightly shabby historical original was kissed by an Italian Art Deco beauty and has blossomed into a new charming face.

**Design:** 2021, Viktor Nübel → p. 480

**Foundry:** Viktor Nübel, Germany, viktornuebel.com → p. 492

**Language support:** Latin, Cyrillic

**OpenType features:** Discretionary Ligatures, Superscript, Subscript, Ordinals, Fractions, Numerator, Denominator, Ornaments, Stylistic Alternates, Stylistic Sets, Localized Forms

**Test version available:** No

**Web font format available:** Yes

→ P. 448, 459

abcdefghijklmnopqrstuvwxyzæfjåçéñöůß
ABCDEFGHIJKLMNOPQRSTUVWXYZÆÇØß
1234567890@.,!?')]§*“”»«/–½©€$£¥&↗Б

абвгдеёжзийклмнопрстуфхцчшщъыьэюя
АБВГДЕЁЖЗИЙКЛМНОПРСТУФХЦЧШЩЪЫ
1234567890@.,!?')]§*“”»«/–½©€$£¥&

Babetta is a family of two styles: Neon and Normal. Neon in three weights: Neon Tube, **Neon, and Neon Case.** Normal in five weights: Thin, Light, Regular, **Medium, and Bold**

# Narcos

## Pablo Escobar

## 1949-1993

Javier Peña Steve Murphy

Gilberto Rodríguez Orejuela

## LOS PEPES

# El Señor

## VIVA COLOMBIA!

Bacalar

Bacalar is inspired by the vernacular typography found on “colectivo buses” used to transport people on the Yucatan peninsula (Mexico). Geometric forms contrast with very thin details and reversed contrast, thanks to which no one will pass by it indifferently. Bacalar consists of ten width styles, which were created by mechanical stretching—because of that, the whole family has a brutalist character.

**Design:** 2022, Mateusz Machalski → p. 479

**Foundry:** The Designers Foundry, New Zeland, thedesignersfoundry.com → p. 491

**Language support:** Latin

**OpenType features:** Tabular Lining, Proportional Lining, Standard Ligatures, Discretionary Ligatures, All Caps, Superscript, Subscript, Contextual Alternates, Arrows

**Test version available:** Yes

**Web font format available:** Yes

→ P. 459

abcdefghijklmnopqrstuvwxyzæœfjåçéñöûß
ABCDEFGHIJKLMNOPQRSTUVWXYZÆÇØẞ
1234567890@.,!?’)]§*“”»«/–©€$£¥&‡

Bacalar is a typeface of ten widths: Turbo Condensed, Ultra Condensed, Extra Condensed, Condensed, Normal, Semi Expanded, Expanded, Extra Expanded, Ultra Expanded, and Turbo Expanded

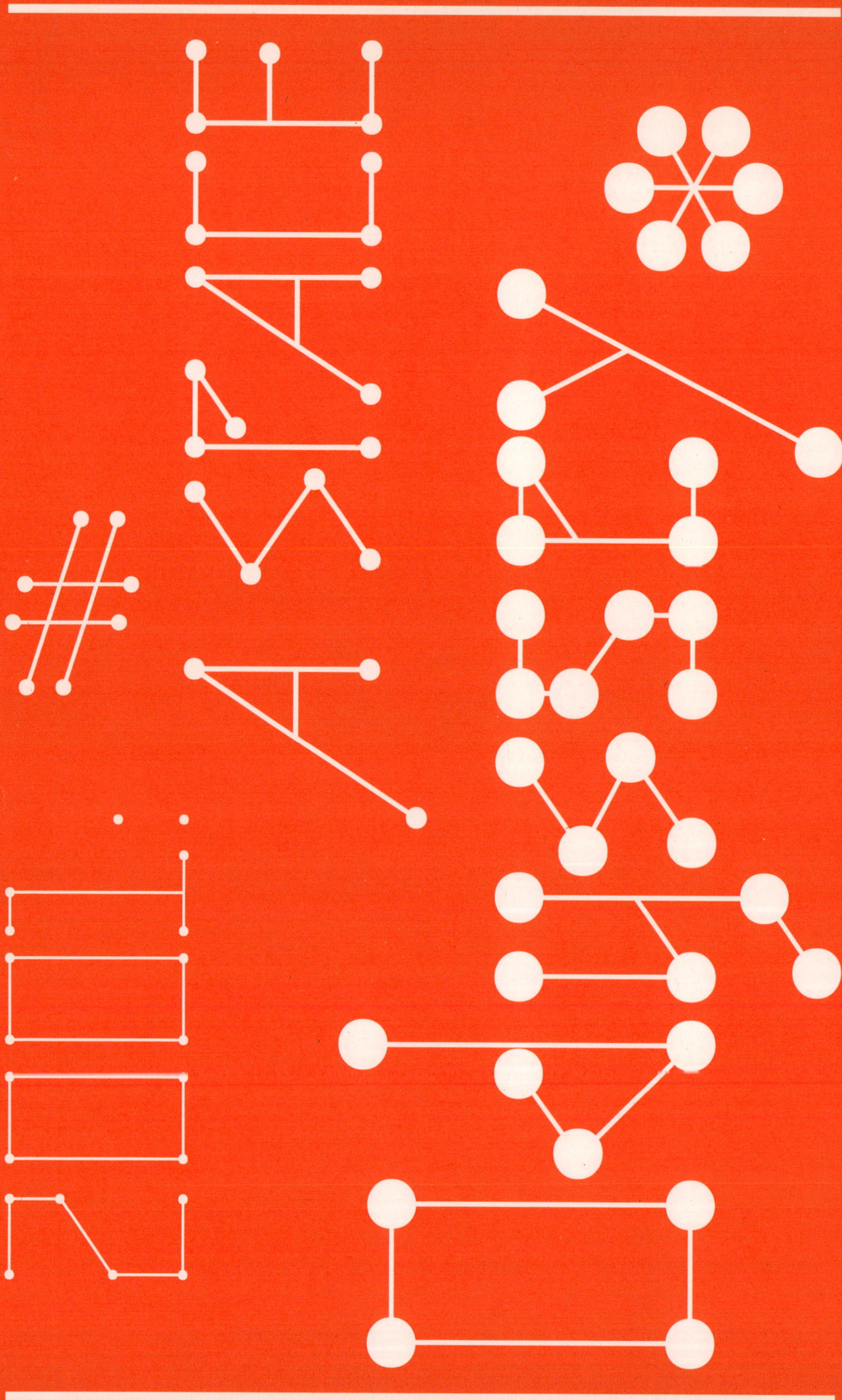


Bagatelle

This typeface is the simple idea of an alphabet constructed with rudimentary geometry, then taken to its extremes aesthetically and technologically. Its idea is rooted in decades-old designer debates about the merits of drawing letterforms with a ruler and a compass, adaptive morphing in variable font technologies, and overall basic transformational subtleties in typography.

**Design:** 2022, Patrick Griffin
→ p. 476

**Foundry:** Canada Type, Canada, canadatype.com → p. 488

**Language support:** Latin Extended, Cyrillic, Greek

**OpenType features:** Superscript, Subscript, Ordinals, Swashes, All Alternates, Contextual Alternates, Fractions, Numerator, Denominator Stylistic Alternates, Stylistic Sets, Historical Forms, Localized Forms, Unicase

**Test version available:** No

**Web font format available:** Yes

→ P. 459

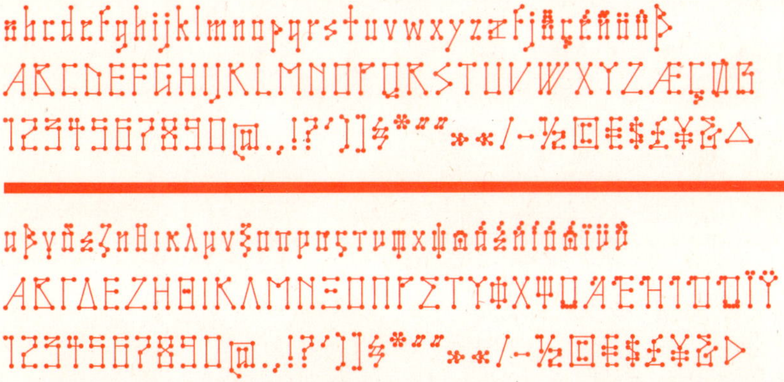

Bagatelle is a typeface of six weights: Thin, Light, Regular, Medium, Bold, and Heavy

# THE END OF THE EARTH WILL NOT BE THE END OF US!

[МЕЖЗВЕЗДНЫЙ]

Bajazzo

Bajazzo is a multi-weight all-around Sans Serif designed by Schriftlabor's Senior Type Designer Lisa Schultz. The early sketches for the letters were inspired by old opera playbills and small adverts found in Viennese newspapers from the 1930s. Bajazzo stands out given its multiple size optimization, making it a versatile font for smaller and big display sizes.

**Design:** 2022, Lisa Schultz
→ p. 482

**Foundry:** Schriftlabor, Austria, schriftlabor.at → p. 491

**Language support:** Latin, Cyrillic, Vietnamese

**OpenType features:** Proportional Oldstyle, Tabular Lining, Proportional Lining, Tabular Oldstyle, Standard Ligatures, Discretionary Ligatures, All Caps, Small Caps, Capitals to Small Caps, Superscript, Subscript, Ordinals, Contextual Alternates, Fractions, Numerator, Denominator, Arrows, Stylistic Alternates, Stylistic Sets, Slashed Zero, Localized Forms, Case Sensitive Forms

**Test version available:** Yes

**Web font format available:** Yes

abcdefghijklmnopqrstuvwxyzæåçéñöûß
ABCDEFGHIJKLMNOPQRSTUVWXYZÆÇØ
12345678900@.,!?')]§*“”»«/–½©€$£¥&↩✿

aăâbcdđeêghiklmnoôơpqrstuưvxyằẻổỵ
AĂÂBCDĐEÊGHIKLMNOÔƠPQRSTUƯVXY
12345678900@.,!?')]§*“”»«/–½©€$£¥&↔♡

Bajazzo is a typeface of three widths: Narrow, Normal, and Expanded, each in nine weights plus *Italics:* Narrow Thin, *Narrow Thin Italic,* Narrow Extra Light, *Narrow Extra Light Italic,* Narrow Light, *Narrow Light Italic,* Regular, *Italic,* Medium, ***Medium Italic,*** **Semi Bold,** ***Semi Bold Italic,*** **Bold,** ***Bold Italic,*** **Expanded Extra Bold,** ***Expanded Extra Bold Italic,*** **Expanded Black, *and Expanded Black Italic***

→ P. 448

**Seven Samurai** → [1954]

Ikiru {1952}☑

**Godzilla** → {50–118,5m high}

“**Годзилла** has turned the heart of Tokyo into a sea of fire.”– **STEVE** MARTIN // <u>Monster co-star(s):</u>

**KING KONG!** MECHAGODZILLA.

Ugetsu (1953){**≈¾**}

**Tokyo Drifter** → ☑ **(1966)**

Francesco Canovaro created Bakemono as a way to explore the design space around the duality of fixed/proportional width. He was also interested in the concept of mono-width design, inherent in monospaced typefaces, that can bring flexibility and ease of use also to proportional type—allowing you to change the weight of a word without losing the text alignment. In his research on fixed width type design, he mixed the lessons of mechanical typewriter technology with the intuitions of an eastern brush.

**Design:** 2021, Francesco Canovaro → p. 473

**Foundry:** Zetafonts, Italy, zetafonts.com → p. 492

**Language support:** Latin, Cyrillic

**OpenType features:** Proportional Oldstyle, Tabular Lining, Proportional Lining, Tabular Oldstyle, Superscript, Subscript, Ordinals, Fractions, Numerator, Denominator, Arrows, Stylistic Alternates, Stylistic Sets, Slashed Zero, Localized Forms, Case Sensitive Forms, Mark Positioning, Optical size, Font Variations

**Test version available:** Yes

**Web font format available:** Yes

abcdefghijklmnopqrstuvwxyzæåçéñö
ABCDEFGHIJKLMNOPQRSTUVWXYZÆÇØ
1234567890Ø@.,!?’)]§*“”»«/–½©€$£¥&↑

абвгдеёжзийклмнопрстуфхцчшщъыьэюя
АБВГДЕЁЖЗИЙКЛМНОПРСТУФХЦЧШЩЪЫЬЭЮЯ
1234567890⓪@.,!?’)]§*“”»«/–½©€$£¥&←

Bakemono is a family of three styles: Mono, Text, and Stereo, each in seven weights: Mono Thin, Mono Extra Light, Mono Light, Mono Regular, **Mono Medium**, **Mono Bold**, **Mono Extra Bold**, Text Thin, Text Extra Light, Text Light, Text Regular, **Text Medium**, **Text Bold**, **Text Extra Bold**, Stereo Thin, Stereo Extra Light, Stereo Light, Stereo Regular, **Stereo Medium**, **Stereo Bold, and Stereo Extra Bold**



→ P. 448, 466

ISN'T IT ROMANTIC? ☺ #AMOUR, 1H 29MIN.

PRÊTE-MOI TA MAIN, 2006

LE GOÛT DES AUTRES— @ AGNÈS JAOUI SEVEN BRIDES FOR SEVEN BROTHRES

Bakerie is a display typeface, designed with letterforms of contrasting widths. Fluid yet sharp, Bakerie is inspired by the elegance of the art and type forms of the late 19th century. Its name references the changing curves of bread dough as it is kneaded, pushed, and pulled into wonderful shapes. Its range of alternative letters and ligatures allow for inventive combinations, ideal for titles and logotypes.

**Design:** 2022, Clément Cases
→ p. 473

**Foundry:** Range Left Shop, United Kingdom, rangeleft.co.uk
→ p. 491

**Language support:** Latin Extended

**OpenType features:** Proportional Oldstyle, Standard Ligatures, Discretionary Ligatures, All Caps, Titling Alternates, Contextual Alternates, Contextual Ligatures, Fractions, Numerator, Stylistic Alternates, Stylistic Sets

**Test version available:** No

**Web font format available:** Yes

→ P. 459

ABCDEFGHIJKLMNOPQRSTUVWXYZÆÅÇÉÑÖÛ
ABCDEFGHIJKLMNOPQRSTUVWXYZÇØ
1234567890(@.,!?')]*""/—½©€$£¥&→☺

BAKERIE IS A TYPEFACE OF ONE
REGULAR WEIGHT

ME BEFORE YOU

2016

# EMILIA CLARKE

AS

LOUISA »LOU« CLARK

Bakewell is the fourth typeface of the *Winslow Type System.* It's a low contrast Sans Serif with ball terminals and a sweet disposition. The typeface includes a wide range of styles, widths, and weights that make it a great addition to any type collection. From Narrow to Wide and Hairline to Bold, the font family offers extended optionality. Packed with OpenType features, users can create one-of-a-kind designs perfectly tailored to their specific needs!

**Design:** 2022, Kimmy Kirkwood → p. 477

**Foundry:** Kimmy Design, United States of America, kimmydesign.com → p. 489

**Language support:** Latin Extended

**OpenType features:** Proportional Oldstyle, Proportional Lining, Discretionary Ligatures, Historical Ligatures, All Caps, Small Caps

**Test version available:** Yes

**Web font format available:** Yes

→ P. 448, 460

abcdefghijklmnopqrstuvwxyzæfjåçéñöûß
ABCDEFGHIJKLMNOPQRSTUVWXYZÆÇØß
1234567890@.,!?')]§*“”»«/–½©€$£¥&

Bakewell is a typeface of four widths: Narrow, Normal, Semi Wide, and Wide, each in seven weights plus *Italics:* Narrow Hairline, *Narrow Hairline Italic,* Narrow Thin, *Narrow Thin Italic,* Thin, *Thin Italic,* Light, *Light Italic,* Regular, *Italic,* **Wide Medium,** ***Wide Medium Italic,*** **Wide Bold,** ***Wide Bold Italic,*** **Wide Heavy, and** ***Wide Heavy Italic***

## (2001)

## Anybody interested in grabbing a couple of burgers and hittin' the cemetery?

↘

# THE ROYAL TENENBAUMS

written by *Wes Anderson*
*& Owen Wilson*

## A WES ANDERSON

# film

Bartok

Sarah Kremer's Bartok redefines the very notion of a type family. Its four styles with their singular designs break with the principle of formal unity usually sought after in such families. Each variant stands out for its expressivity, contributing to the creation of a contrasted whole. The development of Bartok was undertaken in the context of editorial design to propose a multifaceted typeface with only four styles.

**Design:** 2021, Sarah Kremer
→ p. 478

**Foundry:** 205TF, France, 205.tf
→ p. 488

**Language support:** Latin Extended

**OpenType features:** Proportional Oldstyle, Tabular Lining, Proportional Lining, Tabular Oldstyle, Standard Ligatures, All Caps, Superscript, Subscript, Ordinals, Fractions, Numerator, Denominator, Ornaments, Arrows, Slashed Zero, Localized Forms, Case Sensitive Forms

**Test version available:** Yes

**Web font format available:** Yes

abcdefghijklmnopqrstuvwxyzæfjåçéñöûß
ABCDEFGHIJKLMNOPQRSTUVWXYZÆÇØß
1234567890ø@.,!?')]§*“”»«/–½©€$£¥&↔♥

Bartok is a typeface of four weights: Regular, *Italic*, **Highlight, and Poster**

→ P. 449, 454, 460

Benedikt Cumberbatch

Martin Freeman

# Sherlock Holmes

*IT'S NOT A GAME ANYMORE.*

*{2010–2017} London, 221B Baker Street

Benedikt is a stainless Renaissance Antiqua with provocative Italics, derived from monumental roman letterforms and their wax tablet counterparts. Its unique characteristics and subtle details evoke a sense of diversity and humanity which make it ideal for branding and packaging design. The true Small Caps integrate well into the text and qualify this font for any professional use case.

**Design:** 2021, Prof. Hans R. Heitmann → p. 476, Johannes Ammon → p. 472

**Foundry:** Finaltype, Germany, finaltype.de → p. 489

**Language support:** Latin Extended

**OpenType features:** Proportional Oldstyle, Tabular Lining, Proportional Lining, Tabular Oldstyle, Standard Ligatures, Discretionary Ligatures, Small Caps, Capitals to Small Caps, Superscript, Ordinals, All Alternates, Contextual Alternates, Fractions, Stylistic Alternates, Stylistic Sets, Localized Forms, Case Sensitive Forms, Mark Positioning

**Test version available:** Yes

**Web font format available:** Yes

→ P. 454

abcdefghijklmnopqrstuvwxyzæfiåçéñöûß
ABCDEFGHIJKLMNOPQRSTUVWXYZÆÇØẞ
1234567890@.,!?')]§*“”»«/-½©€$£¥&

Benedikt is a typeface of seven weights plus *Italics:* Extra Light, *Extra Light Italic,* Light, *Light Italic,* Regular, *Italic,* Medium, *Medium Italic,* **Semi Bold,** ***Semi Bold Italic,*** **Bold,** ***Bold Italic,*** **Extra Bold,** ***and Extra Bold Italic***

KU'DAMM
'56
**BERLIN**
—WEST
БЕРЛИН
Βερολίνο

↖

**GALANT**

**Berlin Type**

The city of Berlin has a new alphabet. When the German capital recently received a new corporate identity by Jung von Matt, an exclusive typeface was also designed for it. It is quite a challenge for a type designer—especially for a born and bred Berliner—to unite past and present with the city's diversity and flair. One of the reasons is Berlin's unique intercultural mix, its magnificent buildings, and contemporary architecture, alongside diverse cultural offers and an overall easy-going lifestyle.

**Design:** 2020, Hannes von Döhren → p. 475, Bernd Volmer → p. 484

**Foundry:** HvD Fonts, Germany, hvdfonts.com → p. 489

**Language support:** Latin Extended, Cyrillic, Greek

**OpenType features:** Tabular Lining, Proportional Lining, Fractions, Ordinals, Superscript, Subscript, Stylistic Alternates, Arrows, Ornaments

**Test version available:** Yes

**Web font format available:** Yes

→ P. 449, 469

abcdefghijklmnopqrstuvwxyzæfjåçéñöûß
ABCDEFGHIJKLMNOPQRSTUVWXYZÆÇØẞ
1234567890@.,!?')]§*""»«/-½©€$£¥&→☆

αβγδεζηθικλμνξοπρσςτυφχψωάέήίόώϊϋΰ
ΑΒΓΔΕΖΗΘΙΚΛΜΝΞΟΠΡΣΤΥΦΧΨΩΆΈΉΊΌΏΪΫ
1234567890@.,!?')]§*""»«/-½©€$£¥&↘★

Berlin Type is a typeface of two weights: Regular **and Bold**

# Equilibrium

/ CHRISTIAN BALE & TAYE DIGGS — 2002

Blak

Blak is a neoclassical blackletter inspirited display typeface. Its pure geometric shapes and strict grids give the typeface a modern and bold aesthetic. Blak was designed for large display purposes with large impact. The name *Blak* references the creation process of the typeface; the act of removing all unnecessary decorative elements from a classic Blackletter and applying strict styling rules.

**Design:** 2019, Jan Weidemüller → p. 484

**Foundry:** Ultra Kuhl, Germany, ultra-kuhl.com → p. 492

**Language support:** Latin Extended

**OpenType features:** Tabular Lining, Proportional Lining, Contextual Alternates, Stylistic Sets, Case Sensitive Forms, Font Variations

**Test version available:** No

**Web font format available:** Yes

→ P. 460, 468

abcdefghijklmnopqrstuvwxyzæffåçéñöûß
ABCDEFGHIJKLMNOPQRSTUVWXYZÆÇØẞ
1234567890@.,;!?'[]*“”»«/—©€$£&

Blak is a typeface of five widths: Zoom, Wide, Normal, Compact,

←

YOU'VE
GOT
**M@iL**

→

*Kathleen Kelly;
*Shopgirl* {Meg
Ryan}#★
**&** Joe Fox; **NY152**
**[Tom Hanks]** ●

Blatt

TYPE BY Blatt, designed by Fred Smeijers, is a family for editorial use. Its character is undoubtedly digital and Blatt certainly does not hide that. It also performs well as a display face, making it a suitable tool for a wide range of contemporary publications—dynamic or static—requiring a modern editorial touch and covering significant amounts of text in reading sizes.

**Design:** 2019, Fred Smeijers → p. 483

**Foundry:** TYPE BY, Belgium, typeby.com → p. 492

**Language support:** Latin Extended

**OpenType features:** Proportional Oldstyle, Tabular Lining, Proportional Lining, Tabular Oldstyle, Standard Ligatures, Discretionary Ligatures, All Caps, Small Caps, Capitals to Small Caps, Superscript Subscript, Ordinals, All Alternates, Contextual Alternates, Fractions, Numerator, Denominator, Arrows, Stylistic Alternates, Stylistic Sets, Slashed Zero, Localized Forms, Case Sensitive Forms

**Test version available:** No

**Web font format available:** Yes

→ P. 458

abcdefghijklmnopqrstuvwxyzæfjåçéñöûß
ABCDEFGHIJKLMNOPQRSTUVWXYZÆÇØß
12345678900@.,!?')]§*“”»«/–½©€$£¥&→★

Blatt is a typeface of eight weights plus *Italics:* Thin, *Thin Italic,* Light, *Light Italic,* Blond, *Blond Italic,* Normal, *Normal Italic,* **Medium,** ***Medium Italic,*** **Semi Bold,** ***Semi Bold Italic,*** **Bold,** ***Bold Italic,*** **Black,** ***and Black Italic***

»Don’t be so gloomy. *After all it’s not that awful.* Like the fella says, *in Italy for 30 years* under the Borgias *they had warfare, terror, murder,* and bloodshed, but they produced *Michelangelo, Leonardo da Vinci, and the Renaissance.*«

This font family is an ode to the typography scene of New York City and Chicago in the late 1970s, when Ad agencies, design studios, and typesetters used their cameras, geometry sets, drafting boards, and cunning lingo to model an ideal life of consumption and printed it all into a sleek culture everyone thought would last forever.

**Design:** 2021, Patrick Griffin → p. 476

**Foundry:** Canada Type, Canada, canadatype.com → p. 488

**Language support:** Latin Extended

**OpenType features:** Tabular Lining, Proportional Lining, Standard Ligatures, Superscript, Subscript, Ordinals, All Alternates, Fractions, Numerator, Denominator, Stylistic Alternates, Stylistic Sets, Localized Forms

**Test version available:** No

**Web font format available:** Yes

abcdefghijklmnopqrstuvwxyzæfjåçéñöûß
ABCDEFGHIJKLMNOPQRSTUVWXYZÆÇØẞ
1234567890@.,!?')]§*“”»«/–½©€$£¥&

Borax is a typeface of four weights plus *Italics:* Regular, *Italic,* Medium, ***Medium Italic,*** **Bold,** ***Bold Italic,*** **Heavy,** ***and Heavy Italic***

→ P. 455

[1895] LONDON ST JAMES'S THEATRE

WRITTEN BY OSCAR WILDE

# THE IMPORTANCE OF BEING *EARNEST*

*»The very essence of romance is uncertainty.«*

ADAPTED BY

## DAME EDITH EVANS & KURT BAKER & OLIVER PARKER

Bourton Text

Bourton Text is a modern sans serif typeface family, perfect for both text type settings and display purposes.

**Design:** 2022, Kimmy Kirkwood
→ p. 477

**Foundry:** Kimmy Design, USA, kimmydesign.com → p. 489

**Language support:** Latin Extended

**OpenType features:** Tabular Lining, Proportional Lining, All Caps, Small Caps, Capitals to Small Caps, Superscript, Subscript, Contextual Alternates, Contextual Ligatures

**Test version available:** No

**Web font format available:** Yes

→ P. 449, 460

abcdefghijklmnopqrstuvwxyzæåçéñöûß
ABCDEFGHIJKLMNOPQRSTUVWXYZÆÇØẞ
1234567890@.,!?')]§*""»«/–½©€$£¥&

Bourton Text is a family of two styles: Normal and Round, each in three widths: Narrow, Normal, and Wide, each in seven weights plus *Italics:* Hairline Narrow, *Hairline Narrow Italic,* Thin Narrow, *Thin Narrow Italic,* Light, *Light Italic,* Medium, *Medium Italic,* **Semi Bold Wide,** ***Semi Bold Italic Wide,*** **Bold Wide,** ***and Bold Italic Wide.*** Round Hairline Narrow, *Round Hairline Narrow Italic,* Round Thin Narrow, *Round Thin Narrow Italic,* Round Light, *Round Light Italic,* Round Medium, *Round Medium Italic,* **Round Semi Bold Wide,** ***Round Semi Bold Italic Wide,*** **Round Bold Wide,** ***and Round Bold Italic Wide***

**“Frankly, my dear, I don’t give a damn.”**
— Gone with the Wind (1939)

# «بصراحة يا عزيزتي، أنا لا أكترث البتة»

من فيلم ذهب مع الريح (١٩٣٩)

Bree Arabic

Bree Arabic delivers a spirited look and feel for branding and headline usage while retaining a welcoming tone in paragraph text. Since *Bree Latin* is influenced by handwriting, its Arabic counterpart is based on Ruq’ah, the informal handwriting style used for Arabic.

**Design:** 2021, Azza Alameddine → p. 472, Veronika Burian → p. 473, José Scaglione → p. 482, Najla Badran → p. 472, Rabab Charafeddine → p. 473

**Foundry:** TypeTogether, Czech Republic, type-together.com → p. 492

**Language support:** Latin, Arabic, Farsi

**OpenType features:** Proportional Oldstyle, Tabular Lining, Proportional Lining, Tabular Oldstyle, Standard Ligatures, All Caps, Superscript, Subscript, Ordinals, Fractions, Alternative Fractions, Numerator, Denominator, Stylistic Alternates, Stylistic Sets, Historical Forms, Slashed Zero, Localized Forms, Case Sensitive Forms, Required Ligatures, Mark Positioning, Terminal Form, Initial Form, Isolated Form, Medial Form, Font Variations

**Test version available:** Yes

**Web font format available:** Yes

→ P. 449

abcdefghijklmnopqrstuvwxyzœffåçéñöûß
ABCDEFGHIJKLMNOPQRSTUVWXYZÆÇØẞ
1234567890@.,!?’)]§*“”»«/–½©€$£¥&

ء ـا ا أ ـأ إ ـإ آ ـآ ٱ ـٱ ب ببب ت تتت ث ثثث ج ججج ح ححح خ خخخ
د ـد ذ ـذ ر ـر ز ـز س سسس ش ششش ص صصص ض ضضض
ط ططط ظ ظظظ ع ععع غ غغغ ف ففف ق ققق
ك ككك ل للل م ممم ن ننن ه ههه ة ـة و ـو ؤ ـؤ ي ييي
ئ ئئئ ى ـى لا ـلا لأ ـلأ لإ ـلإ لآ ـلآ لٱ ـلٱ ٠١٢٣٤٥٦٧٨٩ ،؛؟

Bree Arabic is a typeface of seven weights: Thin, Light, **Book**, **Regular**, **Semi Bold**, **Bold**, **and Extra Bold**

หนัง
เอเชีย
e
หนัง
หมวด
หนัง: ไทย

Bree Thai

Bree Thai delivers a spirited look and feel for branding and headline usage while retaining a welcoming tone in paragraph text. Since *Bree Latin* is influenced by handwriting, its closest Thai counterpart is the modern loopless style. Not only does this help Bree Thai complement the other established scripts, but it also gives text a lively and approachable appearance in paragraphs with fluid shapes and measured flourishes.

**Design:** 2021, Panuwat Usakulwattana → p. 484, Veronika Burian → p. 473, José Scaglione → p. 782

**Foundry:** TypeTogether, Czech Republic, type-together.com → p. 492

**Language support:** Latin, Thai

**OpenType features:** Proportional Oldstyle, Tabular Lining, Proportional Lining, Tabular Oldstyle, Standard Ligatures, Discretionary Ligatures, All Caps, Superscript, Subscript, Ordinals, Fractions, Alternative Fractions, Numerator, Denominator, Stylistic Alternates, Stylistic Sets, Historical Forms, Slashed Zero, Localized Forms, Mark Positioning, Font Variations

**Test version available:** Yes

**Web font format available:** Yes

→ P. 449

abcdefghijklmnopqrstuvwxyzæﬂåçéñöûß
ABCDEFGHIJKLMNOPQRSTUVWXYZÆÇØ
12345678900@.,!?')]§*“”»«/–½©€$£¥&

กขฃคฅฆงจฉชซฌญฎฏฐฑฒณดตถทธนบปผฝ
พฟภมยรฤลฦวศษสหฬอฮฯะ ัาำ
๑๒๓๔๕๖๗๘๙๐@.,-:;!?')]§*“”«»/–½©€$£¥&ๆ

Bree Thai is a typeface of seven weights plus *Obliques:* Thin, *Thin Oblique,* Light, *Light Oblique,* Book, ***Book Oblique,*** **Regular, *Oblique,* Semi Bold, *Semi Bold Oblique,* Bold, *Bold Oblique,* Extra Bold, *and Extra Bold Oblique***

# BLADE 1982 RUNNER

Broker

Broker is an angular variable display typeface that invites carefree experimentation, but is designed to make a statement. With twelve unique styles and variable controls for thickness, decoration, and shape, Broker is a versatile and expressive shape-shifter that adapts to fit your mood. It can go from slim, mono-weight to edgy stressed angled styles, and full-on style with chunky serif heels. Because it's drawn on a rectangular frame, it's modular, making it particularly easy to lay out and stack.

**Design:** 2022, Michu Benaim → p. 472, Alexander Wright → p. 484, Rodrigo Fuenzalida → p. 475

**Foundry:** In-House International, United States of America / Spain, weareinhouse.com/types → p. 489

**Language support:** Latin

**OpenType features:** Proportional Lining, All Caps, Stylistic Alternates, Case Sensitive Forms

**Test version available:** No

**Web font format available:** Yes

→ P. 460

abcdefghijklmnopqrstuvwxyzéñö
ABCDEFGHIJKLMNOPQRSTUVWXYZ
1234567890@.,;!?'")]§*“”»«/-©€$£¥€

Broker is a family of five styles: Normal, Sans, Serif, Stressed Sans, and Stressed Serif. Normal in one Regular weight. Sans, Serif, Stressed Sans, and Stressed Serif each in three weights: Sans Light, Sans Medium, Sans Bold, Serif Light, Serif Medium, Serif Bold, Stressed Sans Light, Stressed Sans Medium, Stressed Sans Bold, Stessed Serif Light, Stressed Serif Medium, and Stressed Serif Bold

"[...] with great power there must also come— great responsibility!"

« [...] с большой властью должна приходить и большая ответственность!» ¶

PETER PARKER, *SPIDERMAN*

Brutalista

Brutalista is a typeface inspired by the architectural brutalist style, which seeks to use the expression of raw material. The drawing has its roots in grotesque and neo-grotesque sources from the early 20th century, but with a contemporary style. It has a medium x-height, clear counterforms, and low contrasts, which give it versatility and functionality. In some characters, peculiar cuts and drawings are used, giving them personality. It is an ideal font for headlines and brands, but also for when you need to present simple and clear information.

**Design:** 2021, Jorge Cisterna
→ p. 474

**Foundry:** Latinotype, Chile, latinotype.com → p. 490

**Language support:** Latin Extended, Cyrillic

**OpenType features:** Proportional Oldstyle, Proportional Lining, Standard Ligatures, Superscript, Ordinals, Fractions, Stylistic Alternates, Stylistic Sets, Slashed Zero, Localized Forms, Case Sensitive Forms

**Test version available:** No

**Web font format available:** Yes

abcdefghijklmnopqrstuvwxyzæåçéñöûß
ABCDEFGHIJKLMNOPQRSTUVWXYZÆÇØẞ
12345678900@.,!?')]§*“”»«/–½©€$£¥&

абвгдеёжзийклмнопрстуфхцчшщъыьэюя
АБВГДЕЁЖЗИЙКЛМНОПРСТУФХЦЧШЩЪЫЬЭЮЯ
12345678900@.,!?')]§*“”»«/–½©€$£¥&

Brutalista is a family of two styles: Normal and Alt, each in seven weights plus *Italics:* Ultra Light, *Ultra Light Italic,* Light, *Light Italic,* Regular, *Italic,* **Medium,** ***Medium Italic,*** **Semi Bold,** ***Semi Bold Italic,*** **Bold,** ***Bold Italic,*** **Black,** ***Black Italic,*** Alt Ultra Light, *Alt Ultra Light Italic,* Alt Light, *Alt Light Italic,* Alt Regular, *Alt Italic,* **Alt Medium,** ***Alt Medium Italic,*** **Alt Semi Bold,** ***Alt Semi Bold Italic,*** **Alt Bold,** ***Alt Bold Italic,*** **Alt Black,** ***and Alt Black Italic***

→ P. 449

*La Dolce Vita!*

***The sweet life***

Das süße Leben

***Сладкая жизнь!***

*Słodkie życie!*

**The good life!**

*Slatki život!*

**Tatlı Hayat!**

Exactitude and visibility are translated typographically through the reference to sixteenth-century *Garalde* typography and its controlled, highly legible letterforms. To balance this formal rigor, lightness and quickness were added by letting the design be inspired by the calligraphic hand, following the lesson of Gudrun Zapf. The idea of multiplicity was kept central in a range of weights encompassing both display and text use cases.

**Design:** 2021, Andrea Tartarelli
→ p. 483

**Foundry:** Zetafonts, Italy, zetafonts.com → p. 492

**Language support:** Latin Extended, Cyrillic

**OpenType features:** Proportional Oldstyle, Tabular Lining, Proportional Lining, Tabular Oldstyle, Standard Ligatures, Discretionary Ligatures, Superscript, Subscript, Ordinals, Contextual Alternates, Contextual Ligatures, Fractions, Numerator, Denominator, Arrows, Stylistic Alternates, Stylistic Sets, Slashed Zero, Alternate Annotation, Localized Forms, Case Sensitive Forms, Mark Positioning, Optical size

**Test version available:** Yes

**Web font format available:** Yes

→ P. 455

abcdefghijklmnopqrstuvwxyzæffåçéñöûß
ABCDEFGHIJKLMNOPQRSTUVWXYZÆÇØß
1234567890⓪@.,!?')]§*“”»«/-½©€$£¥&↘☀

абвгдеёжзийклмнопрстуфхцчшщъыьэюя
АБВГДЕЁЖЗИЙКЛМНОПРСТУФХЦЧШЩЪЫ
1234567890Ø@.,!?')]§*“”»«/-½©€$£¥&↓☾

Calvino is a family of two styles: Normal and Grande. Normal in eight weights plus *Italics:* Thin, *Thin Italic,* Extra Light, *Extra Light Italic,* Light, *Light Italic,* Book, *Book Italic,* Regular, *Italic,* **Semi Bold,** ***Semi Bold Italic,*** **Bold,** ***Bold Italic,*** **Extra Bold,** ***and Extra Bold Italic.*** Grande in nine weights plus *Italics:* Grande Monoline, *Grande Monoline Italic,* Grande Thin, *Grande Thin Italic,* Grande Extra Light, *Grande Extra Light Italic,* Grande Light, *Grande Light Italic,* Grande Regular, *Grande Italic,* Grande Semi Bold, ***Grande Semi Bold Italic,*** **Grande Bold,** ***Grande Bold Italic,*** **Grande Extra Bold,** ***Grande Extra Bold Italic,*** **Grande Black,** ***and Grande Black Italic***

Capricho

*Little Miss Sunshine*

Pequeña Miss Sunshine

↗

**Una familia en la que ser normal, es sólo apariencia.** ↙

Capricho is a warm, comfy, and pleasantly readable typeface. It unites the virtues of a 17th-century transitional typeface with its own distinctive and individual flavor. Its large descenders and ascenders make for a distinguished appearance. The complementary Italic with its gently flowing ductus is the contrasting counterpoint.

**Design:** 2021, Dieter Hofrichter → p. 476

**Foundry:** Hoftype, Germany, hoftype.com → p. 489

**Language support:** Latin Extended

**OpenType features:** Standard Ligatures, Discretionary Ligatures, Case Sensitive Forms, Small Caps, Historical Forms, Proportional Figures, Tabular OldStyle Figures, Proportional OldStyle Figures, Superscript, Subscript, Ordinals, Subscript Fractions, Subscript Fractions, Slashed Zero

**Test version available:** Yes

**Web font format available:** Yes

→ P. 455

abcdefghijklmnopqrstuvwxyzæfjåçéñöûß
ABCDEFGHIJKLMNOPQRSTUVWXYZÆÇØ
1234567890Ø@.,!?’)]§*“”»«/–½©€$£¥&↗

Capricho is a typeface of nine weights plus *Italics:* Thin, *Thin Italic,* Extra Light, *Extra Light Italic,* Light, *Light Italic,* Regular, *Italic,* Medium, *Medium Italic,* **Semi Bold,** ***Semi Bold Italic,*** **Bold,** ***Bold Italic,*** **Extra Bold,** ***Extra Bold Italic,*** **Black,** ***and Black Italic***

“*Every man* ***dies,*** *not every man* ***really lives.***”

†[♥]

Cardone

Cardone, developed between 2016 and 2021, is a singular interpretation of early so-called Scottish modern faces, later called *Scotch Roman.* Specifically created for editorial design, this Serif typeface seeks an ideal balance between elegance and robustness: its ample curves contrast with the brutality of its lines and the verticality of its axis.

**Design:** 2021, Fátima Lázaro
→ p. 478

**Foundry:** 205TF, France, 205.tf
→ p. 488

**Language support:** Latin Extended

**OpenType features:** Proportional Oldstyle, Tabular Lining, Proportional Lining, Tabular Oldstyle, Standard Ligatures, Discretionary Ligatures, All Caps, Superscript, Subscript, Ordinals, Contextual Alternates, Fractions, Numerator, Denominator, Ornaments, Arrows, Stylistic Sets, Slashed Zero, Localized Forms, Case Sensitive Forms

**Test version available:** Yes

**Web font format available:** Yes

→ P. 455

abcdefghijklmnopqrstuvwxyzæfjåçéñöûß
ABCDEFGHIJKLMNOPQRSTUVWXYZÆÇØ
1234567890Ø@.,!?’)]§*“”»«/–½©€$£¥&↔♥

Cardone is a family of two styles: Normal and **Micro.** Normal in five weights plus *Italics:* Thin, *Thin Italic,* Light, *Light Italic,* Regular, *Italic,* Book, *Book Italic,* **Bold,** ***and Bold Italic.*** Micro in one Regular weight with an *Italic*

Centra Mono

# EX_MACHINA

There is nothing more human than the will to survive.

**Release dates**

December 16th, 2014 “ “ ” ” ‟ ‟
(BFI Southbank)
January 21st, 2015
(United Kingdom)
April 10th, 2015
(United States)

$15 million // $36 million

*108 MINUTES*

Centra Mono is a geometric Sans by Josh Finklea, constrained but not hindered by a fixed-width system. Neither limited by technology or context, it takes its place as a contemporary response to monospace typography. Centra Mono is part of an established conversation between *Centra's* humanistic warmth and modernist rationale, but operates as its own fine-tuned instrument.

**Design:** 2021, Josh Finklea
→ p. 475

**Foundry:** Sharp Type, United States of America, sharptype.co → p. 491

**Language support:** Latin Extended

**OpenType features:** Tabular Lining, Tabular Oldstyle, All Caps, Superscript, Subscript, Ordinals, Fractions, Numerator, Denominator, Arrows, Stylistic Alternates, Stylistic Sets, Localized Forms, Case Sensitive Forms

**Test version available:** Yes

**Web font format available:** Yes

abcdefghijklmnopqrstuvwxyzæåçéñöûß
ABCDEFGHIJKLMNOPQRSTUVWXYZÆÇØß
1234567890@.,!?')]§*“”»«/-½©€$£¥&↖

Centra Mono is a typeface of four weights plus *Italics*: Light, *Light Italic*, Book, *Book Italic*, **Medium**, ***Medium Italic***, **Bold**, ***and Bold Italic***



→ P. 466

# THX 1138

```
*     _----~~(~~-_.
      _{          )   )
    ,    ) -~~- ( ,-' )_
   (  `-,_..`., )-- '_,)
  ( ` _)  (  -~( -_ `,  }
  (_-   _   ~_-~~~~`,  ,' )
    `~ -^(     __;-,((()))
           ~~~~ {_ -_(())
                  `\  }
                    { }
```

The
future
is here.

↖↗↘↙ // 1971

Charte Mono

Charte Mono is a monospaced typeface. It is a playful family that mixes radical shapes like those found in the *M* and *W* with softer curves like the a. It's a family of contrast in shapes. The perpendicular aspect of the f and t give interesting combinations with the very round *r* or *e*.

**Design:** 2022, Nico Inosanto → p. 477

**Foundry:** Nootype, Switzerland, nootype.com → p. 490

**Language support:** Latin Extended, Cyrillic

**OpenType features:** Superscript, Subscript, Ordinals, Fractions, Numerator, Denominator, Arrows, Stylistic Alternates, Stylistic Sets, Slashed Zero, Localized Forms, Case Sensitive Forms

**Test version available:** Yes

**Web font format available:** Yes

→ P. 466

abcdefghijklmnopqrstuvwxyzæflåçéñöûß
ABCDEFGHIJKLMNOPQRSTUVWXYZÆÇØẞ
12345678900@.,!?')]§*“”»«/–½©€$£¥&↙

абвгдеёжзийклмнопрстуфхцчшщъыьэюя
АБВГДЕЁЖЗИЙКЛМНОПРСТУФХЦЧШЩЪЫЬЭЮЯ
12345678900@.,!?')]§*“”»«/–½©€$£¥&↓

Charte Mono is a typeface of six weights: Thin, Light, Regular, **Medium, Bold, and Extra Bold**

# *O Ano da Morte de Ricardo Reis* / ***The Year of the Death of Ricardo Reis***

WRITTEN BY
***José Saramago***

# {directed by}
# *João Botelho*
# LISBON
# #1936/

Chassi is an editorial type family designed for fluency in extended texts. Stylistically it focuses on the elegant roman types of Claude Garamond but without aiming for fidelity. It also takes typefaces into account that were influenced by *Garamond*—like those of Robert Granjon and Jean Jannon—effectively being a revival of *Garamond* as a genre, slightly re-interpreted for our times.

**Design:** 2021, Rui Abreu → p. 472

**Foundry:** R-Typography, Portugal, r-typography.com → p. 491

**Language support:** Latin

**OpenType features:** Proportional Oldstyle, Tabular Lining, Proportional Lining, Tabular Oldstyle, Standard Ligatures, Discretionary Ligatures, All Caps, Small Caps, Capitals to Small Caps, Superscript, Subscript, Fractions, Numerator, Denominator, Stylistic Alternates, Stylistic Sets, Case Sensitive Forms, Optical size

**Test version available:** Yes

**Web font format available:** Yes

abcdefghijklmnopqrstuvwxyzæfjåçéñöûß
ABCDEFGHIJKLMNOPQRSTUVWXYZÆÇØ
1234567890@.,!?')]§*“”»«/–½©€$£¥&

Chassi is a family of three optical sizes: S, M, and L, each in three weights plus *Italics:* S Regular, *S Italic,* **S Medium,** ***S Medium Italic,*** **S Bold,** ***S Bold Italic,*** M Regular, *M Italic,* **M Medium,** ***M Medium Italic,*** **M Bold,** ***M Bold Italic,*** L Regular, *L Italic,* **L Medium,** ***L Medium Italic,*** **L Bold,** ***and L Bold Italic***

→ P. 455, 460

(1942) »«

GARY COOPER

IN

THE PRIDE OF THE YANKEES

(THE LIFE OF LOU GEHRIG)

↤ ↦

Chatham Slab

Chatham Slab is a geometric slab serif typeface that was adapted from historical ephemera of the Chatham Manufacturing Company's heyday in the 1940s. The primary source of inspiration originates from custom company-made embroidered blanket labels and printed packaging design. In order to highlight the historic characteristics of the typeface, the focus was on redrawing the square serif endings, incorporating the condensed width, and emphasizing the Inktraps.

**Design:** 2022, Emily Klaebe → p. 477, Jesse Reed → p. 481

**Foundry:** Order, United States of America, order.design → p. 490

**Language support:** Latin

**OpenType features:** Tabular Lining, Proportional Lining, All Caps, Fractions, Numerator, Denominator, Arrows, Localized Forms, Unicase, Mark Positioning

**Test version available:** No

**Web font format available:** Yes

→ P. 458, 469

ABCDEFGHIJKLMNOPQRSTUVWXYZÅÇÉÑÖÛ
1234567890@.,!?')]§*“”»«/–½©€$£¥&↗

CHATHAM SLAB IS A TYPEFACE OF ONE REGULAR WEIGHT

**Chesna Grotesk**

# **MATT**HEW
# PAIGE**&&&**
# **DAMON**

**Alma mater** Harvard University (*no degree*), born Oct. 8th, 1970 Cambridge, Massachusetts, U.S.

Chesna Grotesk was inspired by typefaces such as *Avenir, Futura,* and *Circular.* It is designed mostly to use on logos, posters, billboards, and branding fields.

**Design:** 201X, Ufuk Aracıoğlu → p. 472

**Foundry:** Horizon Type Foundry, Turkey, horizontype.com → p. 489

**Language support:** Latin Extended

**OpenType features:** Proportional Oldstyle, Tabular Lining, Proportional Lining, Tabular Oldstyle, Standard Ligatures, Discretionary Ligatures, Superscript, Subscript, Fractions, Numerator, Denominator, Stylistic Alternates, Stylistic Sets, Case Sensitive Forms

**Test version available:** Yes

**Web font format available:** Yes

→ P. 449

abcdefghijklmnopqrstuvwxyzæfjåçéñöûß
ABCDEFGHIJKLMNOPQRSTUVWXYZÆÇØ
1234567890@.,!?')]§*""»«/–½©€$£¥&↕

Chesna Grotesk is a typeface of ten weights plus *Italics:* Thin, *Thin Italic,* Extra Light, *Extra Light Italic,* Light, *Light Italic,* Book, *Book Italic,* Regular, *Italic,* Medium, *Medium Italic,* Semi Bold, *Semi Bold Italic,* Bold, ***Bold Italic,*** **Extra Bold,** ***Extra Bold Italic,*** **Black,** ***and Black Italic***

.:인생은≒

한 송이

꽃[:*]이며

dont l'amour est miel

@

AG Choijeongho Minburi Std.

AG Choijeongho Minburi Std. is a Minburi typeface designed by the Hangeul designer Choi Jeong-ho in his later years. While maintaining the characteristics of Choi's hand-drawn style, this typeface is also characterized by its adjusted letter proportions and spacious counters. Like other Minburi types of Choi Jeong-ho, this typeface also has heels, spurs, and hand-drawn curves. AG Choijeongho Minburi Std. is a digital typeface based on the 1.058 letters of the 1.353 original drawings.

**Design:** 2021, Moa Ku → p. 478, Seunghwan Kim → p. 477, Mingyu Park → p. 481, Joachim Müller-Lancé → p. 480, Hyunjin Kim → p. 477

**Foundry:** AG Typography Institute, Republic of Korea, agfont.com/en → p. 488

**Language support:** Latin Extended, Korean

**OpenType features:** Tabular Lining, Proportional Lining, Standard Ligatures, Discretionary Ligatures, Superscript, Subscript, Ordinals, All Alternates, Fractions, Stylistic Alternates, Alternate Annotation, Localized Forms

**Test version available:** Yes

**Web font format available:** Yes

abcdefghijklmnopqrstuvwxyzæåçéñöûß
ABCDEFGHIJKLMNOPQRSTUVWXYZÆÇØß
1234567890@.,!?')]§*"”»«/–½©€$£¥&⇔♣

가냐더례미배세예쟤차캬터히까뗘빠쎄
고뇨두류므보슈쥐최슈쾌훼꽈뚜뱄쓰
폼닌죙왈쉼원휑@.,!?')]§*"”»«/–½©€$£¥&↓⇧

AG Choijeongho Minburi Std. is a typeface of three weights: Regular, Medium, **and Bold**

→ P. 449

when
¤Harry*
»met«
◊SalLy≈

BILLY CHRISTAL
MEG RYAN

© ROB REINER

07
JUL

1987

Claymore

Claymore is a subtly modulated Sans Serif with an equally subtle hint of Gothic inspiration. Its striking image performs exceptionally well across the family's range of weights. The many details have been crafted to deliver an engaging and clear image in text, with a strong individual personality when used at display sizes.

**Design:** 2021, Jeremy Tankard → p. 483

**Foundry:** Jeremy Tankard Typography, United Kingdom, typography.net → p. 489

**Language support:** Latin Extended

**OpenType features:** Proportional Oldstyle, Tabular Lining, Proportional Lining, Tabular Oldstyle, All Caps, Small Caps, Capitals to Small Caps, Superscript, Subscript, Ordinals, Fractions, Alternative Fractions, Numerator, Stylistic Sets

**Test version available:** Yes

**Web font format available:** Yes

→ P. 449

abcdefghijklmnopqrstuvwxyzæåçéñöûß
ABCDEFGHIJKLMNOPQRSTUVWXYZÆÇØẞ
1234567890@.,!?')]§*"">»«/–½©€$£¥&

Claymore is a typeface of eight weights plus *Italics:* Hair, *Hair Italic,* Extra Light, *Extra Light Italic,* Light, *Light Italic,* Regular, *Italic,* **Medium, *Medium Italic,* Bold, *Bold Italic,* Extra Bold, *Extra Bold Italic,* Black, *and Black Italic***

# STEVE McQUEEN {BULLITT}

*"I live for myself and I answer to nobody."*

Cobertura

Ever wondered what would a firmly condensed, script-like typeface with a pointed-nib contrast look like? Please meet Cobertura, designed by Thomas Thiemich and published by TYPE BY. Thomas' designs are famous for their precision and quality: thought out, meticulously designed, and surveyed to the smallest detail. Also in Cobertura, nothing happens accidentally. The result is a design that is unlike others and an all-around delicate but mighty typographic tool.

**Design:** 2019, Thomas Thiemich
→ p. 483

**Foundry:** TYPE BY, Belgium, typeby.com → p. 492

**Language support:** Latin Extended

**OpenType features:** Proportional Oldstyle, Tabular Lining, Proportional Lining, Tabular Oldstyle, Standard Ligatures, Discretionary Ligatures, All Caps, Superscript, Subscript, Ordinals, All Alternates, Contextual Alternates, Fractions, Numerator, Denominator, Arrows, Stylistic Alternates, Stylistic Sets, Slashed Zero, Localized Forms, Case Sensitive Forms

**Test version available:** No

**Web font format available:** Yes

→ P. 449, 460

abcdefghijklmnopqrstuvwxyzæfjåçèñöûß

ABCDEFGHIJKLMNOPQRSTUVWXYZÆÇØß

1234567890Ø@.,!?')]§*""»«/–½©€$£¥&↙

Cobertura is a family of six widths: 01, 02, 03, 04, 05, and 06, each in seven weights plus *Italics:* 01 Thin, *01 Thin Italic*, 02 Light, *02 Light Italic*, 03 Blond, *03 Blond Italic*, 03 Normal, *03 Normal Italic*, **04 Medium**, ***04 Medium Italic***, **05 Semi Bold**, ***05 Semi Bold Italic***, **06 Bold**, ***and 06 Bold Italic***

1999, David Fincher

# FIGHT CLUB

MISCHIEF.
MAYHEM.
SOAP.

¶ $

*

" The first rule of Fight Club is you <u>don't</u> talk about Fight Club! "

A modern take on traditional hand painted signage. Compass Point is effective in providing a retro feel but takes creative liberty in its universal usage and modern applications. Contrast within the letterforms is achieved through the use of a frayed brush to provide a clean outer edge and a gritty textured finish to each stroke. The anatomy of the strokes intends for a stiff feel but is balanced out by subtle looseness in its curves and maintains the natural imperfections of hand lettering.

**Design:** 2021, Derek Campbell → p. 473, Justin Graefer → p. 476

**Foundry:** BLKBK Inc., Canada, blkbk.ink → p. 488

**Language support:** Latin Extended

**OpenType features:** Swashes

**Test version available:** Yes

**Web font format available:** Yes

*abcdefghijklmnopqrstuvwxyzæflàçéñöûß*

*ABCDEFGHIJKLMNOPQRSTUVWXYZÆÇØ*

*1234567890@.,!?')]§*“”»«/- ½©€$£¥¢*

*Compass Point is a typeface of one Regular weight*

→ P. 460, 467

# The Wizard of Oz

∞

Contane is a new font with a classic character. It is high-contrasted and noble in appearance, but still objective and clean. It is predestined for headlines, editorials, and small text applications. All Italic weights also contain Swash Capitals for especially fancy occasions.

**Design:** 2021, Dieter Hofrichter → p. 476

**Foundry:** Hoftype, Germany, hoftype.com → p. 489

**Language support:** Latin Extended

**OpenType features:** Standard Ligatures, Discretionary Ligatures, Case Sensitive Forms, Small Caps, Historical Forms, Proportional Figures, Tabular OldStyle Figures, Proportional OldStyle Figures, Superscript, Subscript, Ordinals, Subscript Fractions, Subscript Fractions, Swash Capitals, Slashed Zero

**Test version available:** Yes

**Web font format available:** Yes

→ P. 455

abcdefghijklmnopqrstuvwxyzæfjåçéñöûß
ABCDEFGHIJKLMNOPQRSTUVWXYZÆÇØ
12345678900@.,!?')]§*"""»«/–½©€$£¥&→

Contane is a typeface of ten weights plus *Italics:* Thin, *Thin Italic,* Extra Light, *Extra Light Italic,* Light, *Light Italic,* Regular, *Italic,* Medium, *Medium Italic,* **Semi Bold,** ***Semi Bold Italic,*** **Bold,** ***Bold Italic,*** **Extra Bold,** ***Extra Bold Italic,*** **Black,** ***Black Italic,*** **Heavy,** ***and Heavy Italic***

# AUDREY TAUTOU

AS / IN:

# «COCO» {AVANT} → CHANEL

2009

Contralto

Contralto is a high contrast sans serif font family, crafted to look elegant but contemporary thanks to soft humanist shapes mixed with sharp geometric details. Contralto comes in 40 styles: 5 weights × Italics × 4 optical sizes, to help optimize contrast and readability. However, you can also use them to fine tune the mood of your graphical composition. Contralto's generous character set and OpenType features let you meet the most demanding layout needs and allow your creativity to fly!

**Design:** 2021, Jan Tonellato
→ p. 483

**Foundry:** Synthview Type Design, France, typography.synthview.com
→ p. 491

**Language support:** Latin Extended

**OpenType features:** Proportional Oldstyle, Tabular Lining, Proportional Lining, Tabular Oldstyle, Standard Ligatures, Discretionary Ligatures, All Caps, Superscript, Subscript, Ordinals, All Alternates, Contextual Ligatures, Fractions, Numerator, Denominator, Arrows, Stylistic Sets, Slashed Zero, Localized Forms, Case Sensitive Forms, Mark Positioning, Optical size

**Test version available:** Yes

**Web font format available:** Yes

abcdefghijklmnopqrstuvwxyzæfiåçéñöûß
ABCDEFGHIJKLMNOPQRSTUVWXYZÆÇØß
12345678900@.,!?')]§*"'"»«/–½©€$£¥&↔

Contralto is a family of four optical sizes: Xsmall, Small, Medium, and Big, each in five weights plus *Italics:* Xsmall Light, *Xsmall Light Italic,* Xsmall Regular, *Xsmall Italic,* **Xsmall Semi Bold,** ***Xsmall Semi Bold Italic,*** **Xsmall Bold,** ***Xsmall Bold Italic,*** **Xsmall Black,** ***Xsmall Black Italic,*** Small Light, *Small Light Italic,* Small Regular, *Small Italic,* **Small Semi Bold,** ***Small Semi Bold Italic,*** **Small Bold,** ***Small Bold Italic,*** **Small Black,** ***Small Black Italic,*** Medium Light, *Medium Light Italic,* Medium Regular, *Medium Italic,* **Medium Semi Bold,** ***Medium Semi Bold Italic,*** **Medium Bold,** ***Medium Bold Italic,*** **Medium Black,** ***Medium Black Italic,*** Big Light, *Big Light Italic,* Big Regular, *Big Italic,* **Big Semi Bold,** ***Big Semi Bold Italic,*** **Big Bold,** ***Big Bold Italic,*** **Big Black,** ***and Big Black Italic***


→ P. 449, 460

# *Tom Hanks is*

OCT — 1994 — 13

*

# Forrest Gump

The world will never be the same
once you've seen it through the eyes of Forrest Gump

The Convey typeface family merges essential features of classical Serifs and Sans Serifs and creates a character with a contemporary and open appearance. The elements of an Antiqua are formally reduced to a minimum while still supporting the eye in keeping lines and maintaining outstanding reading properties. The font was created as a cooperation project with media theorists and designed and perfected through analyzes, reading tests, and the application of media psychology and sociological findings.

**Design:** 2021, Gabriele Lenz → p. 478

**Foundry:** Wannatype, Austria, wannatype.com → p. 492

**Language support:** Latin Extended

**OpenType features:** Tabular Lining, Proportional Lining, Ordinals, Stylistic Alternates

**Test version available:** No

**Web font format available:** Yes

→ P. 455

abcdefghijklmnopqrstuvwxyzæflåçéñöûß
ABCDEFGHIJKLMNOPQRSTUVWXYZÆÇØẞ
1234567890@.,!?')]§*“”»«/–½©€$£¥&

Convey is a typeface of three weights plus *Italics:* Regular, *Italic,* Medium, ***Medium Italic,*** **Bold,** ***and Bold Italic***

# ĦOW TØ Ω LOSE a Guy* in 10 Days:

# ?¿

Cotford

New from the Monotype Studio, Cotford is a contemporary Serif from Creative Type Director Tom Foley. Dynamic, adaptable, and surprising—Cotford is a languid Serif that ranges from delicate thins, bending and reaching like flower stems, to bold heavy weights that command the page and screen with confidence and vintage charm. And as a variable font, Cotford allows designers to explore and refine the design almost endlessly, unearthing its many visual tones and hidden secrets.

**Design:** 2021, Tom Foley → p. 475

**Foundry:** Monotype, United Kingdom, monotype.com → p. 490

**Language support:** Latin Extended

**OpenType features:** Standard Ligatures, Superscript, Subscript, Ordinals, All Alternates, Fractions, Numerator, Denominator, Localized Forms, Case Sensitive Forms, Mark Positioning

**Test version available:** Yes

**Web font format available:** Yes

abcdefghijklmnopqrstuvwxyzæåçéñöûß
ABCDEFGHIJKLMNOPQRSTUVWXYZÆÇØ
1234567890@.,!?')]§*“”»«/–½©€$£¥&

Cotford is a family of two styles: Display and Text. Display in five weights plus *Italics:* Thin, *Thin Italic,* Light, *Light Italic,* Regular, *Italic,* **Bold,** ***Bold Italic,*** **Extra Bold,** ***and Extra Bold Italic.*** Text in three weights plus *Italics:* Light, *Light Italic,* Regular, *Italic,* **Bold,** ***and Bold Italic***

→ P. 455, 460

②⓪①④❷⓿❶❹

THE THE
GRAND GRAND

BUDAPEST
BUDAPEST

HOTEL HOTEL

February 6th, 2014 (BERLINALE)
March 6th, 2014 (GERMANY)
March 7th, 2014 (UNITED STATES)

⟦№ 14⟧
written and directed
by ***Wes Anderson***

Quality Content

↙

92 % TOMATOMETER & 86 % AUDIENCE SCORE

**Delvard Serif**

Delvard Serif is an eccentric, yet very functional old-style typeface. A decade after Nikola Djurek drew *Delvard*—a collection of Sans and Display fonts—comes Delvard Serif, an eye-catching serif typeface in three optical sizes.

**Design:** 2022, Nikola Djurek
→ p. 474

**Foundry:** Typotheque, The Netherlands, typotheque.com
→ p. 492

**Language support:** Latin Extended

**OpenType features:** Proportional Oldstyle, Tabular Lining, Proportional Lining, Tabular Oldstyle, Standard Ligatures, Discretionary Ligatures, All Caps, Small Caps, Capitals to Small Caps, Superscript, Subscript, All Alternates, Fractions, Numerator, Denominator, Stylistic Sets, Slashed Zero

**Test version available:** Yes

**Web font format available:** Yes

abcdefghijklmnopqrstuvwxyzæfjåçéñöû
ABCDEFGHIJKLMNOPQRSTUVWXYZÆÇ
1234567890O@.,!?')]§*“”»«/–½©€$£¥&→∞

Delvard Serif is a family of three styles: Text, Subhead, and Display, each in four weights plus *Italics:* Text Regular, *Text Italic,* **Text Medium,** ***Text Medium Italic,*** **Text Semi Bold,** ***Text Semi Bold Italic,*** **Text Bold,** ***Text Bold Italic,*** Subhead Regular, *Subhead Italic,* **Subhead Medium,** ***Subhead Medium Italic,*** **Subhead Semi Bold,** ***Subhead Semi Bold Italic,*** **Subhead Bold,** ***Subhead Bold Italic,*** Display Regular, *Display Italic,* **Display Medium,** ***Display Medium Italic,*** **Display Semi Bold,** ***Display Semi Bold Italic,*** **Display Bold,** ***and Display Bold Italic***

→ P. 455, 460

Diana Ross
in *Lady*
*sings*
*the* BLLues
*from 1972*

*NoW Playing→
at ***a theater*** or
***drive-in*** near you

**Denton**

Denton is a typeface full of warmth, bringing expressive 70's era design into the 21st century. Inspired by the bold, tightly set headline serif titling from this liberated era, Denton encompasses the style into a modern superfamily that can meet all the needs of today's brands. Tight kerning, the uniform rhythm, and carefully designed letter interaction give Denton a warm, refined personality.

**Design:** 2022, Ellen Luff → p. 479, Tom Watkins → p. 484

**Foundry:** Peregrin Studio, United Kingdom, peregrinstudio.com → p. 491

**Language support:** Latin Extended

**OpenType features:** Proportional Oldstyle, Tabular Lining, Standard Ligatures, Discretionary Ligatures, All Caps, Subscript, Alternative Fractions, Numerator, Arrows, Case Sensitive Forms, Optical size, Font Variations

**Test version available:** Yes

**Web font format available:** Yes

abcdefghijklmnopqrstuvwxyzæfjåçéñöûß
ABCDEFGHIJKLMNOPQRSTUVWXYZÆÇØß
1234567890@.,!?')]§*“”»«/–½©€$£¥&→

Denton is a family of two styles: Normal and Text, both in three widths: Normal, Condensed, and XCondensed, each in seven weights plus *Italics:* Thin, *Thin Italic,* **Medium,** ***Medium Italic,*** **Black,** ***Black Italic,*** Condensed Thin, *Condensed Thin Italic,* **Condensed Medium,** ***Condensed Medium Italic,*** **Condensed Black,** ***Condensed Black Italic,*** Extra Condensed Thin, *Extra Condensed Thin Italic,* **Extra Condensed Medium,** ***Extra Condensed Medium Italic,*** **Extra Condensed Black,** ***Extra Condensed Black Italic,*** Text Thin, *Text Thin Italic,* **Text Medium,** ***Text Medium Italic,*** **Text Black,** ***Text Black Italic,*** Text Condensed Thin, *Text Condensed Thin Italic,* **Text Condensed Medium,** ***Text Condensed Medium Italic,*** **Text Condensed Black,** ***Text Condensed Black Italic,*** Text XCondensed Thin, *Text XCondensed Thin Italic,* **Text XCondensed Medium,** ***Text XCondensed Medium Italic,*** **Text XCondensed Black,** ***and Text XCondensed Black Italic***

→ P. 455, 460

How to steal a *Million*

{*1.000.000}

&

AUDREY HEPBURN PETER O'TOOLE

**Didot Modern**

Didot Modern is the result of a collaboration between Arnaud Chemin and Nouvelle Noire. It is a hybrid typeface consisting of ten weights, combining upright and italic cuts. The proportions refer to the Didones from the French printing tradition, mixed with expressive features invoking geometry and minimalism. Flat endings, sharp triangular serifs, and a multitude of stylistic features bring the Didot legacy into the new digital area where elegance and classicism meet technology and rationalism.

**Design:** 2021, Arnaud Chemin
→ p. 474

**Foundry:** Nouvelle Noire Type Foundry, Switzerland, nouvellenoire.ch → p. 490

**Language support:** Latin Extended

**OpenType features:** Proportional Oldstyle, Tabular Lining, Proportional Lining, Standard Ligatures, Superscript, Subscript, Contextual Alternates, Contextual Ligatures, Fractions, Numerator, Denominator, Arrows, Stylistic Alternates, Stylistic Sets

**Test version available:** Yes

**Web font format available:** Yes

abcdefghijklmnopqrstuvwxyzæfjåçéñöûß
ABCDEFGHIJKLMNOPQRSTUVWXYZÆÇØẞ
1234567890@.,!?’)]§*“”»«/–½©€$£¥&→

Didot Modern is a typeface of five weights plus *Italics:* Light, *Light Italic,* Regular, *Italic,* **Medium,** ***Medium Italic,*** **Bold,** ***Bold Italic,*** **Black,** ***and Black Italic***

→ P. 455

# Percy Jackson & the Lightning Thief

Distel

Distel is a decorative Display font with spiky terminals, based on historical Uncial scripts. For better readability, some of the shapes were adapted to fit contemporary demands and current reading habits. By default, many typical shapes from the Uncial were preserved but can always be swapped with optional alternates. This font works great in headlines but also features unexpected readability even in small sizes—perfect for your next corporate design or packaging project.

**Design:** 2019, Prof. Hans R. Heitmann → p. 476, Johannes Ammon → p. 472

**Foundry:** Finaltype, Germany, finaltype.de → p. 489

**Language support:** Latin Extended

**OpenType features:** Standard Ligatures, Discretionary Ligatures, All Alternates, Contextual Alternates, Fractions, Stylistic Alternates, Stylistic Sets, Localized Forms, Case Sensitive Forms

**Test version available:** Yes

**Web font format available:** Yes

→ P. 460

abcdefghijklmnopqrstuvwxyzæå
ABCDEFGHIJKLMNOPQRSTUVWXYZÆÇ
1234567890@.,!?')]§*“”»«/–½©€$£¥₲

Distel is a typeface of one Regular weight

Paris

*Full Moon in Paris*

**Division**

Division is a script typeface that has its origins in *Berthold Script*. The uppercase letters have been worked with expressive voluptuousness, Serifs in a "chip" spirit, and reveal the approach of a contemporary calligraphic posture. The Inline style offers a simplified drawing, revealing an apparent structure where the loops fade and thus complements the more contrasting Regular style. The typeface is recommended for use in medium to large sizes and in All Caps/Initial Caps.

**Design:** 2022, Alff Rosine → p. 481

**Foundry:** Skrr Type, France, skrr-type.com → p. 491

**Language support:** Latin

**OpenType features:** Standard Ligatures

**Test version available:** No

**Web font format available:** No

abcdefghijklmnopqrstuvwxyzfiçéñöûß

ABCDEFGHIJKLMNOPQRSTUVWXYZ

1234567890@.,:!?')]§*""»«/-©€$£¥₲

Division is a typeface of two weights: Inline and Regular



→ P. 460, 467

2019

ONE × SMALL × STEP

*FOR × LAMB*

# #FAR
# MA
# GED
# DON

**Drafting* Mono**

Monospaced fonts are often used during the production stage of projects. They are used by programmers while coding and film crews while filming. They resemble the rhythm of typewriters and permeate our pre-digital visual landscape. Drafting* Mono aims to capture this still-in-the-works spirit with something neutral and timeless that is also personal and anachronistic. It takes heavy inspiration from typewriters, aiming to capture their spirit and logic rather than mimicking their appearance literally.

**Design:** 2021, Owen Earl → p. 475

**Foundry:** indestructible type*, United States of America, indestructibletype.com → p. 489

**Language support:** Latin Extended

**OpenType features:** Small Caps, Fractions

**Test version available:** Yes

**Web font format available:** Yes

→ P. 466

abcdefghijklmnopqrstuvwxyzæåçéñöûß
ABCDEFGHIJKLMNOPQRSTUVWXYZÆÇØß
12345678900@.,!?')]§*"""»«/–½©€$£¥&

Drafting* Mono is a typeface of seven weights plus *Italics*: Thin, *Thin Italic*, Extra Light, *Extra Light Italic*, Light, *Light Italic*, Regular, *Italic*, **Medium**, ***Medium Italic***, **Semi Bold**, ***Semi Bold Italic***, **Bold**, ***and Bold Italic***

# Please don't tell why his hair turned Green!

… after you've seen:

# (1948)

THE BOY WITH
GREEN HAIR

The underlying grid system behind Edge's simple, rigorous shapes remains the same, while the typeface uses the rational grid in a different way. The typeface is the logical extension of that grid. Edge is playful despite its strict, formal constraints, building on the heritage of pioneers in graphic design, yet it is equally relevant for designers today.

**Design:** 2020, Ermin Međedović
→ p. 479

**Foundry:** Typotheque, The Netherlands, typotheque.com
→ p. 492

**Language support:** Latin

**OpenType features:** Proportional Oldstyle, Tabular Lining, Proportional Lining, Tabular Oldstyle, Standard Ligatures, All Caps, Small Caps, Superscript, Subscript

**Test version available:** Yes

**Web font format available:** Yes

abcdefghijklmnopqrstuvwxyzæfiåçéñöûß
ABCDEFGHIJKLMNOPQRSTUVWXYZÆÇØ
12345678900@.,!?')]§*“”»«/–½©€$£¥&→☛

Edge is a typeface of nine weights plus *Italics:* Thin, *Thin Italic,* Extra Light, *Extra Light Italic,* Light, *Light Italic,* Regular, *Italic,* Medium, *Medium Italic,* **Bold,** ***Bold Italic,*** **Extra Bold,** ***Extra Bold Italic,*** **Black,** ***and Black Italic***



→ P. 458, 460

セン ト チヒロ ノ カミガクシ
2001!!

Chi
hi&
ro

OGINO (HIIRAGI)

No-Face※
KAONASHI
カオナシ →

Ellograph CF

Ellograph CF is a cheerful monospaced typeface with a soft, rounded construction and striking cursive Italics. A generous x-height and short descenders allow for even, flowing lines of text. It is designed as a typeface for use in coding applications, while also charming in logos, headlines, and print.

**Design:** 2020, Connary Fagen → p. 475

**Foundry:** Connary Fagen, Inc., United States of America, connary.com → p. 488

**Language support:** Latin Extended, Japanese Katakana

**OpenType features:** Tabular Lining, Proportional Lining, Fractions, Numerator, Denominator, Arrows, Stylistic Alternates, Stylistic Sets Slashed Zero, Mark Positioning

**Test version available:** Yes

**Web font format available:** Yes

→ P. 466

abcdefghijklmnopqrstuvwxyzæåçéñß

ABCDEFGHIJKLMNOPQRSTUVWXYZÆÇØẞ

1234567890@.,!?')]§*“”»«/–½©€$£&↕☮

アイウエオ　カキクケコ　ガギグゲゴ　サシスセソ　ザジズゼゾ　タチツテト

ダヂヅデド　ナニヌネノ　ハヒフヘホ　バビブベボ　パピプペポ　マミムメモ

ラリルレロ　ワヰヱヲ　ヤユヨ　ンッ

Ellograph CF is a typeface of eight weights plus *Italics*: Thin, *Thin Italic*, Extra Light, *Extra Light Italic*, Light, *Light Italic*, Regular, *Italic*, Demi Bold, *Demi Bold Italic*, **Bold**, ***Bold Italic***, **Extra Bold**, ***Extra Bold Italic***, **Heavy**, ***and Heavy Italic***

**B.B.C. News 6 p.m.**

The Speech of H. M. The King

September 3rd, 39

Information Room

*"In this grave hour, perhaps the most fateful in our history, I send to every household of my peoples, both at home and overseas, this message, spoken with the same depth of feeling for each one of you, as if I were able to cross your threshold and speak to you myself. For the second time in the lives of most of us,* ***we are at war.¶*** *[…]"*

**LD Elsnac**

LD Elsnac is a contemporary roman type family. Its design is based on letterforms coming straight from the chalkboard in Kai Büschl's type and typography courses held for the first years students at the Deutsche Meisterschule für Mode | Designschule München. The font family's fundamental approach is to reduce the letter parts to their very basic forms without forgetting a contemporary look and its own very distinct character.

**Design:** 2020, Kai Büschl → p. 473

**Foundry:** Lazydogs Typefoundry, Germany, lazydogs.de → p. 490

**Language support:** Latin Extended

**OpenType features:** Proportional Oldstyle, Tabular Lining, Proportional Lining, Tabular Oldstyle, Standard Ligatures, All Caps, Small Caps, Capitals to Small Caps, Superscript, Subscript, Ordinals, Fractions, Numerator, Denominator, Arrows, Stylistic Alternates, Stylistic Sets, Localized Forms

**Test version available:** Yes

**Web font format available:** Yes

→ P. 455

abcdefghijklmnopqrstuvwxyzæfjåçéñöûß
ABCDEFGHIJKLMNOPQRSTUVWXYZÆÇØß
1234567890@.,!?')]§*“”»«/–©€$£¥&↘

LD Elsnac is a typeface of five weights plus *Italics:* Light, *Light Italic*, Regular, *Italic*, Medium, *Medium Italic*, **Bold**, ***Bold Italic***, **Heavy**, ***and Heavy Italic***

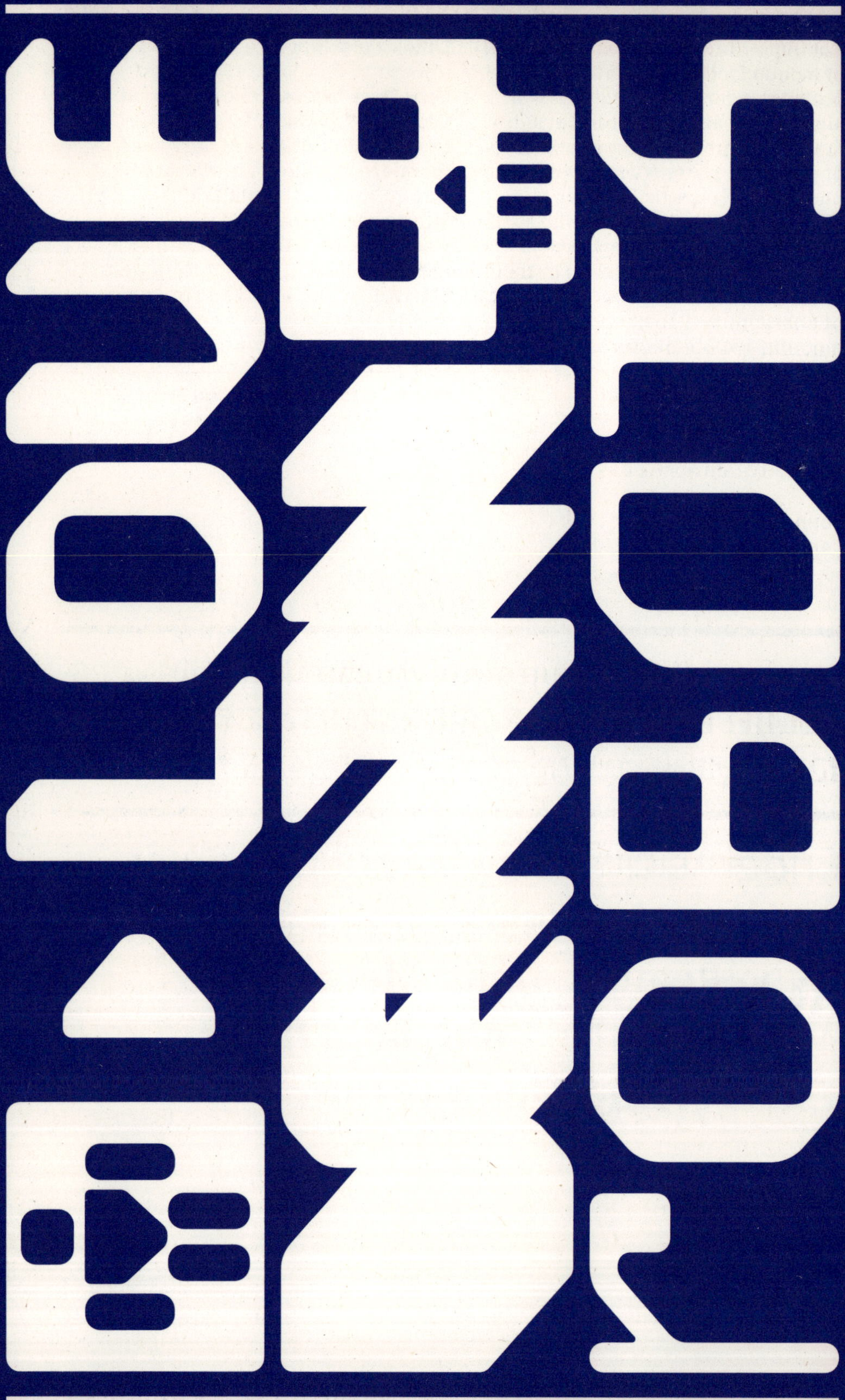

Ender

The Ender family is a culmination of a deep look into the MICR (magnetic ink character recognition) aesthetic, which remained synonymous with futurism for a couple of generations, and its influence on today's modular type design runs very deep. The initial exploration ballooned into a great big adventure and resulted in a series of original fonts with thousands of characters, arrows, icons, border, and grid elements as well as a variety of chromatic stacking possibilities.

**Design:** 2022, Patrick Griffin → p. 476, Robby Woodard → p. 484

**Foundry:** Canada Type, Canada, canadatype.com → p. 488

**Language support:** Latin Extended

**OpenType features:** Proportional Oldstyle, Tabular Lining, Proportional Lining, Standard Ligatures, Discretionary Ligatures, Superscript, Subscript, Ordinals, All Alternates, Fractions, Numerator Denominator, Ornaments, Arrows, Stylistic Alternates, Stylistic Sets, Localized Forms, Case Sensitive, Forms, Unicase

**Test version available:** No

**Web font format available:** Yes

→ P. 461

abcdefghijklmnopqrstuvwxyzœftåçéñöûß
ABCDEFGHIJKLMNOPQRSTUVWXYZÆÇØ
1234567890@@.,!?’)]§*“”»«/–½©€$£¥&

Ender is a family of seven styles:
[illegible] Light, Inline, Regular,
X1, X2, and X3

SCHE
HE
**RA**
ZA
DE

Catherine Zeta-Jones

One Thousand & One Nights

**Ereganto Serif**

Ereganto Serif is a seven-weight typeface that wishes to express a tribute to the gracious and delicate forms of the human body. All seven weights contain character sets that include Uppercase, Lowercase, Numerals, Diacritics, Punctuation, Ligatures, Alternates, and Symbols. Furthermore, it supports more than 60 languages derived from Latin, namely Western, Central, and South Eastern European languages, making it a perfect fit to be used either in titles or other typographic compositions.

**Design:** 2021, Brígida Guerreiro → p. 476

**Foundry:** KOBU Foundry, Portugal, kobufoundry.com → p. 489

**Language support:** Latin Extended

**OpenType features:** Standard Ligatures, Discretionary Ligatures, Historical Ligatures, All Alternates, Contextual Alternates, Contextual Ligatures, Arrows, Stylistic Alternates

**Test version available:** Yes

**Web font format available:** Yes

abcdefghijklmnopqrstuvwxyzæfjåçéñöûß
ABCDEFGHIJKLMNOPQRSTUVWXYZÆÇØß
1234567890@.,!?')]§*""»«/–1/2©€$£¥&↗❦

Ereganto Serif is a typeface of seven weights: Thin, Extra Light, Light, Regular, **Medium, Semi Bold, and Bold**


→ P. 455

2012

# Moonrise Kingdom

Q

Bruce Willis
Edward Norton
Bill Murray
Frances McDormand
Tilda Swinton
Jason Schwartzman
Bob Balaban

Ǽ

Eugenia

Commissioned for the La Repubblica weekly women's magazine D, Eugenia by Miguel Reyes draws on all sorts of bizarre italic and script letterforms that Giambattista Bodoni cut in the 18th century. It was drawn to accompany *Eugenio Serif,* which Miguel drew for La Repubblica in 2018. *Eugenio* and Eugenia were both commissioned by Francesco Franchi.

**Design:** 2021, Miguel Reyes → p. 481, Francesco Franchi → p. 475

**Foundry:** Commercial Type, United States of America, commercialtype.com → p. 488

**Language support:** Latin

**OpenType features:** –

**Test version available:** Yes

**Web font format available:** No

*abcdefghijklmnopqrstuvwxyzæffåçéñöûß*
*ABCDEFGHIJKLMNOPQRSTUVWXYZÆÇ*
*1234567890@.,!?')]§*“”»«/–½©€$£¥&→99*

*Eugenia is a family of two styles: Headline and Poster, each in two weights: Headline Light, **Headline Regular**, Poster Light, **and Poster Regular***

→ P. 467

1924/@ŒÉő~

↑

Ballet Mécanique ♥

Ballet Mécanique ♥

Ballet Mécanique ♥

Ballet Mécanique ♥

Ballet Mécanique ♥

Ballet Mécanique ♥

Ballet Mécanique ♥

↓

by Fernand Léger
& Dudley Murphy

Exposure borrows the eponymous principle from photography, using it to question the possibilities offered by variable fonts in a completely original way. Available in Roman and Italic, Exposure is a remarkable feat—both technically and in terms of drawing—that shows how other ways of exploiting variable font technology are possible. Exposure's axis of variation ranges from -100 to +100, and gives a feeling of adjusting the intensity of the light which the typeface is exposed to.

**Design:** 2022, Federico Parra Barrios → p. 481

**Foundry:** 205TF, France, 205.tf → p. 488

**Language support:** Latin Extended

**OpenType features:** Proportional Oldstyle, Tabular Lining, Proportional Lining, Tabular Oldstyle, Standard Ligatures, All Caps, Superscript, Subscript, Ordinals, Contextual Alternates, Fractions, Numerator, Denominator, Ornaments, Arrows, Slashed Zero, Localized Forms, Case Sensitive Forms, Font Variations

**Test version available:** Yes

**Web font format available:** Yes

abcdefghijklmnopqrstuvwxyzæfjåçéñöûß
ABCDEFGHIJKLMNOPQRSTUVWXYZÆÇØß
1234567890Ø@.,!?')]§*""»«/–½©€$£¥&↙♥

Exposure is a typeface of twenty-one weights plus *Italics:* +100, *+100 Italic,* +90, *+90 Italic* +80, *+80 Italic,* +70, *+70 Italic,* +60, *+60 Italic,* +50, *+50 Italic,* +40, *+40 Italic,* +30, *+30 Italic,* +20, *+20 Italic,* +10, *+10 Italic,* 0, *0 Italic,* -10, *-10 Italic,* -20, *-20 Italic,* -30, *-30 Italic,* -40, *-40 Italic,* -50, *-50 Italic,* -60, *-60 Italic,* -70, *-70 Italic,* -80, *-80 Italic,* -90, *-90 Italic,* -100, *-100 Italic*

→ P. 455, 461

Lucky
Luke

لذا أتيت لأقتل
Lucky Luke
لأسباب خاصة

R KOX

The more you look at it, the more you like it! Felka—which reads "Lucky" in Polish—is the next of Thomas Thiemich's design experiments published by TYPE BY, where the urge for the extremes meets the search for minimalism. But Felka goes further: its Capitals are built on three stacked bars, while its matching lowercase is built out of just two! Letters reduced to the max is no overstatement here. Felka Slab, Brick, Line, and Leaf—what can you do with it? Display typography, of course!

**Design:** 2020, Thomas Thiemich → p. 483

**Foundry:** TYPE BY, Belgium, typeby.com → p. 492

**Language support:** Latin Extended, Arabic

**OpenType features:** Proportional Oldstyle, Proportional Lining, All Caps, Ordinals, Arrows, Stylistic Alternates, Stylistic Sets, Localized Forms

**Test version available:** No

**Web font format available:** Yes

→ P. 461

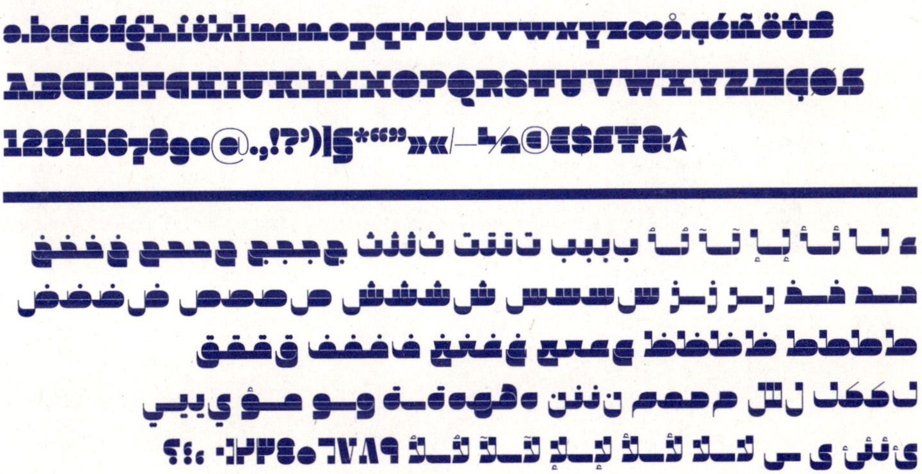

Felka is a family of four styles: Line, Slab, Brick, AND LEAF

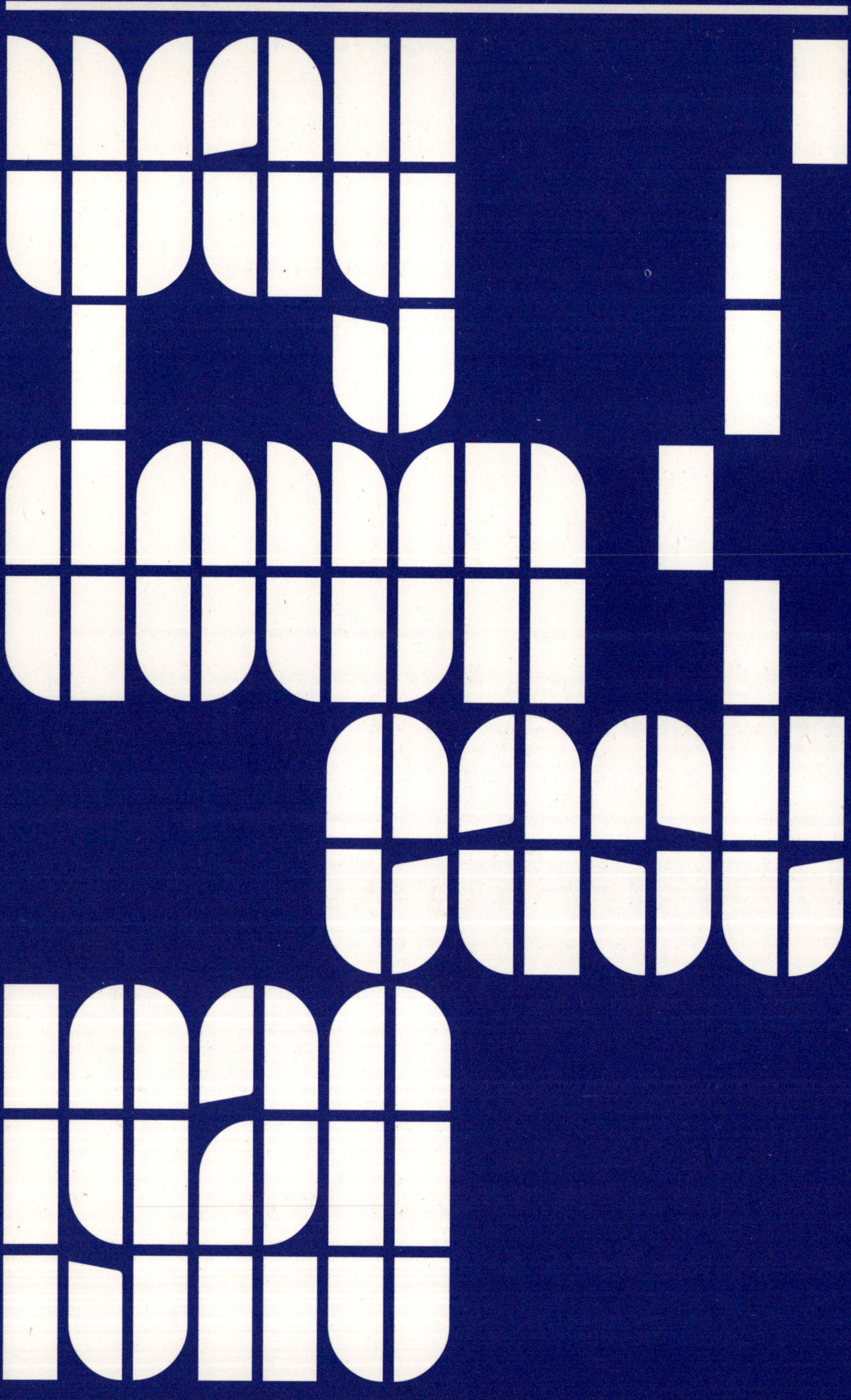

Fernhout

For the new Dutch Design Week brand identity, Thonik gave the almost 20-year-old logo, DDW's tulip, a second life by styling it as the *W* in the event name. DDW's tulip is a constellation of rectangles and quarter circles. These elements were also used in typographic experiments from the 1920's that were revised in 1963 by the late Wim Crouwel for the poster he created for painter Edgar Fernhout. It is this poster that studio Thonik took as inspiration for the new Dutch Design Week brand identity.

**Design:** 2021, Studio Thonik → p. 483, Wim Crouwel → p. 474

**Foundry:** The Foundry Types, United Kingdom, thefoundrytypes.com → p. 491

**Language support:** Latin Extended

**OpenType features:** Uppercase, Lowercase, Ligatures, Figures, Mathematic Symbols, Ordinals, Punctuation

**Test version available:** Yes

**Web font format available:** Yes

→ P. 461, 469

abcdefghijklmnopqrstuvwxyzfj

1234567890@.,:!?'[]×“”

fernhout is a typeface of one regular weight

# Owen Wilson:

** November 18th, 1968*
*Dallas, Texas,*
**U.S.A.**

**Wow!**

Wow?

**WOW**

*Wow!?*

**№7 ⟶**

Firelli

Firelli is an original family of 14 styles including 7 weights and Italics, delighting from Thin to Black, italic Swash Caps, Ligatures, and neat Alternate Characters. Big headlines will love Firelli's incorruptible details. Longer texts will benefit from a wide-ranging family with its solid posture. Go, use everything Firelli has to offer, to design your contentful magazines, powerful annual reports, or even bedtime stories and fairy tales.

**Design:** 2020, Teddy Derkert → p. 474

**Foundry:** Typejockeys, Austria, typejockeys.com → p. 492

**Language support:** Latin Extended

**OpenType features:** Proportional Oldstyle, Tabular Lining, Proportional Lining, Standard Ligatures, All Caps, Small Caps, Capitals to Small Caps, Superscript, Subscript, Ordinals, Swashes, Contextual, Swashes, Contextual Alternates, Fractions, Numerator, Denominator, Arrows, Localized Forms, Required Ligatures, Font Variations

**Test version available:** Yes

**Web font format available:** Yes

→ P. 458

abcdefghijklmnopqrstuvwxyzæfkåçéñöûß
ABCDEFGHIJKLMNOPQRSTUVWXYZÆß
1234567890@.,!?')]§*“”»«/–½©€$£¥&↔⌘

Firelli is a typeface of seven weights plus *Italics:* Thin, *Thin Italic,* Light, *Light Italic,* Regular, *Italic,* **Semi Bold,** ***Semi Bold Italic,*** **Bold,** ***Bold Italic,*** **Extra Bold,** ***Extra Bold Italic,*** **Black,** ***and Black Italic***

2011

*∫∫

# BLACK SWAN

**CZARNY ŁABĘDŹ**
**LE CYGNE NOIR**

*Natalie Portman ↘*
*Vincent Cassel · Mila Kunis ↗*

Fizz

Derived from Branzczyk's flamboyant display family *FEZ*, Fizz is conceived as the counterpart for running text. Its sturdier construction does the work in small sizes but retains the outgoing character of its display sibling. The flared terminals and strongly asymmetric counters translate into the Italic, which is drawn to be a strong visual contrast to the Roman while keeping a similar texture. In addition to the Sans, a Slab Serif companion adds typographic versatility to the family.

**Design:** 2021, Alexander Branczyk → p. 473, Sebastian Carewe → p. 473

**Foundry:** Face2Face, Germany, czyk.de → p. 489

**Language support:** Latin Extended, Cyrillic

**OpenType features:** Proportional Oldstyle, Tabular Lining, Proportional Lining, Tabular Oldstyle, Standard Ligatures, Discretionary Ligatures, Small Caps, Capitals to Small Caps, Superscript, Subscript, Ordinals, All Alternates, Fractions, Numerator, Denominator, Arrows, Stylistic Alternates, Stylistic Sets, Slashed Zero, Case Sensitive Forms

**Test version available:** Yes

**Web font format available:** Yes

abcdefghijklmnopqrstuvwxyzæåçéñöûß
ABCDEFGHIJKLMNOPQRSTUVWXYZÆÇØẞ
1234567890Ø@.,!?')]§*"“»«/–½©€$£¥&→

абвгдеёжзийклмнопрстуфхцчшщъыьэюя
АБВГДЕЁЖЗИЙКЛМНОПРСТУФХЦЧШЩЪЫЬЭ
1234567890Ø@.,!?')]§*"“»«/–½©€$£¥&↕

Fizz is a family of two styles: Normal and Slab, each in eight weights plus *Italics:* Extra Light, *Extra Light Italic,* Light, *Light Italic,* Regular, *Italic,* Medium, *Medium Italic,* **Semi Bold,** ***Semi Bold Italic,*** **Bold,** ***Bold Italic,*** **Extra Bold,** ***Extra Bold Italic,*** **Black,** ***Black Italic,*** Slab Extra Light, *Slab Extra Light Italic,* Slab Light, *Slab Light Italic,* Slab Regular, *Slab Italic,* Slab Medium, *Slab Medium Italic,* **Slab Semi Bold,** ***Slab Semi Bold Italic,*** **Slab Bold,** ***Slab Bold Italic,*** **Slab Extra Bold,** ***Slab Extra Bold Italic,*** **Slab Black,** ***and Slab Black Italic***

→ P. 449, 458

# « week

**TITRE :** WEEK-END
**RÉALISATEUR :** *Jean-Luc Godard*
**ASSISTANT-RÉALISATEUR :** *Claude Miller*
**MUSIQUE :** *Antoine Duhamel*

**FORMAT :** couleur par Eastmancolor — 35 mm — 1.66:1 — son monophonique
**GENRE :** COMÉDIE NOIRE
**DURÉE :** *95 MINUTE* **DATES DE SORTIE :** France 27 décembre 1967, Italie 13 avril 1968

# end »

Flecha

Flecha is a sharp and streamlined old-style typeface made for editorial design. On the whole, Flecha has a sturdy and mechanized appearance with its rigid letterforms, square terminals, and geometrically simplified strokes. Nevertheless, Flecha manages to be delicate and reminiscent of the broad nib pen. Made for editorial design, the family is divided into three optical sizes: S for body text, M for medium-sized headlines, and L for large headlines and titles.

**Design:** 2019, Rui Abreu → p. 472

**Foundry:** R-Typography, Portugal, r-typography.com → p. 491

**Language support:** Latin Extended

**OpenType features:** Proportional Oldstyle, Tabular Lining, Proportional Lining, Tabular Oldstyle, Standard Ligatures, Discretionary Ligatures, All Caps, Small Caps, Capitals to Small Caps, Superscript, Subscript, Fractions, Numerator, Denominator, Stylistic Alternates, Stylistic Sets, Case Sensitive Forms, Optical size

**Test version available:** Yes

**Web font format available:** Yes

abcdefghijklmnopqrstuvwxyzæfjåçéñöûß

ABCDEFGHIJKLMNOPQRSTUVWXYZÆÇØ

1234567890@.,!?')]§*“”»«/–½©€$£¥&»→

Flecha is a family of two widths: Normal and Brônzea. Normal in three optical sizes: S, M, and L, each in six weights plus *Italics:* S Extra Light, *S Extra Light Italic,* S Regular, *S Italic,* **S Bold,** ***S Bold Italic,*** M Light, *M Light Italic,* **M Medium,** ***M Medium Italic,*** **M Black,** ***M Black Italic,*** L Extra Light, *L Extra Light Italic,* L Regular, *L Italic,* **L Bold,** ***and L Bold Italic.*** Brônzea in two optical sizes: M and L, each in six weights plus *Italics:* M Extra Light, *M Extra Light Italic,* M Regular, *M Italic,* **M Bold,** ***M Bold Italic,*** L Light, *L Light Italic,* **L Medium,** ***L Medium Italic,*** **L Black,** ***and L Black Italic***



→ P. 455, 461

**CARPE DIEM.**
MAKE *YOUR* LIVES
**EXTRA**ORDINARY.

// ***Seize the day, boys. [#YOLO]***

Fontanella is a typeface designed by Guisela Mendoza, which emerged from calligraphy and manual drawings exploring the skeleton and classic proportions of Roman capital letters. The initial process later gave rise to a sans serif family composed of nine weights and its Italic variants. The slightly enlarged x-height makes it perfect for composing short texts in editorial, fashion, branding, magazine, television, window display, and other media projects. Fontanella a classic spirit reinterpreted in a contemporary language.

**Design:** 2022, Guisela Mendoza → p. 479

**Foundry:** Latinotype, Chile, latinotype.com → p. 490

**Language support:** Latin Extended

**OpenType features:** Proportional Oldstyle, Proportional Lining, Standard Ligatures, Small Caps Capitals to Small Caps, Ordinals, Fractions, Stylistic Alternates, Stylistic Sets, Localized Forms, Case Sensitive Forms

**Test version available:** No

**Web font format available:** Yes

abcdefghijklmnopqrstuvwxyzæåçéñöûß
ABCDEFGHIJKLMNOPQRSTUVWXYZÆÇØß
1234567890@.,!?')]§*""»«/–½©€$£¥&

Fontanella is a typeface of nine weights plus *Italics:* Thin, *Thin Italic,* Extra Light, *Extra Light Italic,* Light, *Light Italic,* Regular, *Italic,* **Medium,** ***Medium Italic,*** **Semi Bold,** ***Semi Bold Italic,*** **Bold,** ***Bold Italic,*** **Extra Bold,** ***Extra Bold Italic,*** **Black,** ***and Black Italic***

→ P. 449, 461

Life’s too short to be a background character.*

Free Guy!@

Free Guy!@

Free Guy!@

Free Guy!@

Free Guy!@

Free Guy!@

Free Guy!@

**Formulate**

Formulate began as a model alphabet for children who are just learning to read and write. The letterforms are closely related to how letters are written in early education while incorporating letter-construction methods from type design tradition. Multiplexed styles add a lot of utility to this typeface. Styles can be easily layered and weights can be changed without reflowing text. This creates fun opportunities for creating custom looks or interesting animations.

**Design:** 2021, Alanna Munro
→ p. 480

**Foundry:** Alanna Munro Type Foundry, Canada, alannamunro.com
→ p. 488

**Language support:** Latin

**OpenType features:** Proportional Lining, Stylistic Sets, Mark Positioning

**Test version available:** Yes

**Web font format available:** Yes

→ P. 461, 467

abcdefghijklmnopqrstuvwxyzæçéñöû
ABCDEFGHIJKLMNOPQRSTUVWXYZÆÇ
1234567890@.,!?')]*“”»«/-©$&

Formulate is a family of three styles: Outline, Inline, and Normal. Outline in eight weights: Outline Light, Outline Light Arrows, Outline Light Dots, Outline Light Inline, Outline Bold, Outline Bold Arrows, Outline Bold Dots, and Outline Bold Inline. Inline in three weights: Inline Dots, Inline, and Inline Arrows. Normal in six weights: Extra Light Dots, Extra Light, Light, Regular, **Medium, and Bold.**

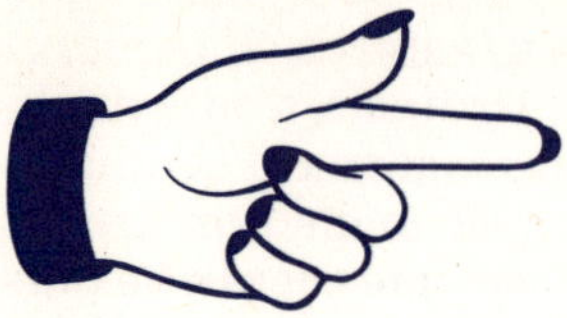

This is Benjamin.

He's a little worried about his future.

ANNE BRANCROFT
& DUSTIN HOFFMAN
KATHARINE ROSS

THE GRADUATE
1967

PP Fragment

PP Fragment is born from vintage lettering and signs, bridging 19th century letterforms and contemporary typography. Pangram Pangram's 35th release uses the latest technology, gracefully oscillating between an elegant, highly contrasted Serif face, a revival mid-serif called *Glare*, and a strong Sans, each with a distinct features yet perfectly complementary.

**Design:** 2022, Mathieu Desjardins → p. 474, Francesca Bolognini → p. 472

**Foundry:** Pangram Pangram, Canada, pangrampangram.com → p. 491

**Language support:** Latin Extended

**OpenType features:** Proportional Oldstyle, Standard Ligatures, Discretionary Ligatures, Superscript, Subscript, Ordinals, Contextual Alternates, Contextual Ligatures, Numerator, Denominator, Arrows, Stylistic Alternates, Stylistic Sets, Slashed Zero, Case Sensitive Forms

**Test version available:** Yes

**Web font format available:** Yes

# PP Fragment

→ P. 449, 456

abcdefghijklmnopqrstuvwxyzæffåçéñöûß
ABCDEFGHIJKLMNOPQRSTUVWXYZÆÇØẞ
1234567890@.,!?')]§*""»«/—½©€$£¥&⇔☞

PP Fragment is a family of four styles: Glare, Sans, Serif, **and Text.** Glare, Sans, and Serif each in eight weights: Glare Thin, Glare Extra Light, Glare Light, Glare Regular, **Glare Medium, Glare Bold, Glare Extra Bold, Glare Black,** Sans Thin, Sans Extra Light, Sans Light, Sans Regular, **Sans Medium, Sans Bold, Sans Extra Bold, Sans Black,** Serif Thin, Serif Extra Light, Serif Light, Serif Regular, **Serif Medium, Serif Bold, and Serif Extra Bold.** Text in four weights: Light, Regular, **Medium, and Bold**

ANCHORMAN

gg

“I’m not even ↙↗

MÆD

Это потрясающе!”

WWW

Franzi

Franzi typeface family—as neutral as can be, but at the same time individual and striking. Its unmistakable character lies in its details, with no effect pushing itself to the fore. As a wide-running typeface with a relatively large x-height, it is perfectly suited for small text sizes, but its elegant details leave nothing to be desired in display applications either.

**Design:** 2022, Ekke Wolf → p. 484

**Foundry:** Wannatype, Austria, wannatype.com → p. 492

**Language support:** Latin Extended, Cyrillic, Greek

**OpenType features:** Proportional Oldstyle, Tabular Lining, Proportional Lining Tabular Oldstyle Standard Ligatures, Discretionary Ligatures, All Caps, Small Caps, Capitals to Small Caps Superscript Subscript, Ordinals, Swashes, Contextual Alternates Fractions, Numerator, Denominator, Arrows, Stylistic Alternates, Stylistic Sets, Historical Forms, Slashed Zero, Localized Forms

**Test version available:** No

**Web font format available:** Yes

abcdefghijklmnopqrstuvwxyzæfʒåçéñöûß
ABCDEFGHIJKLMNOPQRSTUVWXYZÆÇØẞ
1234567890@.,!?')]§*""»«/–½©€$£¥&↙🚲

αβγδεζηθικλμνξοπρσςτυφχψωάέήίόώϊϋΰ
ΑΒΓΔΕΖΗΘΙΚΛΜΝΞΟΠΡΣΤΥΦΧΨΩΆΈΉΊΌΏΪΫ
12345678900@.,!?')]§*""»«/–½©€$£¥&↗🚲

Franzi is a family of ten weights plus *Italics:* Hairline, Hairline Italic, Extra Light, *Extra Light Italic,* Ultra Light, *Ultra Light Italic,* Light, *Light Italic,* Regular, *Italic,* Medium, *Medium Italic,* **Semi Bold,** ***Semi Bold Italic,*** **Bold,** ***Bold Italic,*** **Extra Bold,** ***Extra Bold Italic,*** **Black,** ***and Black Italic***

→ P. 449

Watch for
the Sensation of the
Season!

The SCARLET
LADY
{1928} U.S.A.

STARRING LYA de PUTTI * DON ALVARDO * WARNER OLAND
A COLUMBIA SUPER-SPECIAL

Futura Now

# Futura Now

For nearly 90 years, Paul Renner's *Futura* has been as popular as it is versatile—from children's books to fashion magazines to the plaque on the Moon. Futura is a typographic icon.

**Design:** 2020, Terrance Weinzierl → p. 484, Juan Villanueva→ p. 484, Steve Matteson → p. 479

**Foundry:** Monotype, United Kingdom, monotype.com → p. 490

**Language support:** Latin Extended, Cyrillic, Greek

**OpenType features:** Standard Ligatures, Discretionary Ligatures, Superscript, Subscript, Ordinals, All Alternates, Contextual Alternates, Fractions, Numerator Denominator, Ornaments, Stylistic Alternates, Localized Forms, Case Sensitive, Forms, Mark Positioning

**Test version available:** Yes

**Web font format available:** Yes

abcdefghijklmnopqrstuvwxyzæfjåçéñöûß
ABCDEFGHIJKLMNOPQRSTUVWXYZÆÇØ
1234567890@.,!?')]§*""»«/–½©€$£¥&↘

*абвгдеёжзийклмнопрстуфхцчшщъыьэюя*
*АБВГДЕЁЖЗИЙКЛМНОПРСТУФХЦЧШЩЪЫЬЭЮЯ*
*1234567890@.,!?')]§*""»«/–½©€$£¥&*

Futura Now is a family of eight styles: Text, Display, Headline, **INLINE, OUTLINE, SHADOW, Stencil,** *and Script.* Text in two widths: Normal and Condensed, each in nine weights plus *Italics:* Light, ***Medium Italic,*** **Condensed Bold, *and Condensed Extra Black Italic.*** Display in six weights plus *Italics:* Light, *Italic,* **Bold, *and Black Italic.*** Headline in two widths: Normal and Condensed, each in nine weights plus *Italics:* Light, ***Medium Italic,*** **Condensed Bold, *and Condensed Extra Black Italic.*** **SHADOW AND INLINE EACH IN THREE WEIGHTS: INLINE NORMAL, INLINE BOLD,** AND SHADOW FILL. OUTLINE IN SIX WEIGHTS: THIN, EXTRA LIGHT, LIGHT, **REGULAR, BOLD,** AND FILL. **Stencil in one Regular weight.** *Script in five weights: Extra Light, Light, Regular, **Bold, and Extra Bold***

→ P. 450, 461, 467

BF Garant Prot

GATTACA

# Как вы прячетесь, когда бежите от себя?

BF Garant Pro elegantly balances geometric design with dynamic character! The strict architecture combines open counters, tapered spurs, and diagonal cut ascenders/descenders that create a lively character without denying the straightness of geometry. The large x-height, unique details, and humanist-inspired alternates make it a contemporary, highly legible design tool, ideal for branding use and also for contemporary editorial design. For projects far, far away, the Galactic Credits sign is available!

**Design:** 2022, Guido Schneider
→ p. 482

**Foundry:** BrassFonts, Germany, brass-fonts.de → p. 488

**Language support:** Latin Extended, Cyrillic, Greek

**OpenType features:** Proportional Oldstyle, Tabular Lining, Proportional Lining, Tabular Oldstyle, Standard Ligatures, Discretionary Ligatures, All Caps, Small Caps, Capitals to Small Caps, Superscript, Subscript, Ordinals, All Alternates, Fractions, Alternative Fractions, Numerator, Denominator, Ornaments, Arrows, Stylistic Alternates, Stylistic Sets, Slashed Zero, Localized Forms, Case Sensitive Forms

**Test version available:** Yes

**Web font format available:** Yes

abcdefghijklmnopqrstuvwxyzæfjåçéñöûß
ABCDEFGHIJKLMNOPQRSTUVWXYZÆÇØẞ
1234567890ø@.,!?')]§*“”»«/–½©€$£¥&☮

αβγδεζηθικλμνξοπρσςτυφχψωάέήίόώϊϋΰ
ΑΒΓΔΕΖΗΘΙΚΛΜΝΞΟΠΡΣΤΥΦΧΨΩΆΈΉΊΌΏΪΫ
1234567890Ø@.,!?')]§*“”»«/–½©€$£¥&

BF Garant Pro is a typeface of ten weights plus *Italics:* Thin, *Thin Italic,* Extra Light, *Extra Light Italic,* Light, *Light Italic,* Semi Light, *Semi Light Italic,* Regular, *Italic,* Medium, *Medium Italic,* **Semi Bold,** ***Semi Bold Italic,*** **Bold,** ***Bold Italic,*** **Extra Bold,** ***Extra Bold Italic,*** **Black,** ***and Black Italic***


→ P. 450

The Terminal—

# Life is waiting.

Mehran Karimi Nasseri

↘ *Paris-Charles de Gaulle Airpot*

*coup d'état!*

1988 → 2006

**TERMINAL 1**

Tom Hanks as ↘

Viktor Navorski

from → Krakozhia ↙

to ↘ *John F. Kennedy International Airport*

↘ ↑ ↓ ↙ ↗ → ← ↖

↘ ↑ ↓ ↙ ↗ → ← ↖

**Garino**

Garino is a modern Sans Serif typeface. It gains its expressive character from a dynamic sweep in the curves and highcontrast transitions. The thinner and thicker weights are particularly suitable for strong headlines, while the middle weights can be used for typographic challenges and body text. As a result, it can be used in a reserved as well as an expressive way. Thanks to an extensive character collection, it becomes a real workhorse. A versatile allrounder that is up to all challenges.

**Design:** 2021, Julien Fincker → p. 475

**Foundry:** Julien Fincker, Germany, julienfincker.com → p. 489

**Language support:** Latin Extended

**OpenType features:** Proportional Oldstyle, Tabular Lining, Proportional Lining, Tabular Oldstyle, Standard Ligatures, Discretionary Ligatures, Small Caps, Superscript Subscript, Ordinals, Contextual Alternates, Fractions, Numerator, Denominator, Arrows, Stylistic Alternates, Stylistic Sets, Case Sensitive Forms, Mark Positioning

**Test version available:** Yes

**Web font format available:** Yes

→ P. 450

abcdefghijklmnopqrstuvwxyzæfjåçéñöûß
ABCDEFGHIJKLMNOPQRSTUVWXYZÆÇØẞ
1234567890@.,!?')]§*“”»«/–⅓©€$£¥&↘

Garino is a typeface of ten weights plus *Obliques:* Thin, *Thin Oblique,* Extra Light, *Extra Light Oblique,* Light, *Light Oblique,* Book, *Book Oblique,* Regular, *Regular Oblique,* **Medium,** ***Medium Oblique,*** **Bold,** ***Bold Oblique,*** **Extra Bold,** ***Extra Bold Oblique,*** **Black,** ***Black Oblique,*** **Heavy,** ***and Heavy Oblique***

Call me by your name!

Genie

Genie is an embodiment of dynamism. A mix of brutalism and illegibility, the typographic movement represents both perfection and imperfection in the beauty of calligraphy. Rare kinks are incorporated to give the realism of organic handwriting. Superfluous, as people said, an additional set of Astrological glyphs was designed, that nobody asked for.

**Design:** 2021, Jiahui Tan → p. 483

**Foundry:** Fable Type Foundry, Singapore, fable.design/typefaces → p. 488

**Language support:** Latin

**OpenType features:** –

**Test version available:** No

**Web font format available:** No

→ P. 461, 468

abcdefghijklmnopqrstuvwxyz
ABCDEFGHIJKLMNOPQRSTUVWXYZ
1234567890@.,!?')}§*"" ></-€$£&>∞

Genie is a typeface of one Regular weight

# CRY MACHO

**A story of being lost ...
and found.**

CLINT
EASTWOOD

—†‡†—

SEPTEMBER
17-2021

**Geometrico Slab**

Geometrico Slab. Round with strong serifs. Should it express power? Geometric and with slab serifs: a relatively rare combination. Geometrico Slab takes its cue from Herb Lubalin's typeface family of the same name, and by using optical corrections with restraint, it looks a touch more uncompromising. The flexible, partly asymmetrical arrangement of the Serifs avoids an overly heavy effect. The typeface family is suitable for both headlines and small point sizes. Curious? Try Geometrico Slab free of charge.

**Design:** 2022, Filippo Salmina → p. 482

**Foundry:** FSdesign, Switzerland, geometrico.ch → p. 489

**Language support:** Latin Extended

**OpenType features:** Tabular Lining, Proportional Lining, Standard Ligatures, Superscript, Subscript, Ordinals, Fractions, Numerator, Denominator

**Test version available:** Yes

**Web font format available:** Yes

→ P. 458

abcdefghijklmnopqrstuvwxyzœfjåçéñöûß
ABCDEFGHIJKLMNOPQRSTUVWXYZÆÇØ
1234567890@.,!?']]§*“”»«/–½©€$£¥&

Geometrico Slab is a typeface of eleven weights: Ultra Light, Extra Light, Thin, Light, Regular, **Medium, Demi Bold, Bold, Black, Extra Black, and Ultra Black**

Boy, have we got a vacation for you ... ↵

: D

**... where nothing can *possibly* go**

**w r o n g !**

&&& G♡ &&&

Geóso

Geóso is a humanist Sans Serif with a geometric feel. Beautifully handcrafted, with a focus on legibility in small sizes—and elegance in large ones. Thanks to its precise letterspacing, Geóso looks smooth and balanced when set in all caps. The uniwidth system comes in handy where space is limited and precision is required. Digital applications, such as hover effects and animations, are a natural match for Geóso, which is also available as variable font.

**Design:** 2019, Prof. Hans R. Heitmann → p. 476, Johannes Ammon → p. 472

**Foundry:** Finaltype, Germany, finaltype.de → p. 489

**Language support:** Latin Extended

**OpenType features:** Proportional Oldstyle, Tabular Lining, Proportional Lining, Tabular Oldstyle, Standard Ligatures, Discretionary Ligatures, Small Caps, Capitals to Small Caps, Superscript, Subscript, Ordinals, All Alternates, Contextual Alternates, Fractions, Numerator, Denominator, Arrows, Stylistic Alternates, Stylistic Sets, Localized Forms, Case Sensitive Forms

**Test version available:** Yes

**Web font format available:** Yes

→ P. 450

abcdefghijklmnopqrstuvwxyzæfiåçéñöûß
ABCDEFGHIJKLMNOPQRSTUVWXYZÆÇØẞ
1234567890@.,!?')]§*""»«/–½©€$£¥&↕ ☺

Geóso is a family of nine weights plus *Italics:* Thin, *Thin Italic,* Ultra Light, *Ultra Light Italic,* Light, *Light Italic,* Regular, *Italic,* **Medium,** ***Medium Italic,*** **Demi Bold,** ***Demi Bold Italic,*** **Bold,** ***Bold Italic,*** **Extra Bold,** ***Extra Bold Italic,*** **Heavy,** ***and Heavy Italic***

Seeing is believing
*Seeing is believing*
*Seeing is believing*
*Seeing is believing*
**Seeing is believing**
***Seeing is believing***
**Seeing is believing**
***Seeing is believing***
**Seeing is believing**
***Seeing is believing***

**Ghost**

Ghost is a rediscovery of the humanist Sans. Working backwards from the genre's origin in Roman inscriptional lettering, Ghost harmonizes key elements of the genre's most compelling exemplars into a distinctly contemporary aesthetic. By abandoning the looseness and organic qualities characteristic of the genre, Ghost conceives of these motifs as mechanically constructed expressions of calligraphic form. Ghost is connected to the human hand not by imitation, but by representation.

**Design:** 2022, Lucas Sharp
→ p. 482

**Foundry:** Sharp Type, United States of America, sharptype.co → p. 491

**Language support:** Latin Extended

**OpenType features:** Proportional Oldstyle, Tabular Lining, Proportional Lining, Tabular Oldstyle, Standard Ligatures, All Caps, Superscript, Subscript, Ordinals, Fractions, Numerator, Denominator, Arrows, Stylistic Alternates, Stylistic Sets, Localized Forms, Case Sensitive Forms

**Test version available:** Yes

**Web font format available:** Yes

→ P. 450

abcdefghijklmnopqrstuvwxyzæfiåçéñöûß
ABCDEFGHIJKLMNOPQRSTUVWXYZÆÇØẞ
1234567890@.,!?')]§*“”»«/–½©€$£¥&&♠

Ghost is a typeface of five weights plus *Italics:* Light, *Light Italic,* Regular, *Italic,* **Medium,** ***Medium Italic,*** **Bold,** ***Bold Italic,*** **Extra Bold,** ***and Extra Bold Italic***

**5** strangers.

**4** secrets.

**3** schemes.

**2** best friends.

# SMOKE /1995

&

**1** neighborhood hangout where *the world still makes sense.*

**Gineto**

Gineto is a clean and airy contemporary Grotesque, tailored for small sizes. The design concept developed from the brevier size of Gothic no. 4, a nineteenth-century design by the New York type foundry Farmer, Little & Co.. This brevier features slightly narrow shapes with generous letter-spacing and long ascenders and descenders. Gineto's design echoes the spacious and ventilated construction of Gothic no.4 with unambiguous letterforms for enhanced clarity in small sizes.

**Design:** 2021, Rui Abreu → p. 472

**Foundry:** R-Typography, Portugal, r-typography.com → p. 491

**Language support:** Latin Extended

**OpenType features:** Tabular Lining, Proportional Lining, All Caps, Superscript, Subscript, Fractions, Numerator, Denominator, Slashed Zero, Case Sensitive Forms

**Test version available:** Yes

**Web font format available:** Yes

→ P. 450

abcdefghijklmnopqrstuvwxyzæflåçéñöûß
ABCDEFGHIJKLMNOPQRSTUVWXYZÆÇØ
12345678900@.,!?')]§*“”»«/–½©€$£¥&→

Gineto is a family of two styles: Normal and Fit, each in four weights plus *Italics:* Regular, *Italic,* **Medium,** ***Medium Italic,*** **Bold,** ***Bold Italic,*** **Black,** ***and Black Italic,*** Fit Regular, *Fit Italic,* Fit Medium, ***Fit Medium Italic,*** **Fit Bold,** ***Fit Bold Italic,*** **Fit Black,** ***and Fit Black Italic***

the **perks** of being a ***wall*** « ***flower***

Logan Lerman **&** Emma Watson **&** Ezra Miller

**/ WE ARE INFINITE**

**Goldplay**

Goldplay is based on *Isidora Sans,* yet features rounded shapes. Its rounded, soft terminals give it a friendly and expressive look, and its modern and contemporary style, as well as its classic proportions, make it an excellent choice for diverse use. One of its key features is a large x-height which make it look elegant and classy. The standard sans serif version—fresh, clean, and contemporary—is a perfect choice for editorial and corporate design, headlines, books, magazines, or any other piece of graphic design.

**Design:** 2019, Enrique Hernandez → p. 476

**Foundry:** Latinotype, Chile, latinotype.com → p. 490

**Language support:** Latin Extended

**OpenType features:** Standard Ligatures, Discretionary Ligatures, Ordinals, Fractions, Stylistic Alternates, Stylistic Sets, Localized Forms, Case Sensitive Forms

**Test version available:** No

**Web font format available:** Yes

abcdefghijklmnopqrstuvwxyzæﬂåçéñöûß
ABCDEFGHIJKLMNOPQRSTUVWXYZÆÇØß
1234567890@.,!?')]§*“”»«/–½©€$£¥&

Goldplay is a family of two styles: Normal and Alt, each in seven weights plus *Italics:* Thin, *Thin Italic,* Light, *Light Italic,* Regular, *Italic,* Medium, *Medium Italic,* **Semi Bold,** ***Semi Bold Italic,*** **Bold,** ***Bold Italic,*** **Black,** ***Black Italic,*** Alt Thin, *Alt Thin Italic,* Alt Light, *Alt Light Italic,* Alt Regular, *Alt Italic,* Alt Medium, *Alt Medium Italic,* **Alt Semi Bold,** ***Alt Semi Bold Italic,*** **Alt Bold,** ***Alt Bold Italic,*** **Alt Black,** ***and Alt Black Italic***



→ P. 450, 461

Good2Type has been created in the process of a new brand identity for G2K Group, an AI service provider. The identity was designed to—visually—disrupt the AI/Tech sector and needed to stand out, which is why the designers chose a modernistic approach. Since they couldn't find a typeface that matched their requirements for the Corporate Identity, they drew one by themselves. The result—Good2Type—is used as a display typeface on the G2K Group's website and other marketing collaterals.

**Design:** 2020, Jan Erlinghagen → p. 475

**Foundry:** CRU Brand Consultancy, Germany, madebycru.com → p. 488

**Language support:** Latin

**OpenType features:** –

**Test version available:** No

**Web font format available:** Yes

# Good2Type

→ P. 461, 469

ABCDEFGHIJKLMNOPQRSTUVWXYZ

1234567890@.,!?')§*"'/-€$£¥&

GOOD2TYPE IS A TYPEFACE OF TWO WEIGHTS: REGULAR **AND BOLD**

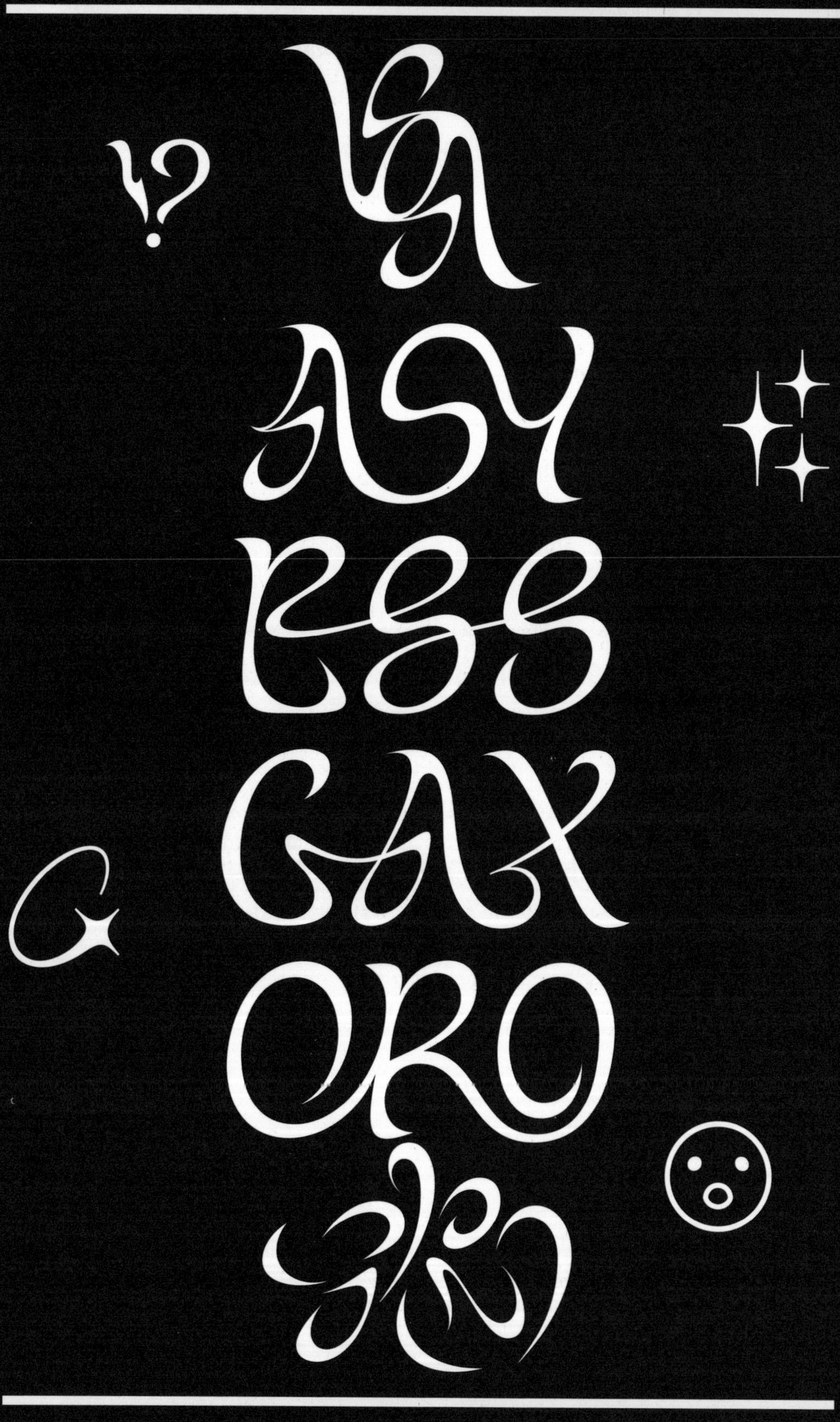

Gosna

Gosna was released as the designer's first display font. The designs came very intuitively, probably because the designer projected his ideal handwriting onto it. The main challenge for the design was to draw expressive and curvy glyphs while making sure that the overall font feels stable and systematic. Another point of focus is the ligatures, which emphasize the calligraphic flow of Gosna. Similar to musicians playing multiple notes in the span of a single breath, threaded glyphs seem to build up a sense of momentum.

**Design:** 2021, Dae Huen Lee
→ p. 478

**Foundry:** Quicknap.zzz, France, instagram.com/quicknap.zzz
→ p. 491

**Language support:** Latin

**OpenType features:** Tabular Oldstyle, Standard Ligatures, Discretionary Ligatures, All Caps, Contextual Ligatures, Fractions, Ornaments, Arrows, Stylistic Alternates, Stylistic Sets

**Test version available:** Yes

**Web font format available:** Yes

abcdefghijklmnopqrstuvwxyzæffåçéñöû
ABCDEFGHIJKLMNOPQRSTUVWXYZÆÇØ
1234567890@.,!?')]§*“”»«/–½©€$£¥&→G

Gosna is a typeface of one Regular weight


→ P. 461, 468

MR AND
MRS. ♡
SMITH ▶

PLANET DER
∞ AFFEN /

QUESTIONS?

♠ ZZORRO!

Granit Display

The inspiration for Granit was various vernacular letterforms from the realm of 19th and 20th-century tombstones (including from the notorious Père-Lachaise cemetery). Granit inherits its distinctive personality from a very specific stencil-like feature, often found on letters such as *a, g, n, r,* and *y.* While giving us a glimpse of the by-gone charm of traditional stone carving techniques, these subtleties empower Granit's palette with a more eccentric and optimistic character tailored for titling.

**Design:** 2021, Alex Chavot → p. 474

**Foundry:** Apex Type Foundry, France, apextypefoundry.com → p. 488

**Language support:** Latin Extended

**OpenType features:** Proportional Oldstyle, Tabular Lining, Proportional Lining, Tabular Oldstyle, Standard Ligatures, Discretionary Ligatures, Historical Ligatures, All Caps, Small Caps, Capitals to Small Caps, Superscript, Subscript, Ordinals, Contextual Alternates, Fractions, Numerator, Denominator, Arrows, Stylistic Sets, Historical Forms, Slashed Zero, Localized Forms, Case Sensitive Forms

**Test version available:** Yes

**Web font format available:** Yes

abcdefghijklmnopqrstuvwxyzæfjåçéñöûß
ABCDEFGHIJKLMNOPQRSTUVWXYZÆÇØß
1234567890Ø@.,!?')]§*""»«/–½©€$£¥&↗★

Granit Display is a typeface of one Regular weight plus *Italics*

→ P. 456, 461

»The curious fish gets caught!«

Grato Marker

Grato Marker is the handwritten expression of geometric ideas. An authentic companion to Grato Classic and Grotesk, Grato Marker is a playful hybrid of geometry and informality: it lets vertical strokes tilt and its baseline bounce as it plays with letter sizing. Its hand-made forms can feel charmingly wobbly, but they remain clear and legible, even in small sizes.

**Design:** 2022, Teja Smrekar → p. 483, Jakob Runge → p. 482

**Foundry:** TypeMates, Germany, typemates.com → p. 492

**Language support:** Latin Extended, Cyrillic, Greek

**OpenType features:** Proportional Oldstyle, Tabular Lining, Proportional Lining, Tabular Oldstyle, Standard Ligatures, Superscript, Subscript, Ordinals, Contextual Alternates, Fractions, Numerator, Denominator, Ornaments, Arrows, Stylistic Alternates, Stylistic Sets, Slashed Zero, Localized Forms, Case Sensitive Forms, Mark Positioning

**Test version available:** Yes

**Web font format available:** Yes

# Grato Marker

→ P. 468

abcdefghijklmnopqrstuvwxyzæijåçéñöûß

ABCDEFGHIJKLMNOPQRSTUVWXYZÆÇØ

123456789oo@.,!?')]§*""»«/-©€$£¥&↘

абвгдеёжзийклмнопрстуфхцчшщъыьэюя

АБВГДЕЁЖЗИЙКЛМНОПРСТУФХЦЧШЩЪЫЬЭЮЯ

1234567890O@.,!?')]§*""»«/-©€$£¥&↔

Grato Marker is a typeface of four weights: Light, Regular, **Medium, and Bold**

(film technique)

*Found footage is a cinematic technique in which all or a substantial part of the work is presented as if it were discovered film or video recordings.

Found

*footage

Greenstone is a double homage by Connor Davenport: first to *Ogg's* vernacular lettering style; the second to the stone carving of American John Howard Benson and British David Kindersley. This tribute is a synecdochic acknowledgment of the dialogue between the American and British type industries of the 19th to 20th centuries. While perfectly serviceable as a model alphabet for stone carving, Greenstone is a typographic expression of an ancient tradition of lettering.

**Design:** 2021, Connor Davenport
→ p. 474

**Foundry:** Sharp Type, United States of America, sharptype.co → p. 491

**Language support:** Latin Extended

**OpenType features:** Proportional Oldstyle, Proportional Lining, All Caps, Superscript, Subscript, Swashes, Contextual Alternates, Contextual Ligatures, Fractions, Numerator, Denominator, Arrows, Stylistic Alternates, Stylistic Sets, Localized Forms, Case Sensitive Forms

**Test version available:** Yes

**Web font format available:** Yes

→ P. 456

abcdefghijklmnopqrstuvwxyzæåçéñöûß
ABCDEFGHIJKLMNOPQRSTUVWXYZÆÇØẞ
1234567890@.,!?')]§*“”»«/–½©€$£¥&↗☾

Greenstone is a typeface of one Regular weight plus *Italics*

* A MOVIE DAVID ANDREW LEO FINCHER
(BORN AUGUST 28TH, 1962)

# The Curious Case of BENJAMIN BUTTON (2008)¶

BRAD PITT & CATE BLANCHETT

The basic visual idea of Grunt was to create a serif text typeface with (mostly) inverted diagonal contrast. First draft of the typeface was made with the Letterink app, that uses skeleton based stroke drawing. Later it was redrawn in outlines to reduce some too dominant and distracting calligraphic features. With variable font technology it is possible to slightly modify its weight and width to create the desired "typographic color" on the page.

**Design:** 2021, Michal Tornyai → p. 483

**Foundry:** Michal Tornyai, Slovakia, tornyai.sk → p. 490

**Language support:** Latin

**OpenType features:** Proportional Oldstyle, Proportional Lining, Standard Ligatures, Discretionary Ligatures, Contextual Alternates, Font Variations

**Test version available:** No

**Web font format available:** No

abcdefghijklmnopqrstuvwxyzflåéöß
ABCDEFGHIJKLMNOPQRSTUVWXYZ
1234567890@.,!?')*“”/–©€$&

Grunt is a typeface of one Regular weight

→ P. 456, 469

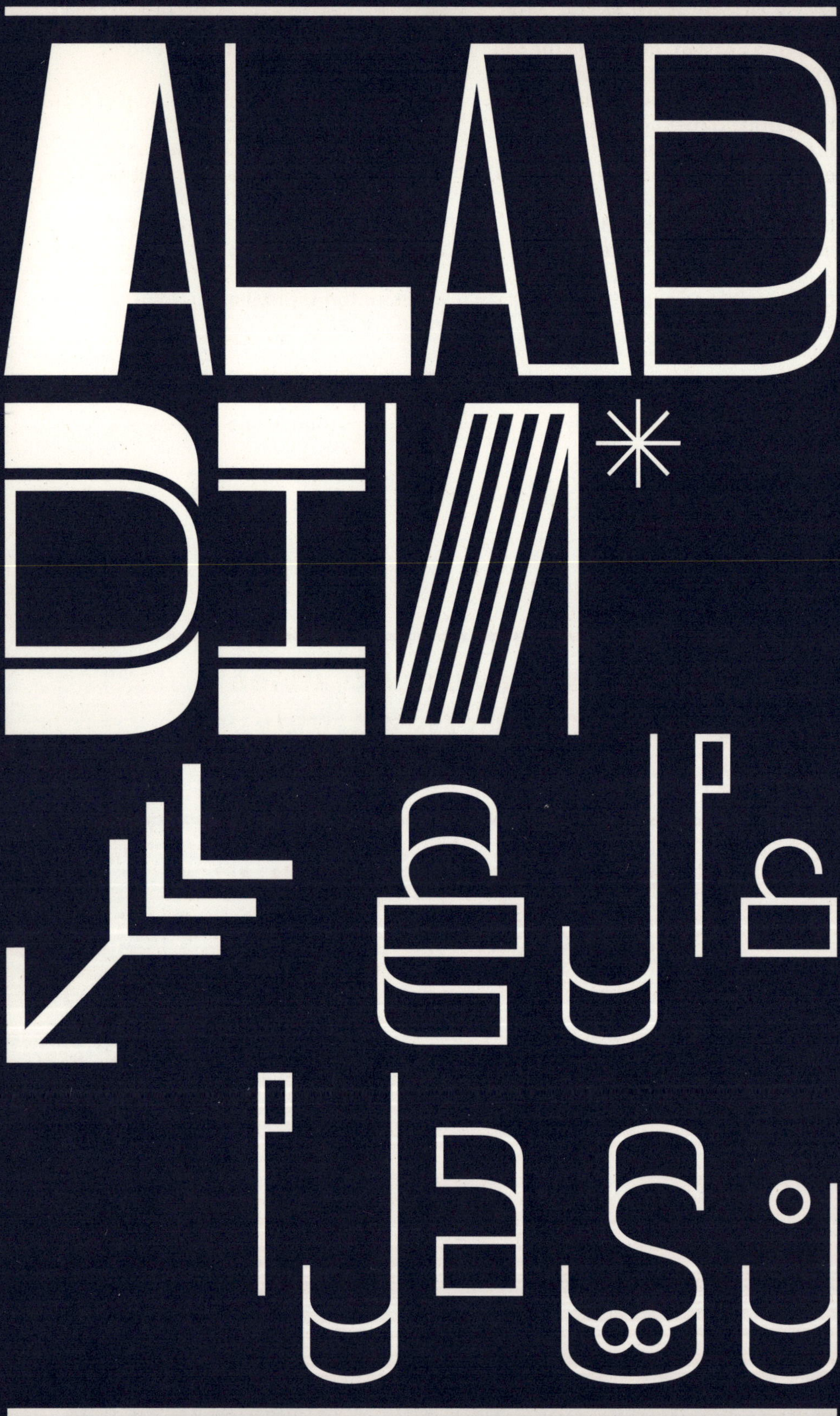


Gustella

Gustella is a rare cherry on the pie—this could be its shortest and most eloquent description. Designed by Thomas Thiemich for TYPE BY, it was conceived to catch and endear the graphic designer's eye, and it succeeds with brio. Its extreme reverse-contrast design has many qualities: precise, juicy, and innovative. And it shines in Latin and Arabic of every variant, from the Solid to Boxed, Inline, and the spectacular Stripes version.

**Design:** 2019, Thomas Thiemich → p. 483

**Foundry:** TYPE BY, Belgium, typeby.com/ → p. 492

**Language support:** Latin Extended, Arabic

**OpenType features:** Tabular Lining, Proportional Lining, Ordinals, All Alternates, Contextual Alternates, Fractions, Stylistic Alternates, Stylistic Sets, Slashed Zero, Localized Forms, Case Sensitive Forms, Required Ligatures, Terminal Form, Initial Form, Isolated Form, Medial Form

**Test version available:** No

**Web font format available:** Yes

→ P. 461

abcdefghijklmnopqrstuvwxyzææåçéñöûß
ABCDEFGHIJKLMNOPQRSTUVWXYZÆÇØẞ
1234567890Ø@.,:!?')]§*“”»«/–½©€$£¥§→★

ء ا أ إ آ ٱ ب ببب ت تتت ث ثثث ج ججج ح ححح خ خخخ
د ـد ذ ـذ ر ـر ز ـز س سسس ش ششش ص صصص ض ضضض
ط ططط ظ ظظظ ع ععع غ غغغ ف ففف ق ققق
ك ككك ل للل م ممم ن ننن ه ههه ة ـة و ـو ؤ ـؤ ي ييي
ئ ئئئ ى ـى لا ـلا لأ ـلأ لإ ـلإ لآ ـلآ لٱ ـلٱ ٠١٢٣٤٥٦٧٨٩ ،؛؟

Gustella is a family of four styles: Boxed, Striped, Inline, and Solid, each in four weights: Boxed Thin, Boxed Light, Boxed Normal, Boxed Bold, Striped Thin, Striped Light, Striped Normal, Striped Bold, Inline Thin, Inline Light, Inline Normal, Inline Bold, Solid Thin, Solid Light, Solid Normal, and Solid Bold

Sunday, 05:00 a.m.    한여름 새벽

# Another
# Day
# of
# Sunshine
# 햇살

**Happiness Sans**

Happiness Sans is a custom font for Hyundai Department Store, embracing its brand mission "Bring happiness to customers and flourish the world." It delivers cheerful happiness through the curve of the apex and ascending curve at the end of the stroke where you can feel the aesthetics of handwriting. For the Latin type, we reinterpreted the early grotesque style, reproduced the curved feature of Hangeul, and set the position and size of the baseline so it blends well with Hangeul.

**Design:** 2022, Moa Ku → p. 478, Jookyeong Kim → p. 477, Seunghwan Kim → p. 477, Noheul Lee → p. 478, Eerang Park → p. 481, Hyunsong Lee → p. 478

**Foundry:** AG Typography Institute, South Korea, agfont.com/en → p. 488

**Language support:** Latin Extended, Korean

**OpenType features:** Tabular Lining, Proportional Lining, Standard Ligatures, Discretionary Ligatures, Superscript, Subscript, Ordinals, All Alternates, Fractions, Numerator, Denominator, Stylistic Sets, Slashed Zero, Localized Forms, Case Sensitive Forms, Font Variations

**Test version available:** Yes

**Web font format available:** Yes

abcdefghijklmnopqrstuvwxyzæfjåçéñöûß
ABCDEFGHIJKLMNOPQRSTUVWXYZÆÇØẞ
12345678900@.,!?')]§*""»«/-½©€$£¥&↕♭

가냐더레미배세예재차캬터히까떠빠쎄
쨰고뇨두류므보슈쥐최슈쾌훼꽈뚜뾰쓰
12345678900@.,!?')]§*""»«/-½©€$£¥&→♂

Happiness Sans is a typeface of three weights: Regular, **Bold, and Title**

→ P. 450, 461, 469

*The*

SCRANTON BUSINESS PARK
1725 SLOUGH AVENUE
SCRANTON, PA.

Office.

Dunder
Mifflin INC,
*Paper*
*Company*

**Haultin**

When examining Pierre Haultin's original work, the research mostly relies on prints, as actual typographic material left nowadays is scarce. So Smeijers distilled his own interpretation of a Haultin-ic roman and italic based on the only originals left. Smeijers' Haultin design is an efficient text face, but it is not a revived digital version of the historical material. Haultin is a thoroughly contemporary typeface—that respects its primary historical sources—and is a formidable design tool.

**Design:** 2019, Fred Smeijers → p. 483

**Foundry:** TYPE BY, Belgium, typeby.com → p. 492

**Language support:** Latin Extended

**OpenType features:** Proportional Oldstyle, Tabular Lining, Proportional Lining, Tabular Oldstyle, Standard Ligatures, Discretionary Ligatures, All Caps, Small Caps, Capitals to Small Caps, Superscript, Subscript, Ordinals, All Alternates, Contextual Alternates, Contextual Ligatures, Fractions Numerator, Denominator, Arrows, Stylistic Alternates, Stylistic Sets, Historical Forms, Slashed Zero, Localized Forms, Case Sensitive Forms

**Test version available:** No

**Web font format available:** Yes

abcdefghijklmnopqrstuvwxyzæfjåçéñöûß
ABCDEFGHIJKLMNOPQRSTUVWXYZÆÇØß
12345678900@.,!?')]§*“”»«/–½©€$£¥&←★

Haultin is a typeface of twelve weights plus *Italics:* Thin, *Thin Italic,* Extra Light, *Extra Light Italic,* Light, *Light Italic,* Blond, *Blond Italic,* Normal Light, *Normal Light Italic,* Normal, *Italic,* Normal Dark, *Normal Dark Italic,* Medium, *Medium Italic,* **Semi Bold,** ***Semi Bold Italic,*** **Bold,** ***Bold Italic,*** **Extra Bold,** ***Extra Bold Italic,*** **Black, and** ***Black Italic***



→ P. 456

# 2001 OCEAN'S 11 ELEVEN

Born as a space-optimizing typeface, Heading Now provides a full spectrum of type solutions to your design problems. It can be used in its compressed widths to manage space on the printed page and the screen: excels in titles and subheadings, timetables, infographics, and in situations of exuberant and excessive copywriting. On the other side of the width spectrum, you can find extended width variants, ready to be used for titling where style and energy matter more than pixel or paper economy.

**Design:** 2021, Francesco Canovaro → p. 473

**Foundry:** Zetafonts Foundry, Italy, zetafonts.com → p. 492

**Language support:** Latin Extended, Cyrillic, Greek

**OpenType features:** Proportional Oldstyle, Tabular Lining, Proportional Lining, Tabular Oldstyle, Standard Ligatures, Discretionary Ligatures, Small Caps, Superscript, Subscript, Ordinals, Fractions, Numerator, Denominator, Arrows, Stylistic Sets, Slashed Zero, Case Sensitive Forms

**Test version available:** Yes

**Web font format available:** Yes

abcdefghijklmnopqrstuvwxyzæffåçéñöûß
ABCDEFGHIJKLMNOPQRSTUVWXYZÆÇØß
1234567890Ø@.,!?’)]§*“”»«/–½©€$£¥&→☀

αβγδεζηθικλμνξοπρσςτυφχψωάέήίόώϊϋΰ
ΑΒΓΔΕΖΗΘΙΚΛΜΝΞΟΠΡΣΤΥΦΧΨΩΆΈΉΊΌΏΪΫ
12345678900@.,!?’)]§*“”»«/–½©€$£¥&↗♲

Heading Now is a typeface of ten widths: 01, 10, 20, 30, 40, 50, 60, 70, 80, and 90, each in eight weights plus *Italics:* 01 Thin, *12 Light Italic,* 23 Book, ***34 Regular Italic,*** *44 Regular Italic,* **55 Medium, 65 Medium,** ***76 Bold Italic,*** **87 Extra Bold,** ***and 98 Heavy Italic***



→ P. 450, 462

# HÔTEL DU NØRD

Heliuum

Heliuum is not just a single font, it's a playful typographic program. Behind simple but strong and determined shapes, this typeface contains seven different character sets. Three ranges of uppercases evolve on three different heights. Four ranges of small capitals are standing on four different baselines aligned from the bottom to the top of the taller uppercases.

**Design:** 2021, Damien Gautier
→ p. 476

**Foundry:** 205TF, France, 205.tf
→ p. 488

**Language support:** Latin Extended

**OpenType features:** Proportional Oldstyle, Tabular Lining, Proportional Lining, Tabular Oldstyle, Standard Ligatures, Discretionary Ligatures, Small Caps, Superscript, Subscript, Contextual Alternates, Fractions, Ornaments, Arrows, Stylistic Sets, Localized Forms, Case Sensitive Forms, Font Variations

**Test version available:** Yes

**Web font format available:** Yes

→ P. 450

ABCDEFGHIJKLMNOPQRSTUVWXYZÆÅÇĒÑŌŪß
ABCDEFGHIJKLMNOPQRSTUVWXYZÆÇØß
1234567890@.,!?')]§*"'"»«/–½©€$£¥&→♥

HELIUUM IS A TYPEFACE OF TWO WEIGHTS: EXTRA LIGHT **AND REGULAR**

# The Phantom of the Opera

Helsa

→ P. 456, 462

Helsa is a slim and eccentric Serif typeface. It's a free interpretation of the narrow elzevirs of the beginning of the 20th century for use in titles and short texts. Due to its narrow proportions and high contrast, it doesn't take up much space in the line and allows you to increase the point size freely.

**Design:** 2022, Nick Nedashkovskiy → p. 480

**Foundry:** Paratype, Russia, paratype.ru → p. 491

**Language support:** Latin Extended, Cyrillic Extended, Greek

**OpenType features:** Proportional Oldstyle, Tabular Lining, Proportional Lining, Tabular Oldstyle, Standard Ligatures, Discretionary Ligatures, All Caps, Superscript, Subscript, Ordinals, Titling Alternates, Fractions, Numerator, Denominator, Arrows, Stylistic Alternates, Stylistic Sets, Localized Forms, Case Sensitive Forms, Mark Positioning

**Test version available:** No

**Web font format available:** Yes

abcdefghijklmnopqrstuvwxyzæﬀåçéñöûß
ABCDEFGHIJKLMNOPQRSTUVWXYZÆÇØß
1234567890@.,!?')]§*“”»«/-½©€$£¥&↕◌

абвгдеёжзийклмнопрстуфхцчшщъыьэюяӝқӵӧлӳғҗҙкќө
АБВГДЕЁЖЗИЙКЛМНОПРСТУФХЦЧШЩЪЫЬЭӜҚӴӦЛӲҒҖҘКЌӨ
1234567890@.,!?')]§*“”»«/-½©€$£¥&↘♣

Helsa Display is a typeface of one Regular weight

Beauty & the Beast

Disney's 1991 animated film

*

The most beautiful love story ever told

*

Hernandez Bros

Hernandez Bros is a typeface designed by Daniel and Eli Hernández. It was born in the midst of the Covid pandemic, from a collaborative spirit where everything called them to work together as a family in order to obtain better results in such trying times. The Hernández siblings started a ping pong of drawings based on Bulfinch found in the 1912 ATF catalog. From this exercise, Hernandez Bros–a modern Sans Serif–was designed. It is an elegant font with beautiful and harmonious contrasts, which make it ideal for titles, brands, editorial design, and magazines among others.

**Design:** 2022, Daniel Hernandez → p. 476, Elizabeth Hernandez → p. 476

**Foundry:** Latinotype, Chile, latinotype.com→ p. 490

**Language support:** Latin Extended

**OpenType features:** Standard Ligatures, Superscript, Ordinals, Fractions, Stylistic Alternates, Stylistic Sets, Localized Forms, Case Sensitive Forms

**Test version available:** No

**Web font format available:** Yes

→ P. 456, 462

abcdefghijklmnopqrstuvwxyzæfiåçéñöûß
ABCDEFGHIJKLMNOPQRSTUVWXYZÆÇØß
1234567890@.,!?')]§*“”»«/–½©€$£¥&

Hernandez Bros is a typeface of eight weights: Extra Light, Light, Regular, **Medium, Semi Bold, Bold, Extra Bold, and Black**

Because there is a law such as

# GRAVITY

the universe can & will create itself from

∞

вселенная

Hubble is being released to commemorate the Hubble Space Telescope’s 30 years of viewing the wonders of space, created by Posterizer KG Font Foundry in 2020. The starting idea was to make a strong, but rhythmic and dynamic black Display typeface with a monumental and authentic appearance. Pretty short ascenders and descenders, thorny serifs, and tiny space between and inside the glyphs make it suitable for typographic creations with compact and closely packed texts.

**Design:** 2020, Lazar Dimitrijević
→ p. 474

**Foundry:** Posterizer KG, Serbia, myfonts.com/foundry/PosterizerKG
→ p. 491

**Language support:** Latin, Cyrillic

**OpenType features:** Standard Ligatures

**Test version available:** Yes

**Web font format available:** Yes

→ P. 462, 468

abcdefghijklmnopqrstuvwxyzæfiåçéñöôß
ABCDEFGHIJKLMNOPQRSTUVWXYZÆÇØ
1234567890@.,!?’)]§*“”»«/–½©€$£¥&

абвгдеёжзийклмнопрстуфхцчшщъыьэюя
АБВГДЕЁЖЗИЙКЛМНОПРСТУФХЦЧШЩЪЫЬЭ
1234567890@.,!?’)]§*“”»«/–½©€$£¥&

Hubble is a typeface of one Regular weight

†

*no*

GOD!

*Please*

*NOO!!*

≈

Immortel

Immortel is a type family with four variants developed according to the Hippocratic theory of humors that explains these latter through the presence of one of the four principal fluids. Each one is the cause behind the development of a character trait: phlegm represents a lymphatic, sluggish, slow character (Infra); yellow bile, an angry and prideful character (Colera); blood, a jovial and warm character (Vena); and black bile provokes hopelessness and melancholy (Acedia).

**Design:** 2021, Clément Le Tulle-Neyret → p. 484

**Foundry:** 205TF, France, 205.tf → p. 488

**Language support:** Latin Extended

**OpenType features:** Proportional Oldstyle, Tabular Lining, Proportional Lining, Tabular Oldstyle, Standard Ligatures, Discretionary Ligatures, All Caps, Small Caps, Capitals to Small Caps, Superscript, Subscript, Ordinals, Contextual Alternates, Fractions, Numerator, Denominator, Ornaments, Arrows, Stylistic Sets, Slashed Zero Localized Forms, Case Sensitive Forms, Font Variations

**Test version available:** Yes

**Web font format available:** Yes

→ P. 456

abcdefghijklmnopqrstuvwxyzæfjåçéñöûß
ABCDEFGHIJKLMNOPQRSTUVWXYZÆÇØß
12345678900@.,!?')]§*“”»«/–©€$£¥&↗♥

Immortel is a family of four styles: Infra, Acedia, Colera, and Vena. Infra and Vena each in one Roman weight plus *Median and Italic:* Infra Roman, *Infra Median, Infra Italic,* Vena Roman, *Vena Median, and Vena Italic.* Acedia and Colera each in one Roman weight plus *Italic:* Acedia Roman, *Acedia Italic,* Colera Roman, *and Colera Italic*

THE

**_Beautiful_**

SECRET

**things**

LIFE

***don't***

OF

**ask**

WALTER

for

MITTY

*

{~}

MNKY Jane

MNKY Jane is a contemporary take on early 20th century American Grotesk typefaces such as *Franklin Gothic, Trade Gothic,* and *Monotype Grotesque.* The typeface is intended to be a workhorse, but enough character is embedded to work well in a branding context.

**Design:** 2022, Mitch Paone
→ p. 481

**Foundry:** Monkey Type, United States of America/Switzerland, monkeytype.xyz → p. 490

**Language support:** Latin Extended

**OpenType features:** Standard Ligatures, Ordinals, Fractions

**Test version available:** Yes

**Web font format available:** Yes

→ P. 450

abcdefghijklmnopqrstuvwxyzæijåçéñöûß
ABCDEFGHIJKLMNOPQRSTUVWXYZÆÇØẞ
1234567890@.,!?')]§*“”»«/–½©€$£¥&↘

MNKY Jane is a typeface of seven weights plus *Italics:* Thin, *Thin Italic,* Light, *Light Italic,* Book, *Book Italic,* Regular, *Italic,* **Medium,** ***Medium Italic,*** **Semi Bold,** ***Semi Bold Italic,*** **Bold,** ***and Bold Italic***

# The Ħø̄©̄Ħ

# *man who*

# ***made*** a

# FRANKENSTEIN'S

# **MONSTER**

®

Directed by
James Whale

**1931**

Produced by
Carl Laemmle

**Kaybuts**

The thinner and bolder weights of Kaybuts are designed to be used for elements that you want to stand out. The middleweights are designed to be optimal for use with text. Incidentally, the typeface was designed under the influence of, or with Mary Shelley's novel *Frankenstein* in mind.

**Design:** 2022, Shuji Kikuchi → p. 477

**Foundry:** sugargliderz, Japan, sugargliderz.com → p. 491

**Language support:** Latin Extended

**OpenType features:** Proportional Oldstyle, Standard Ligatures, Discretionary Ligatures, Small Caps, Superscript, Subscript, Ordinals, Fractions, Numerator, Denominator, Case Sensitive Forms

**Test version available:** No

**Web font format available:** Yes

abcdefghijklmnopqrstuvwxyzæfjåçéñöûß
ABCDEFGHIJKLMNOPQRSTUVWXYZÆÇØ
1234567890@.,!?')]§*""»«/-©€$£¥&

Kaybuts is a family of three styles: Sans, Semi Serif, and Serif, each in six weights plus *Italics:* Sans Extra Light, *Sans Extra Light Italic*, Sans Light, *Sans Light Italic*, Sans, *Sans Italic*, Sans Medium, *Sans Medium Italic*, **Sans Bold**, ***Sans Bold Italic***, **Sans Extra Bold**, ***Sans Extra Bold Italic***, Semi Serif Extra Light, *Semi Serif Extra Light Italic*, Semi Serif Light, *Semi Serif Light Italic*, Semi Serif Regular, *Semi Serif Italic*, Semi Serif Medium, *Semi Serif Medium Italic*, **Semi Serif Bold**, ***Semi Serif Bold Italic***, **Semi Serif Extra Bold**, ***Semi Serif Extra Bold Italic***, Serif Extra Light, *Serif Extra Light Italic*, Serif Light, *Serif Light Italic*, Serif, *Serif Italic*, Serif Medium, *Serif Medium Italic*, **Serif Bold**, ***Serif Bold Italic***, **Serif Extra Bold**, and ***Serif Extra Bold Italic***

→ P. 450, 456, 462

22 attachEvent("onreday-
23 statechange",H),e.funtion
24 F(e)§
25 t= _[e]={};break ≈}
2ð promise(). done(n.resolve).
28 /Name("**SOURCE CODE**")
29 style.cssText = 2011
30
31 } [©],r.
32 }
34 directed by=**Duncan Jones**
35 if (x == "") {¶
3ð
37 gggggggggggggggg
38 function setcookie(cname
39 }}};
4Ø alert ("Jake GYLLENHAAL
41

Keratine explores the impossible territory between Antiqua and Blackletter, as a way to re-discover and empower an unexpected and contemporary dynamism. Using contemporary digital aesthetics to combine the proportions of humanistic type with the gestural energy of Fraktur letterforms, it develops a "digitally carved," quasi-pixelated appearance (clearly stressed in the Italics) that allows an unexpected balance between small-size readability and display-size personality.

**Design:** 2022, Cosimo Lorenzo Pancini → p. 480

**Foundry:** Zetafonts Foundry, Italy, zetafonts.com → p. 492

**Language support:** Latin Extended

**OpenType features:** Proportional Oldstyle, Ordinals, Stylistic Alternates, Historical Forms

**Test version available:** Yes

**Web font format available:** Yes

→ P. 462

abcdefghijklmnopqrstuvwxyzæåçéñöûß
ABCDEFGHIJKLMNOPQRSTUVWXYZÆÇØß
1234567890@.,!?')]§*“”»«/–©€$£¥&

Keratine is a typeface of eight weights plus *Italics:* Light, *Light Italic,* Book, *Book Italic,* **Regular,** ***Italic,*** **Semi Bold,** ***Semi Bold Italic,*** **Bold,** ***Bold Italic,*** **Extra Bold,** ***Extra Bold Italic,*** **Heavy,** ***Heavy Italic,*** **Black,** **and** ***Black Italic***

/ TRUTH /

happy face «

put on a

KRN / KRN

krn / krn

put on a

happy face «

/ FEAR /

Kjell

Kjell—a synthesis of opposites. Kjell is a conceptual display typeface balancing between its two extremes. The typeface combining two different faces—the *Fear* and *Truth* weight, which are made out of one stem. Inspired by the 14th tarot card of temperance, Kjell understands itself as a synthesis of its two opposites, which are representing a process of harmonization.

**Design:** 2021, Armin Brenner → p. 473, Markus John → p. 477

**Foundry:** NEW LETTERS, Germany, new-letters.de → p. 490

**Language support:** Latin

**OpenType features:** Standard Ligatures, All Caps, Small Caps, Fractions, Arrows, Required Ligatures

**Test version available:** Yes

**Web font format available:** Yes

→ P. 462

abcdefghijklmnopqrstuvwxyzæåçéñ

ABCDEFGHIJKLMNOPQRSTUVWXYZ

1234567890@.,!?')]§*“”»«/–©€$£¥&

**Kjell is a typeface of two weights: Fear and Truth**

# The KISSING BOOTH №2

Klub

Designed by Pierre Pané-Farré and published by TYPE BY, Klub is a formidable contemporary design tool. As a superfamily of characterful, heavy-contrast fonts spanning across eleven widths and six weights, Klub features impressive perfect-imperfect glyph details and a flair of poster wood type. Jovial and assertive, Klub invites you to embrace its power (also remarkable in color use) and mix its letterforms, styles, and weights for bold, playful, and—above all—impactful typography.

**Design:** 2019, Pierre Pané-Farré → p. 481

**Foundry:** TYPE BY, Belgium, typeby.com → p. 492

**Language support:** Latin Extended

**OpenType features:** Proportional Oldstyle, Tabular Lining, Proportional Lining, Tabular Oldstyle, Standard Ligatures, Discretionary Ligatures, All Caps, Superscript, Subscript, Ordinals, All Alternates, Fractions, Numerator, Denominator, Arrows, Stylistic Alternates, Stylistic Sets, Slashed Zero, Localized Forms

**Test version available:** No

**Web font format available:** Yes

→ P. 450, 462

abcdefghijklmnopqrstuvwxyzœfjåçéñöûß
ABCDEFGHIJKLMNOPQRSTUVWXYZÆÇØ
1234567890Ø@.,!?')]§*“”»«/–½©€$£¥&→★

Klub is a family of eleven widths: 01, 02, 03, 04, 05, 06, 07, 08, 09, 10, and 11, each in six weights: 01 Blond, 02 Normal, 03 Medium, 04 Medium, 05 Semi Bold, 06 Semi Bold, 07 Bold, 08 Bold, 09 Black, and 11 Black

# Stroszek

*Werner Herzog*

Ballad of Bruno S**

Ⓟ **1977**

FT Kunst Grotesk

The idea of searching for a typeface with a 1950s atmosphere dates back to 2014: the project remained in stasis for a few years, only to re-emerge in 2017 with a new approach, now including more contemporary touches in an attempt to bridge past and present. As such, Kunst Grotesk looks at mid-20th-century historical faces for inspiration but incorporates subtle details and a certain digital feeling that make it perfectly suitable for modern use.

**Design:** 2022, Piero Di Biase
→ p. 472

**Foundry:** Formula Type, Italy, formulatype.com → p. 489

**Language support:** Latin Extended

**OpenType features:** Tabular Lining, Proportional Lining, Standard Ligatures, Discretionary Ligatures, Superscript, Subscript, Ordinals, All Alternates, Contextual Alternates, Fractions, Numerator, Denominator, Arrows, Stylistic Sets, Slashed Zero, Localized Forms, Case Sensitive Forms

**Test version available:** Yes

**Web font format available:** Yes

→ P. 450

abcdefghijklmnopqrstuvwxyzæfjåçéñöûß
ABCDEFGHIJKLMNOPQRSTUVWXYZÆÇØẞ
12345678900@.,!?')]§*“”»«/–½©€$£¥&↪☆

FT Kunst Grotesk is a typeface of five weights plus *Italics:* Light, *Light Italic,* Regular, *Italic,* **Medium,** ***Medium Italic,*** **Bold,** ***Bold Italic,*** **Black,** ***and Black Italic***

marvel *universe*
**marvel** *universe*
marvel **universe**
**marvel** ***universe***
***marvel*** *universe*
marvel ***universe***
marvel universe
marvel ***universe***
***marvel*** universe
*marvel* universe
**marvel** *universe*
marvel **universe**
*marvel* ***universe***
***marvel*** *universe*

The Legit Superfamily is a massive collection of text fonts sharing the same metrics throughout all weights. Legit features both optimal readability in small sizes as well as elegant aesthetics in display use. Finaltype quality spacing provides optimal type color, even in All Caps typesetting. The sophisticated uniwidth system is the result of 30+ years of experience by Prof. Hans R. Heitmann. All 102 styles are 100 % compatible in width and remain swappable without altering the layout.

**Design:** 2022, Prof. Hans R. Heitmann → p. 476, Johannes Ammon → p. 472

**Foundry:** Finaltype, Germany, finaltype.de → p. 489

**Language support:** Latin Extended

**OpenType features:** Tabular Lining, Proportional Lining, Standard Ligatures, Discretionary Ligatures, Superscript, Ordinals, All Alternates, Contextual Alternates, Fractions, Stylistic Alternates, Stylistic Sets, Localized Forms, Case Sensitive Forms, Mark Positioning

**Test version available:** Yes

**Web font format available:** Yes

abcdefghijklmnopqrstuvwxyzæffåçéñöûß
ABCDEFGHIJKLMNOPQRSTUVWXYZÆÇ
1234567890@.,!?')]§*""»«/–½©€$£¥&↗

Legit Superfamily is a family of seven styles: Sans, Sans Soft, Slab, Slab Soft, Serif, Serif Soft, and Didone. Sans, Sans Soft, Slab, and Slab Soft, each in nine weights plus *Italics:* Sans Thin, *Sans Ultra Light Italic,* Sans Light, *Sans Italic,* Sans Medium, ***Sans Semi Bold Italic,*** **Sans Bold,** ***Sans Extra Bold Italic,*** **Sans Black,** *Sans Soft Thin Italic,* Sans Soft Ultra Light, *Sans Soft Light Italic,* Sans Soft Medium, ***Sans Soft Semi Bold Italic,*** **Sans Soft Extra Bold,** ***Sans Soft Black Italic,*** Slab Thin, *Slab Ultra Light Italic,* Slab Regular, *Slab Medium Italic,* **Slab Bold,** ***Slab Extra Bold Italic,*** **Slab Black,** *Slab Soft Thin Italic,* Slab Soft Light, *Slab Soft Italic,* **Slab Soft Semi Bold,** ***Slab Soft Bold Italic,*** **Slab Soft Black,** Serif, Serif Soft, and Didone, each in five weights *plus Italics:* Serif Light, *Serif Italic,* **Serif Semi Bold,** ***Serif Bold Italic,*** Serif Soft Light, *Serif Soft Italic,* **Serif Soft Semi Bold,** ***Serif Soft Bold Italic,*** Didone Light, *Didone Italic,* **Didone Semi Bold,** ***and Didone Bold Italic***

→ P. 450, 456, 458

Charlie

&

the

Chocolate

Factory

Lingerie Wild Pro

Lingerie Wild Pro is the most playful font ever designed, ready to take the professional world by storm. Lingerie Wild Pro's high-impact design will immediately draw attention to luxury brands and fashion magazines, and assist design studios in creating incredibly unique typography without the extra effort. You simply won't be able to tear your eyes away.

**Design:** 2019, Moshik Nadav → p. 480

**Foundry:** Moshik Nadav Typography, United States of America, moshik.net → p. 490

**Language support:** Latin Extended

**OpenType features:** Standard Ligatures, Swashes, Contextual Swashes, All Alternates, Contextual Alternates, Contextual Ligatures, Required Ligatures, Custom Ready-Made Words, Alternate Ligatures, Alternate Ampersand, Custom Ready-Made Names

**Test version available:** No

**Web font format available:** Yes

→ P. 462

abcdefghijklmnopqrstuvwxyzæijåçéñöûß
ABCDEFGHIJKLMNOPQRSTUVWXYZÆÇØ
1234567890@.,!?')]§*“”»«/–½©€$£¥&&

Lingerie is a family of four styles: Visage X, Chimera, Chimera X, and Visage

# Who Are You Polly Maggoo?

Lingerie XO, a seductive typeface by Moshik Nadav Typography. After they released Lingerie Typeface, they continued to challenge themselves in creating an even sexier typeface. They deconstructed each letter to completely redesign the form, perfecting each curve and line.

**Design:** 2019, Moshik Nadav → p. 480

**Foundry:** Moshik Nadav Typography, United States of America, moshik.net → p. 490

**Language support:** Latin Extended

**OpenType features:** Standard Ligatures, Swashes, Contextual Swashes, All Alternates, Contextual Alternates, Contextual Ligatures, Required Ligatures, Custom Ready-made Words, Custom Ready-Made names, Custom Alternate Glyphs, Alternate Ampersands, Alternate Ligatures

**Test version available:** No

**Web font format available:** Yes

→ P. 462

abcdefghijklmnopqrstuvwxyzæfjåçéñöûß
ABCDEFGHIJKLMNOPQRSTUVWXYZÆÇØ
1234567890@.,!?')]§*“”»«/–½©€$£¥&

Lingerie XO is a family of two styles: Light Calligraphic and Light Dreamline

# NEON GENESIS EVANGELION

# VOLUME:VI

Longinus

Longinus is a display serif typeface with a modern and aggressive approach inspired by Hideaki Anno's Neon Genesis Evangelion anime series and the last film of the franchise which was released while the type was in progress, helping to define the last details of Longinus. The width and tight kerning can bring tension and drama to a wide variety of display applications.

**Design:** 2021, Domenico Barreto
→ p. 472

**Foundry:** Type Department, United Kingdom, type-department.com
→ p. 492

**Language support:** Latin Extended, Cyrillic

**OpenType features:** Proportional, Lining, Standard Ligatures, All Caps, Fractions, Arrows

**Test version available:** Yes

**Web font format available:** Yes

ABCDEFGHIJKLMNOPQRSTUVWXYZÆÅÇÉÑÖÛ
1234567890@.,!?')]§*“”»«/-½©€$£¥&→

АБВГДЕЁЖЗИЙКЛМНОПРСТУФХЦЧШЩЪЫЬЭЮЯ
1234567890@.,!?')]§*“”»«/-½©€$£¥&↓

LONGINUS IS A TYPEFACE OF ONE REGULAR WEIGHT

→ P. 462

# The » Virgïn Sųicides

What we have here
is a dreamer.

MAY 1999

*Someone completely*
*out of touch*
*with reality.*

**Loretta**

Loretta is an elegant contemporary serif typeface for body text. It has roots in expressive calligraphic motions, compelled into stable typographic shapes. Loretta is perfect for editorial use in books and on the web because it has low contrasts and open shapes that give it ideal legibility. The Italic is vibrant and complements the Regular with style.

**Design:** 2020, Joana Correia → p. 474, Abel Martins → p. 479

**Foundry:** Nova Type Foundry, Portugal, novatypefoundry.com → p. 490

**Language support:** Latin Extended, Vietnamese

**OpenType features:** Proportional Oldstyle, Proportional Lining, Tabular Oldstyle, Standard Ligatures, Discretionary Ligatures, All Caps, Ordinals, Fractions

**Test version available:** Yes

**Web font format available:** Yes

→ P. 456

abcdefghijklmnopqrstuvwxyzæåçéñöûß
ABCDEFGHIJKLMNOPQRSTUVWXYZÆÇØ
1234567890@.,!?')]§*""»«/–½©€$£¥&↑

aăâbcdđeêghiklmnoôơpqrstuưvxyằẻổỵ
AĂÂBCDĐEÊGHIKLMNOÔƠPQRSTUƯVXY
1234567890@.,!?')]§*""»«/–½©€$£¥&‡

Loretta is a typeface of six weights plus *Italics:* Light, *Light Italic,* Regular, *Italic,* Medium, ***Medium Italic,*** **Semi Bold, *Semi Bold Italic,* Bold, *Bold Italic,* Extra Bold, *and Extra Bold Italic***

Don't Look UP

**TR Lox Compressed**

How do you design a versatile type family that combines rigorous forms with a distinctive and friendly expression? Lox bridges the gap between geometric grotesque shapes and contemporary Sans Serifs. To generate versatile tones, an expressive rounded stylistic set has been designed for characters containing diagonals, such as *A* and *M* as well as *w* and *x*. *TR* Lox-Compressed fits especially well in the world of display applications. LoxCompressed is part of an upcoming super family and variable fonts.

**Design:** 2022, Peter Mohr → p. 479, Gilmar Rodrigues → p. 481

**Foundry:** Typerotation, Germany, typerotation.com → p. 492

**Language support:** Latin Extended

**OpenType features:** Proportional Oldstyle, Tabular Lining, Proportional Lining, Tabular Oldstyle, Standard Ligatures, Discretionary Ligatures, All Caps, Superscript, Subscript, Ordinals, All Alternates, Fractions, Numerator, Denominator, Arrows, Stylistic Alternates, Stylistic Sets, Slashed Zero, Font Variations

**Test version available:** Yes

**Web font format available:** Yes

→ P. 451, 462

abcdefghijklmnopqrstuvwxyzæŋåçéñöûß
ABCDEFGHIJKLMNOPQRSTUVWXYZÆÇØẞ
1234567890ø@.,!?’)]§*“”»«/–½©€$£¥&↕

TR Lox Compressed is a typeface of eleven weights *plus Semi Italics and Italics:* Air, *Air Semi Italic, Air Italic,* Extra Thin, *Extra Thin Semi Italic, Extra Thin Italic,* Thin, *Thin Semi Italic, Thin Italic,* Light, *Light Semi Italic, Light Italic,* Regular, *Semi Italic, Italic,* Medium, *Medium Semi Italic, Medium Italic,* Semi Bold, *Semi Bold Semi Italic, Semi Bold Italic,* Bold, *Bold Semi Italic, Bold Italic,* Extra Bold, *Extra Bold Semi Italic, Extra Bold Italic,* Black, *Black Semi Italic, Black Italic,* Extra Black, *Extra Black Semi Italic,* and *Extra Black Italic*

# *Knives Out!*↗

## CENA CON DELITTO

Hell, *any* of them ¿ could have done it.

Lucius

The Lucius type family began as an attempt to reproduce the *Princípios Methodicos para as Letras Aldina e Romana–Typo Portuguez.* The result of the first attempts was bleak, mild, and uninteresting. By mercilessly changing the direction, the designers decided to move forward with the design of a Sans based on the structure of a Serif. This shift allowed drawing a Serif from a different perspective, while maintaining some of the features of a Sans.

**Design:** 2022, Dino dos Santos → p. 482

**Foundry:** DSType Foundry, Portugal, dstype.com → p. 488

**Language support:** Latin Extended

**OpenType features:** Proportional Oldstyle, Tabular Lining, Proportional Lining, Tabular Oldstyle, Standard Ligatures, Superscript, Subscript, Ordinals, Contextual Alternates, Fractions, Numerator, Denominator, Ornaments, Arrows, Stylistic Alternates, Stylistic Sets, Historical Forms, Slashed Zero, Localized Forms, Case Sensitive Forms

**Test version available:** Yes

**Web font format available:** Yes

abcdefghijklmnopqrstuvwxyzæfiåçéñöûß
ABCDEFGHIJKLMNOPQRSTUVWXYZÆÇØ
1234567890Ø@.,!?')]§*“”»«/–½©€$£¥&↗❖

Lucius is a family of two styles: Normal and Sans, each in seven weights plus *Italics:* Thin, *Thin Aldina,* Light, *Light Aldina,* Book, *Book Aldina,* Medium, ***Medium Aldina,*** **Demi Bold,** ***Demi Bold Aldina,*** **Bold,** ***Bold Aldina,*** **Heavy,** ***Heavy Aldina,*** Sans Thin, *Sans Thin Aldina,* Sans Light, *Sans Light Aldina,* Sans Book, *Sans Book Aldina,* Sans Medium, ***Sans Medium Aldina,*** **Sans Demi Bold,** ***Sans Demi Bold Aldina,*** **Sans Bold,** ***Sans Bold Aldina,*** **Sans Heavy,** ***and Sans Heavy Aldina***

→ P. 451, 456

Maax Unicase

# Fast & Furious: Tokyo ◊ Drift.

Maax Unicase is a new extension of the Maax type family. It is clearly a titling variant that asserts a certain originality by having only capital letters which occasionally borrow from the forms of minuscule letters. Available in two weights, this version presents a design that is particular in a number of areas, and whose use will not go unnoticed.

**Design:** 2022, Damien Gautier
→ p. 476

**Foundry:** 205TF, France, 205.tf
→ p. 488

**Language support:** Latin Extended

**OpenType features:** Tabular Lining, Proportional Lining, Standard Ligatures, Discretionary Ligatures, Superscript, Subscript, Contextual Alternates, Fractions, Numerator, Denominator, Ornaments, Arrows, Stylistic Sets, Slashed Zero, Localized Forms, Case Sensitive Forms, Font Variations

**Test version available:** Yes

**Web font format available:** Yes

→ P. 462

abcdefghijklmnopqrstuvwxyzœæåçß
12345678900@.,;!?')]§*""»«/–½©€$£¥&→

maax unicase is a typeface of two weights: bold and black

# DER PRINZ AUS / »ZAMUNDA*

by & with

**EDDIE MURPHY**

**Madley**

Madley is a contemporary slab serif typeface. Featuring monolinear Stems, elongated block Serifs, and teardrop Terminals, the type family goes from a delicate Hairline weight to a heavy Black weight. Because of its range in weights and extensive OpenType features, it's a perfect font for both text and display text settings.

**Design:** 2021, Kimmy Kirkwood → p. 477

**Foundry:** Kimmy Design, United States of America, kimmydesign.com → p. 489

**Language support:** Latin Extended

**OpenType features:** Standard Ligatures, Discretionary Ligatures, All Caps, Small Caps, Swashes, Contextual Swashes, Contextual Alternates, Stylistic Alternates, Stylistic Sets

**Test version available:** Yes

**Web font format available:** Yes

→ P. 458

abcdefghijklmnopqrstuvwxyzæfjåçéñöûß
ABCDEFGHIJKLMNOPQRSTUVWXYZÆÇØ
1234567890@.,!?')]§*""»</-½©€$£¥&

Madley is a typeface of six weights plus *Italics:* Hairline, *Hairline Italic,* Light, *Light Italic,* Regular, *Italic,* **Medium,** ***Medium Italic,*** **Bold,** ***Bold Italic,*** **Black,** ***and Black Italic***

# HOUSE

# (1977 film)

# EXPERIMENTAL/COMEDY HORROR/

*directed by Nobuhiko Obayashi*

Mantar

Mantar is a psychedelic Scotch Roman designed by Cem Eskinazi. After stumbling upon a phototypesetting specimen, Cem was inspired by the warmth of the letters. Mantar is a soft display face with curvy and elongated endings. It comes in 12 styles, including a funky Ultra weight

**Design:** 2021, Cem Eskinazi → p. 475

**Foundry:** Occupant Fonts, United States of America, occupantfonts.com → p. 490

**Language support:** Latin Extended

**OpenType features:** Proportional Lining, Standard Ligatures, Fractions, Numerator, Denominator, Localized Forms, Case Sensitive Forms

**Test version available:** Yes

**Web font format available:** Yes

→ P. 456, 462

abcdefghijklmnopqrstuvwxyzæfjåçéñöûß
ABCDEFGHIJKLMNOPQRSTUVWXYZÆÇØ
1234567890@.,!?')]§*“”»«/–½©€$£¥&↑

Mantar is a typeface of six weights plus *Italics:* Extra Light, *Extra Light Italic,* Light, *Light Italic,* Regular, *Italic,* **Bold,** ***Bold Italic,*** **Black,** ***Black Italic,*** **Ultra,** ***and Ultra Italic***

“Cô ấy **vẫn** là điểm *xoay* **chuyển** *thế giới.*”

DIRECTED BY SOPHIA COPPOLA

**Margit**

The award-winning Margit family is a highly compressed Display typeface, where more weight equals more width. Use Margit's inventive and clear shapes for making your titles, posters, and brandings more expressive. Profit from its vast language support in both Latin and Cyrillic.

**Design:** 2021, Miriam Surányi → p. 483

**Foundry:** Schriftlabor, Austria, schriftlabor.at → p. 491

**Language support:** Latin, Cyrillic, Vietnamese

**OpenType features:** Tabular Lining, Proportional Lining, Standard Ligatures, Discretionary Ligatures, All Caps, Superscript, Subscript, Ordinals, Contextual Alternates, Fractions, Numerator, Denominator, Stylistic Sets, Localized Forms, Case Sensitive Forms

**Test version available:** Yes

**Web font format available:** Yes

abcdefghijklmnopqrstuvwxyzæfjåçéñöûß
ABCDEFGHIJKLMNOPQRSTUVWXYZÆÇØ
1234567890@.,!?’)]§*“”»«/-½©€$£¥₢↖„

aăâbcdđeêghiklmnoôơpqrstuưvxyẳẻổỵ
AĂÂBCDĐEÊGHIKLMNOÔƠPQRSTUƯVXY
1234567890@.,!?’)]§*“”»«/-½©€$£¥₢↔⁎

Margit is a typeface of nine weights plus *Italics:* Thin, *Thin Italic,* Light, *Light Italic,* Regular, *Italic,* Medium, ***Medium Italic,*** **Semi Bold,** ***Semi Bold Italic,*** **Bold,** ***Bold Italic,*** **Extra Bold,** ***Extra Bold Italic,*** **Black,** ***Black Italic,*** **Heavy,** ***and*** **Heavy** ***Italic***

→ P. 451, 462

{Elfriede}

# Effi Briest

EST.D 1896

WRITTEN BY THEODOR FONTANE

Marlide Display

Marlide Display is a contemporary typeface classified around the groups of Romain Elzevir and Latins with elegant roundly bracketed Serifs and a considerable thick to thin contrast. The letterforms are condensed and embrace both curves and pointy elements that create an interlocking rhythm with a lively texture. Marlide Display aims to exercise restraint by going all out on curves, yet attempting to control excessiveness and amplification. This type shines in large letter sizes.

**Design:** 2022, Sibylle Hagmann → p. 476

**Foundry:** Kontour, United States of America, kontour.com → p. 489

**Language support:** Latin Extended

**OpenType features:** Proportional Oldstyle, Tabular Lining, Proportional Lining, Standard Ligatures, Discretionary Ligatures, Superscript, Subscript, Ordinals, Fractions, Alternative Fractions, Numerator, Denominator, Ornaments, Arrows, Stylistic Alternates, Stylistic Sets, Slashed Zero, Localized Forms

**Test version available:** Yes

**Web font format available:** Yes

→ P. 456, 463

abcdefghijklmnopqrstuvwxyzæftåçéñöûß
ABCDEFGHIJKLMNOPQRSTUVWXYZÆÇØß
1234567890Ø@.,!?')]§*""»«/–½©€$£¥&→*

Marlide Display is a typeface of six weights: Light, Regular, **Medium, Bold, Extra Bold, and Heavy**

JENNIFER **ANISTON**

# THE

# &

# SWITCH

JASON **BATEMAN**

**Marlon Pro**

Marlon Pro—a rounded font family for all kinds of projects, characterized by its round and modern appearance. It provides advanced typographical support and comes in nine weights with corresponding Italics. Marlon Pro has true Italics with an extended character set to support Central and Eastern European as well as Western European languages. It provides advanced OpenType functions with features such as Case Sensitive Forms, Small Caps, Standard Ligatures, and many more.

**Design:** 2019, Olivier Gourvat
→ p. 476

**Foundry:** Mostardesign Type Foundry, France, motyfo.com
→ p. 490

**Language support:** Latin Extended

**OpenType features:** Proportional Oldstyle, Tabular Lining, Proportional Lining, Tabular Oldstyle, Standard Ligatures, Discretionary Ligatures, All Caps, Small Caps, Capitals to Small Caps, Superscript, Subscript, Ordinals, All Alternates, Fractions, Numerator, Denominator, Arrows, Stylistic Alternates, Stylistic Sets, Slashed Zero, Localized Forms, Case Sensitive Forms, Mark Positioning

**Test version available:** Yes

**Web font format available:** Yes

abcdefghijklmnopqrstuvwxyzæfjåçéñöûß
ABCDEFGHIJKLMNOPQRSTUVWXYZÆÇØß
1234567890Ø@.,!?')]§*“”»«/–½©€$£¥&↑

Marlon Pro is a typeface of nine weights plus *Italics:* Thin, *Thin Italic,* Extra Light, *Extra Light Italic,* Light, *Light Italic,* Book, *Book Italic,* Regular, *Italic,* Medium, *Medium Italic,* **Bold,** ***Bold Italic,*** **Ultra Bold,** ***Ultra Bold Italic,*** **Heavy,** ***and Heavy Italic***

→ P. 451, 458

# Pirates* of the Caribbean

№1 ▶ THE CURSE OF THE BLACK PEARL

((2003))

Maro—a razor-sharp stencil typeface for expressive text. It is an organically created stencil typeface that follows the logical contrast principles of letter construction until the shape is fractured at its narrowest point.

**Design:** 2021, Nikola Djurek
→ p. 474

**Foundry:** Typotheque,
The Netherlands, typotheque.com
→ p. 492

**Language support:** Latin Extended

**OpenType features:** Proportional Oldstyle, Tabular Lining, Proportional Lining, Tabular Oldstyle

**Test version available:** Yes

**Web font format available:** No

abcdefghijklmnopqrstuvwxyzæfjåçéñöûß
ABCDEFGHIJKLMNOPQRSTUVWXYZÆÇØ
12345678900@.,!?')]$*“”»«/–©€$£¥&→☞

Maro is a typeface of four weights plus *Italics:* Light, *Light Italic,* Regular, *Italic,* **Medium,** ***Medium Italic,*** **Bold,** and ***Bold Italic***

→ P. 463, 467

# LITTLE

∞

# 작은 아씨들

인생은
모두가
**한 편의**
**소설이다**

# WOMEN

* * * * * *

2019

own
your
story

**Maru Buri**

Naver Hangeul Campaign shared the beauty of Hangeul for years. We started the "Maru Project" with Director Ahn Sang-soo, to guide where Hangeul should go in a rapidly changing digital environment. Maru Buri is a Buri (Serif) font that brings warmths to a screen filled with Minburi various visual choices suitable for digital media. It is a young, dignified, and bright-looking font, designed so that all elements of the Hangeul font can be optimized and displayed beautifully on the screen.

**Design:** 2021, Moa Ku → p. 478, Eunyou Noh → p. 480, Noheul Lee → p. 478

**Foundry:** AG Typography Institute, Republic of Korea, agfont.com/en → p. 488

**Language support:** Latin Extended, Korean

**OpenType features:** Tabular Lining, Proportional Lining, Standard Ligatures, Discretionary Ligatures, Superscript, Subscript, Ordinals, All Alternates, Fractions, Numerator, Denominator, Case Sensitive Forms, Scientific Inferiors, Full width, Vertical Writing, Vertical Alternates and Rotation, Glyph Composition / Decomposition

**Test version available:** Yes

**Web font format available:** Yes

abcdefghijklmnopqrstuvwxyzæfiåçéñöûß
ABCDEFGHIJKLMNOPQRSTUVWXYZÆÇØß
1234567890@.,!?')]§*“”»«/–½©€$£¥&↔♧

가냐더례미배세예쟤차캬터히까뗘빠쎄
쨰고뇨두류므보슈쥐최슈쾌훼꽈뚜뾰쓰
1234567890@.,!?')]§*“”»«/–½©€$£¥&↖♂

Maru Buri is a typeface of five weights: Extra Light, Light, Regular, **Semi Bold, and Bold**

→ P. 456, 469

80%

→ Sofia Coppola

→ Wes Ander-son

20%

MNKY Maurice

MNKY Maurice is a brutal geometric sans serif typeface. Inspired by an old sign found on a storefront on the outskirts of Palermo, Italy, spelling out the name "Salotti." The sign letters felt reminiscent of the *Erbar* and *Futura* typefaces but cruder in their shape. Despite its brutal construction, the font's character has a unique fashionable quality making it a great contemporary alternative to classic geometric typefaces like *Futura* or *Avant-Garde.*

**Design:** 2022, Mitch Paone
→ p. 481

**Foundry:** Monkey Type, United States of America / Switzerland, monkeytype.xyz → p. 490

**Language support:** Latin Extended

**OpenType features:** Standard Ligatures, Ordinals, Fractions, Stylistic Sets

**Test version available:** Yes

**Web font format available:** Yes

→ P. 451

abcdefghijklmnopqrstuvwxyzæflåçéñöûß
ABCDEFGHIJKLMNOPQRSTUVWXYZÆÇØẞ
1234567890@.,!?')]§*'"'"»«/–½©€$£¥&↕

MNKY Maurice is a typeface of seven weights plus *Italics:* Extra Light, *Extra Light Italic,* Light, *Light Italic,* **Regular,** ***Italic,*** **Medium,** ***Medium Italic,*** **Semi Bold,** ***Semi Bold Italic,*** **Bold,** ***Bold Italic,*** **Black, *and Black Italic***

× A BANKSY FİLM &

# EXIT THROUGH THE GIFT SHOP

MBI DCMNT-15

MBI–DCMNT15 is a custom typeface that was designed for the documenta fifteen, curated by ruangrupa (Jakarta). Based on the principle of lumbung, the curatorial principle of documenta fifteen, MBI-DMNT15 displays the ideas of processuality, collectiveness, and shared resources. The typeface works as a hybrid between woodcut letters and handwriting, with stylistic alternatives that depict the idea of common authorship and challenges the idea of a fixed visual identity through an ever changing outcome, that gives space for accidents and non-conformity.

**Design:** 2021, Fabian Maier-Bode → p. 479, Angga Reksha Ramadhan → p. 481, Larasati Fildzah Kinanti → p. 475, Louisiana Wattimena → p. 484, Rosyid Mahfuzh → p. 479, André van Rueth → p. 482

**Foundry:** MB Intl., Germany, fabianmaierbode.de → p. 490, studio4oo2, Indonesia, instagram.com/studio4oo2 → p. 491, Stan Hema, Germany, stanhema.com → p. 491

**Language support:** Latin Extended

**OpenType features:** Contextual Alternates, Stylistic Alternates, Stylistic Sets, Font Variations

**Test version available:** No

**Web font format available:** No

ABCDEFGHIJKLMNOPQRSTUVWXYZÆFJÅÇÉÑÖÜ
1234567890@.,!?’)]§*“”»«/–©€$¥&

MBI DCMNT-15 IS A TYPEFACE OF ONE REGULAR WEIGHT



→ P. 463, 469

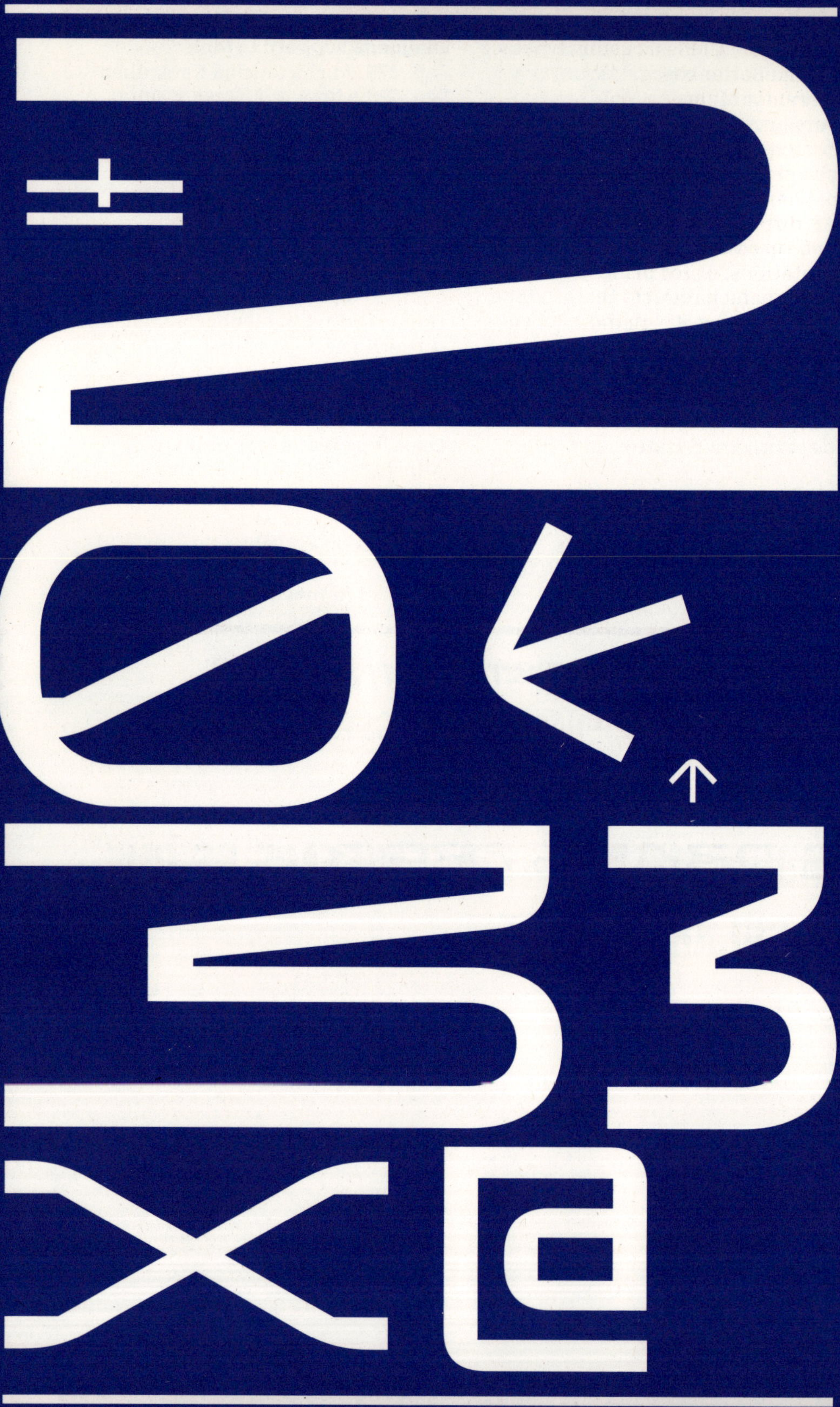

Merantix NUM

Merantix NUM is a custom typeface for the Berlin-based AI-company Merantix Momentum. It's a numbers and symbols only typeface and designed as an addition to their brand identity to be used for displaying results and numbers. The six different widths are designed to be used on their website, in presentations, or for printed material. The typeface reflects the headline typeface used within their branding (At Haüss Aero), but is also different and distinct in its look and feel. It has a modern, humanistic and edgy look that meets the company's claim in a corporate world.

**Design:** 2022, Jan Erlinghagen → p. 475, Elena Schneider → p. 482

**Foundry:** CRU Brand Consultancy, Germany, madebycru.com → p. 488

**Language support:** Latin

**OpenType features:** Superscript, Subscript, Arrows

**Test version available:** No

**Web font format available:** Yes

→ P. 469

1234567890@

.,/–½€$£¥&↔

1234567890

# NO GOATS, NO GLORY

GEORGE CLOONEY
EWAN McGREGOR

& GOAT

JEFF BRIDGES
KEVIN SPACEY

Mersey

TYPE BY Mersey is a display design that stands out through several distinct qualities—watch the masterful "straight diagonals" and stylistic sets. The designers get a free hand in creating powerful display designs: posters or headlines, printed or digital. But Mersey will also keep its beat in medium-length texts and captions, where minimal space meets maximum readability. And perhaps Mersey's strongest feature is its confident "Now"—a firmly contemporary design, not a 19th century throwback.

**Design:** 2019, Fred Smeijers
→ p. 483

**Foundry:** TYPE BY, Belgium, typeby.com → p. 492

**Language support:** Latin Extended

**OpenType features:** Tabular Lining, Proportional Lining, All Caps, Superscript, Subscript, Ordinals, All Alternates, Contextual Alternates, Fractions, Numerator, Denominator, Arrows, Stylistic Alternates, Stylistic Sets, Slashed Zero, Localized Forms, Case Sensitive Forms

**Test version available:** No

**Web font format available:** Yes

abcdefghijklmnopqrstuvwxyzæfjåçéñöûß
ABCDEFGHIJKLMNOPQRSTUVWXYZÆÇØß
1234567890Ø@.,!?')]§*""»«/–½©€$£¥&➶★

Mersey is a family of seven widths: 01, 02, 03, 04, 05, 06, and 07, each in seven weights: 01 Thin, 02 Light, 03 Blond, 04 Normal, 05 Semi Bold, 06 Bold, and 07 Black

→ P. 451, 463

fĩ

*Who lives in a pineapple deep in the sea?*

**Thaddæus ¿**
**Patrick ?**

ŕí

**Method Mono**

Method Mono explores the possibilities of contemporary Monospace with geometric shapes. The main characteristic of Method Mono lies in the conception of its numerous ligatures. Their design differs from common monospace fonts, where several characters are forced to fit together in a single box. Here the ligatures are more open, the ligated glyphs seem to be holding hands, catching the surrounding boxes. This makes the reading of this typography much more dynamic and playful.

**Design:** 2021, Fabien Coupas
→ p. 474

**Foundry:** Slow Fonts, France, slowfonts.xyz → p. 491

**Language support:** Latin Extended

**OpenType features:** Proportional Oldstyle, Tabular Lining, Proportional Lining, Tabular Oldstyle, Standard Ligatures, Discretionary Ligatures, Superscript, Subscript, Ordinals, Contextual Alternates, Contextual Ligatures, Fractions, Numerator, Denominator, Arrows, Stylistic Sets, Slashed Zero, Localized Forms, Case Sensitive Forms

**Test version available:** Yes

**Web font format available:** Yes

abcdefghijklmnopqrstuvwxyzæfjåçéñöûß
ABCDEFGHIJKLMNOPQRSTUVWXYZÆÇØẞ
12345678900@.,!?')]§*""»«/-½©€$£¥&→

Method Mono is a typeface of four weights plus *Italics:* Light, *Light Italic*, Regular, *Italic*, **Bold**, ***Bold Italic***, **Black**, ***and Black Italic***

→ P. 466

# (1988)

AGATHA CHRISTIE'S

# *Ραντεβού με τον → Θάνατο*

**Appointment with** → *Death*

# Hercules Poirot

**Miasma**

Miasma is a type family designed for both long running text and large titles. It comes in two styles (one with soft and another with sharp serifs) each one in four weights and corresponding Italics, together with a grotesque variation that follows the same x-height and character width ratios to be easily used as a companion to its seriffed counterpart. The two contrasted variations come with two sets of capital Greek letters: one with and one without serifs.

**Design:** 2020, George Triantafyllakos → p. 484

**Foundry:** Atypical, Greece, atypical.gr → p. 488

**Language support:** Latin Extended, Greek

**OpenType features:** Stylistic Sets

**Test version available:** Yes

**Web font format available:** Yes

abcdefghijklmnopqrstuvwxyzæåçéñöûß
ABCDEFGHIJKLMNOPQRSTUVWXYZÆÇØ
1234567890@.,!?')]§*“”»«/–©€$£¥&↔

αβγδεζηθικλμνξοπρσςτυφχψωάέήίόώϊϋΰ
ΑΒΓΔΕΖΗΘΙΚΛΜΝΞΟΠΡΣΤΥΦΧΨΩΆΈΉΊΌΏΪΫ
01234567890@.,!?')]§*“”»«/–©€$£¥&↓

Miasma is a family of three styles: Normal, Sharp, and Grotesque. Normal and Sharp in four weights plus *Italics:* Light, *Light Italic,* Regular, *Italic,* Medium, ***Medium Italic,*** **Semi Bold,** ***Semi Bold Italic,*** Sharp Light, *Sharp Light Italic,* Sharp Regular, *Sharp Italic,* **Sharp Medium,** ***Sharp Medium Italic,*** **Sharp Semi Bold,** ***Sharp Semi Bold Italic.*** Grotesque in four weights: Light, Regular, **Medium, and Semi Bold**

→ P. 451, 457

"I believe whatever doesn't **kill** you, simply makes you **... stranger.**"

Milligram

The Milligram main family is Display oriented, with tight spacing and a very high x-height, allowing a very compact typesetting and an effective usage of space in titling, headings, and logos. For long body text typesetting, a text subfamily has been developed, offering a slightly wider set of proportions, looser spacing, and more open counter spaces. On the other side of the spectrum is the "super-display" Milligram Macro subfamily, featuring ultra tight spacing and design, optimized for the best effect in logos and big-size titling.

**Design:** 2022, Cosimo Lorenzo Pancini → p. 480

**Foundry:** Zetafonts, Italy, zetafonts.com → p. 492

**Language support:** Latin, Cyrillic

**OpenType features:** Proportional Oldstyle, Tabular Lining, Proportional Lining, Tabular Oldstyle, Superscript, Subscript, Ordinals, Fractions, Numerator, Denominator, Arrows, Stylistic Alternates, Stylistic Sets, Slashed Zero, Localized Forms, Case Sensitive Forms, Mark Positioning, Optical size, Font Variations

**Test version available:** Yes

**Web font format available:** Yes

→ P. 451

abcdefghijklmnopqrstuvwxyzæåçéñöûß
ABCDEFGHIJKLMNOPQRSTUVWXYZÆÇØ
1234567890Ø@.,!?')]§*""»«/–½©€$£¥&↘

абвгдеёжзийклмнопрстуфхцчшщъыьэюя
АБВГДЕЁЖЗИЙКЛМНОПРСТУФХЦЧШЩЪЫЬЭЮЯ
1234567890Ø@.,!?')]§*""»«/–½©€$£¥&↓

Milligram is a family of three styles: Normal, Macro, and Text. Normal and Macro in seven weights plus *Italics:* Thin, *Thin Italic,* Light, *Light Italic,* Regular, *Italic,* Medium, ***Medium Italic,*** **Bold,** ***Bold Italic,*** **Extra Bold,** ***Extra Bold Italic,*** **Heavy,** ***Heavy Italic,*** Macro Thin, *Macro Thin Italic,* Macro Light, *Macro Light Italic,* Macro Regular, *Macro Italic,* **Macro Medium,** ***Macro Medium Italic,*** **Macro Bold,** ***Macro Bold Italic,*** **Macro Extra Bold,** ***Macro Extra Bold Italic,*** **Macro Heavy,** ***and Macro Heavy Italic.*** Text in four weights plus *Italics:* Book, *Book Italic,* Regular, *Italic,* **Medium,** ***Medium Italic,*** **Bold,** ***and Bold Italic***

# MAKING

$$$$$$the$$$$$$
$$$$Billion$$$$
$$$$Dollar$$$$$
$$$$$$$$$$$$$$

# Code

[2021]

↵ {"Hello, World!"}

$$$$$$$$$$$$$$
$$$$$$$$$$$$$$
%%%%%%%%%%%%%%%

Monoflow

Monoflow is a fixed-width font with a human character for those who care about aesthetics and functionality. It stands out due to its stunning readability, even in small sizes—perfect for writing code and ready for use in corporate and graphic design. It comes with a unique trick that improves spacing while remaining fixed-width: During typing, Monoflow repositions individual letters within their fixed-width bounding box. The words stay monospace while the letters shift in context.

**Design:** 2019, Prof. Hans R. Heitmann → p. 476, Johannes Ammon → p. 472

**Foundry:** Finaltype, Germany, finaltype.de → p. 489

**Language support:** Latin Extended

**OpenType features:** Standard Ligatures, Discretionary Ligatures, Superscript, Ordinals, All Alternates, Contextual Alternates, Fractions, Stylistic Alternates, Stylistic Sets, Slashed Zero, Localized Forms, Case Sensitive Forms, Mark Positioning

**Test version available:** Yes

**Web font format available:** Yes

→ P. 466

abcdefghijklmnopqrstuvwxyzæåçéñöûß
ABCDEFGHIJKLMNOPQRSTUVWXYZÆÇØẞ
12345678900@.,!?’)]§*“”»«/–½©€$£¥&↵

Monoflow is a typeface of four weights plus *Italics:* Light, *Light Italic,* Regular, *Italic,* **Medium,** ***Medium Italic,*** **Bold,** ***and Bold Italic***

Isabelle HUPPERT *in* **L'IVRESSE DU POUVOIR** *by* Claude CHABROL

**Muoto**

Muoto, designed in collaboration between Matthieu Cortat, Anthony Franklin, and Sander Vermeulen (Base Design), is the synthesis of a sensitive and human approach to modernist design. This variable Sans Serif font combines full curves and solid stems, showing that functionalism can actually be warm and softly effective. With its robust structure and subdued proportions, it evokes organic forms dear to Finnish architect Alvar Aalto.

**Design:** 2021, Matthieu Cortat
→ p. 474

**Foundry:** 205TF, France, 205.tf
→ p. 488

**Language support:** Latin Extended

**OpenType features:** Tabular Lining, Proportional Lining, Standard Ligatures, All Caps, Superscript, Subscript, Ordinals, Contextual, Alternates, Fractions, Alternative Fractions, Numerator, Denominator, Ornaments, Arrows, Stylistic Alternates, Stylistic Sets, Slashed Zero, Localized Forms, Case Sensitive Forms, Required Ligatures, Font Variations

**Test version available:** Yes

**Web font format available:** Yes

→ P. 451

abcdefghijklmnopqrstuvwxyzæfjåçéñöûß
ABCDEFGHIJKLMNOPQRSTUVWXYZÆÇØẞ
12345678900@.,!?')]§*“”»«/–½©€$£¥&→♥

Muoto is a typeface of six weights plus *Italics:* Thin, *Thin Italic,* Light, *Light Italic,* Regular, *Italic,* **Medium,** ***Medium Italic,*** **Bold,** ***Bold Italic,*** **Black,** ***and Black Italic***

NOW PLAYING IN A THEATER NEAR YOU:

# QU'EST-CE QU'ON A FAIT *AU* ☟ BON DIEU ?

CHRISTIAN CLAVIER

CHANTAL LAUBY • ÉMILIE CAEN

FRÉDÉRIC CHAU • FRÉDÉRIQUE BEL

► comédie française ◄

Murtaugh & Riggs

Murtaugh & Riggs, a duo of complementary typeface families. With Murtaugh & Riggs, designer Nikola Djurek has taken a new approach to building families, basing this project not on stroke widths, but the idea of age. His Murtaugh is the senior partner of the team, seasoned and grounded but hardly ready for retirement, thank you very much. Riggs is the young gun, trendy, driven, and ready to get at it. And while there is a generational tension between them, there is also a palpable synergy, each drawing from the other as they strike a creative balance.

**Design:** 2020, Nikola Djurek
→ p. 474

**Foundry:** Typotheque, The Netherlands, typotheque.com
→ p. 492

**Language support:** Latin Extended

**OpenType features:** Proportional Oldstyle, Tabular Lining, Proportional Lining, Tabular Oldstyle, Standard Ligatures, All Caps, Small Caps, Capitals to Small Caps, Superscript, Subscript, Fractions, Numerator, Denominator, Slashed Zero

**Test version available:** Yes

**Web font format available:** Yes

abcdefghijklmnopqrstuvwxyzæfjåçéñöû
ABCDEFGHIJKLMNOPQRSTUVWXYZÆÇØ
12345678900@.,!?')]§*“”»«/–½©€$£¥&↙☝

Murtaugh & Riggs is a family of two styles: Murtaugh and Riggs. Murtaugh in two widths: Condensed and Normal, each in six weights plus *Italics:* Condensed Light, *Condensed Light Italic,* **Condensed Medium,** ***Normal Medium Italic,*** **Normal Bold,** ***Normal Bold Italic, and*** **Normal Black.**
Riggs in three widths: Condensed, Normal, and Extended, each in six weights plus *Italics:* Condensed Extra Light, *Condensed Extra Light Italic,* Regular, *Italic,* **Extended Semi Bold,** ***and Extended Semi Bold Italic***


→ P. 451, 463

Shuffleboard
KKings*2011

***Grab life by the rocks!***

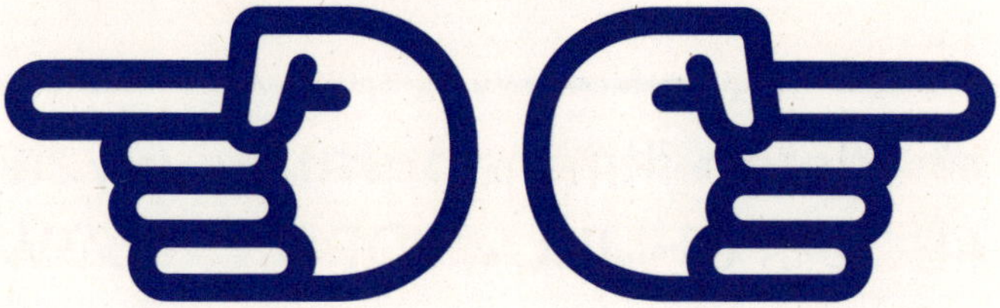

SHORT

**2nd**

**Natom Pro**

Natom Pro is a sans serif and geometric font family adapted to the professional requirements of graphic designers, web designers, and mobile application developers. Comprised of 19 styles including eight styles designed especially for the design of headlines, Natom Pro is a very versatile family of fonts that can be used in many communication projects. This font, with a resolutely contemporary aspect, also hides a unique typographic design, since it has two distinct styles (Title and Roman).

**Design:** 2021, Olivier Gourvat
→ p. 476

**Foundry:** Mostardesign Type Foundry, France, motyfo.com
→ p. 490

**Language support:** Latin Extended

**OpenType features:** Proportional Oldstyle, Tabular Lining, Proportional Lining, Tabular Oldstyle, Standard Ligatures, All Caps, Small Caps, Capitals to Small Caps, Superscript, Subscript, Titling Alternates, All Alternates, Contextual Alternates, Fractions, Numerator, Denominator, Arrows, Stylistic Alternates, Stylistic Sets, Slashed Zero, Case Sensitive Forms

**Test version available:** Yes

**Web font format available:** Yes

abcdefghijklmnopqrstuvwxyzæfjåçéñöûß
ABCDEFGHIJKLMNOPQRSTUVWXYZÆÇØß
1234567890Ø@.,!?')]§*"""»«/–½©€$£¥&↕⊛

Natom Pro is a family of two styles: Normal and TITLE. Normal in six weights plus *Italics:* Extra Light, *Extra Light Italic,* Light, *Light Italic,* Regular, *Italic,* **Medium,** ***Medium Italic,*** **Bold,** ***Bold Italic,*** **Black,** ***and Black Italic.*** TITLE IN SIX WEIGHTS: TITLE EXTRA LIGHT, TITLE LIGHT, TITLE REGULAR, **TITLE MEDIUM, TITLE BOLD, AND TITLE BLACK**


→ P. 451, 463

* From the Director of “PIRATES OF THE CARRIBEAN” *

Johnny Depp is

Rango

X

HéRoS (Pas) Très discret

The Neptun superfamily is an exploration of early German Sans Serif typefaces, using inspiration from various sources and creating a typographic bridge to modern times. The family is split into two subfamilies, taking that approach in different manners: Neptun Nord with a friendly and retro aesthetic, extreme proportions, pointed terminals, and narrow widths. Neptun Süd is on the modern side with wider forms and familiar proportions, but punctual breakouts.

**Design:** 2021, Fabian Dornhecker → p. 475

**Foundry:** LA BOLDE VITA, Germany, laboldevita.com → p. 489

**Language support:** Latin Extended

**OpenType features:** Tabular Lining, Proportional Lining, Standard Ligatures, Discretionary Ligatures, Superscript, Subscript, Swashes, Contextual Alternates, Fractions, Numerator, Denominator, Stylistic Alternates, Stylistic Sets, Slashed Zero, Localized Forms, Case Sensitive Forms

**Test version available:** Yes

**Web font format available:** Yes

→ P. 451

abcdefghijklmnopqrstuvwxyzæfiåçéñöûß
ABCDEFGHIJKLMNOPQRSTUVWXYZÆÇØẞ
12345678900@.,!?')]§*“”»«/–½©€$£¥&↖

Neptun is a family of two styles: Nord and Süd. Nord in three widths: Condensed, Semi Condensed, and Normal, each in seven weights: Nord Condensed Light, **Nord Condensed Regular, Nord Condensed Medium, Nord Semi Condensed Semi Bold, Nord Semi Condensed Bold, Nord Extra Bold, and Nord Black.** Süd in four widths: Normal, Wide, Extra Wide, and Extended, each in seven weights: Süd Light, Süd Regular, **Süd Wide Medium, Süd Extra Wide Semi Bold, Süd Extra Wide Bold, Süd Extended Extra Bold, and Süd Extended Black**

# The Hidden Life of Pets.

BOW *WOWS* &
*PURR*-FECT
PETS! → MEET
***AMAZING***
**CREATURES FROM AROUND THE WORLD AND DIG INTO THE LATEST SCIENCE ON OUR ANIMAL FRIENDS'**
***SENSES & SKILLS.***

**Neue Rational**

Neue Rational is the complete rework of the original *Rational* family. It is the designer's answer to the Neo Grotesk genre con-taining new widths (Condensed and Narrow) and a hybrid between proportional and non-proportional spac-ing called Mix.

**Design:** 2022, René Bieder
→ p. 472

**Foundry:** Studio Rene Bieder, Germany, renebieder.com → p. 491

**Language support:** Latin

**OpenType features:** Tabular Lining, Discretionary Ligatures, Super-script, Subscript, Ordinals, Contextual Alternates, Fractions, Numerator, Denominator, Arrows, Stylistic Alternates, Stylistic Sets, Localized Forms, Case Sensitive Forms

**Test version available:** Yes

**Web font format available:** Yes

→ P. 451, 466

abcdefghijklmnopqrstuvwxyzæflåçéñöûß
ABCDEFGHIJKLMNOPQRSTUVWXYZÆÇØß
1234567890@.,!?')]§*""»«/–½©€$£¥&↑♥

Neue Rational is a family of three styles: Normal, Mix, and Mono. Normal in three widths: Condensed, Narrow, and Normal, each in nine weights plus *Italics:* Condensed Thin, *Condensed Thin Italic,* Condensed Extra Light, *Condensed Extra Light Italic,* Condensed Light, *Condensed Light Italic,* Narrow Regular, *Narrow Regular Italic,* Narrow Medium, *Narrow Medium Italic,* **Narrow Semi Bold,** ***Narrow Semi Bold Italic,*** **Bold,** ***Bold Italic,*** **Black,** ***and Black Italic.*** Mix and Mono in four weights plus *Italics:* Mix Regular, *Mix Regular Italic,* Mix Medium, *Mix Medium Italic,* **Mix Semi Bold,** ***Mix Semi Bold Italic,*** **Mix Bold,** ***Mix Bold Italic,*** Mono Regular, *Mono Regular Italic,* Mono Medium, *Mono Medium Italic,* **Mono Semi Bold,** ***Mono Semi Bold Italic,*** **Mono Bold,** ***and Mono Bold Italic***

… BOMBED OUT
IN SPACE ⟷
↙ WITH A
SPACED OUT ↘
↓BOMB!?

# DARK STAR!

THE SPACED-OUT SPACE SHIP

**MD Nichrome**

A display typeface referencing the typography of science fiction paperbacks from the 70s and early 80s. Many of the typefaces from this time and genre, originally drawn for dry transfer or phototypesetting, were never digitized as carefully as they deserved—MD Nichrome seeks to remedy this for modern technologies and styles, not by reviving any single typeface, but by capturing elements of many.

**Design:** 2021, Rutherford Craze
→ p. 474

**Foundry:** Mass-Driver, The Netherlands, mass-driver.com
→ p. 490

**Language support:** Latin Extended

**OpenType features:** Tabular Lining, Proportional Lining, Superscript, Subscript, Ordinals, Contextual Alternates, Fractions, Numerator, Denominator, Arrows, Stylistic Alternates, Stylistic Sets, Localized Forms, Case Sensitive Forms, Font Variations, Barless Fractions

**Test version available:** Yes

**Web font format available:** Yes

→ P. 451, 463

abcdefghijklmnopqrstuvwxyzæåçéñöûß
ABCDEFGHIJKLMNOPQRSTUVWXYZÆÇØẞ
1234567890@.,!?’)]§*“”»«/–½©€$£¥&↕

MD Nichrome is a typeface of eight weights plus *Obliques:* Infra, *Infra Oblique,* Thin, *Thin Oblique,* Light, *Light Oblique,* Regular, *Oblique,* Dark, *Dark Oblique,* Bold, *Bold Oblique,* Black, *Black Oblique,* Ultra Black, *and Ultra Black Oblique*

# YIPPEE-KI-YAY, MOTHER-{*%!} :)

OPS Noise Abroad

OPS Noise Abroad is designed by OPS Type and Jan Egbers and is published by Our Polite Society Type. OPS Noise Abroad is as rough and ready as the Internet and fits well for headlines. Its style is inspired by old West wood type that has lost its serifs. A modern boot for the new Wild West.

**Design:** 2022, Jens Schildt → p. 482, Jan Egbers → p. 475

**Foundry:** Our Polite Society Type, The Netherlands / Sweden, ourpolitesocietytype.net → p. 491

**Language support:** Latin Extended

**OpenType features:** All Alternates, Case-Sensitive Forms, Denominators, Fractions, Localized Forms, Numerators, Proportional Figures, Scientific Inferiors, Stylistic Sets, Subscript, Superscript, Tabular Figures

**Test version available:** Yes

**Web font format available:** Yes



→ P. 451

abcdefghijklmnopqrstuvwxyzæåçéñöûß
ABCDEFGHIJKLMNOPQRSTUVWXYZÆÇØ
1234567890@.,!?')]§*“”»«/–½©€$£¥&

# OPS Noise Abroad is a typeface of one Regular weight

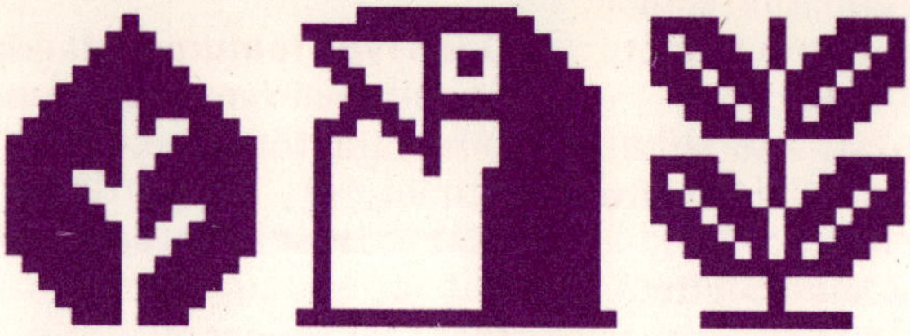

# The Year Earth Changed

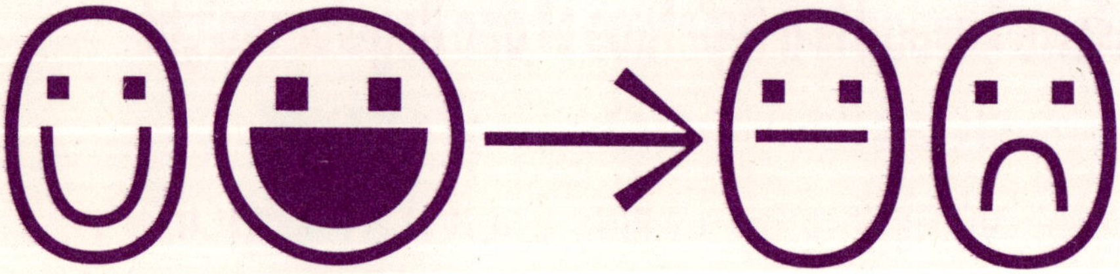

**NARRATED BY:**
@Sír David
Attênborough
**48 mins**

Non Natural is a sans serif typeface with subtle details that endow it with a distinctive personality. The objective was to create a typeface with legibility and good contrast between black and white, making it suitable for different sizes. The typeface has specific features that help in reading and reproduction, the Inktraps are just the right size for the text to be functional. The geometric shapes and structure reflect the inspiration and influence of mid-century Swiss Typography.

**Design:** 2020, Rodrigo Vejar Suarez → p. 483, Jona Saucedo → p. 482

**Foundry:** Non Foundry, Mexico, nonfoundry.com → p. 490

**Language support:** Latin Extended

**OpenType features:** Standard Ligatures, Fractions, Numerator, Denominator, Arrows

**Test version available:** Yes

**Web font format available:** Yes

abcdefghijklmnopqrstuvwxyzæfjåçéñöûß
ABCDEFGHIJKLMNOPQRSTUVWXYZÆÇØß
1234567890@.,!?')]§*“”»«/–½©€$£¥&↗

Non Natural is a family of two styles: Grotesk and Mono. Grotesk in five weights: Thin, Light, **Regular,** **Medium, and Bold.** Mono in four weights: Thin, Light, **Regular, and Medium**

→ P. 452, 466

The *Hundred* Year Old Man who Climbed out @ window

&

*disappeared*

Non Sans is a grotesque sans serif typeface. It was created in 2019, Jona Saucedo's design emphasized in a typeface dense, sturdy appearance and legit text block. In the typeface you can see the Swiss design inspiration of the early 1960's. With its new revision (2022) it has a more unified set of heights and widths, plus it now includes an italic version that functions optimally. The typeface is more contemporary and the shapes of the characters appear better spaced and more legible—even on small electronic devices.

**Design:** 2020, Rodrigo Vejar Suarez → p. 483, Jona Saucedo → p. 482

**Foundry:** Non Foundry, Mexico, nonfoundry.com → p. 490

**Language support:** Latin Extended

**OpenType features:** Standard Ligatures, Fractions, Numerator, Denominator, Arrows

**Test version available:** Yes

**Web font format available:** Yes

abcdefghijklmnopqrstuvwxyzæfjåçéñöûß
ABCDEFGHIJKLMNOPQRSTUVWXYZÆÇØẞ
1234567890@.,!?')]§*""»«/–½©€$£¥&↗

Non Sans is a typeface of five weights plus *Italics:* Light, *Light Italic*, Book, *Book Italic*, Regular, *Italic*, **Medium**, ***Medium Italic***, **Bold**, ***and Bold Italic***

→ P. 452

MEGHE DHAKA TARA (মেঘে ঢাকা তারা MĒGHĒ ḌHĀKĀ TĀRĀ, LIT. THE CLOUD-CAPPED STAR)

# “Brother, I want to survive (দাদা, আমি বাঁচতে চাই।).”

Noort is a modern script pairing of Bengali and Latin, brimming with expressiveness and designed for branding, comfortable book and magazine layouts, and dynamic posters and advertising. From the beginning of Noort's design, the Bengali was always planned as part of the family. Noort Bengali and Noort Latin each needed to have their own DNA, purpose, and aesthetic value, while equally sharing the spotlight. It exudes warmth and energy on screens and in print.

**Design:** 2021, Juan Bruce → p. 473, Veronika Burian → p. 473

**Foundry:** TypeTogether, Czech Republic, type-together.com → p. 492

**Language support:** Latin, Bengali

**OpenType features:** Proportional Oldstyle, Tabular Lining, Proportional Lining, Tabular Oldstyle, Standard Ligatures, Discretionary Ligatures, All Caps, Small Caps, Capitals to Small Caps, Superscript, Subscript, Ordinals, Swashes, Contextual Alternates, Fractions, Alternative Fractions, Numerator, Denominator, Ornaments, Arrows, Stylistic Alternates, Stylistic Sets, Historical Forms, Slashed Zero, Localized Forms, Case Sensitive Forms, Initial Form

**Test version available:** Yes

**Web font format available:** Yes

abcdefghijklmnopqrstuvwxyzæfjåçéñöûß
ABCDEFGHIJKLMNOPQRSTUVWXYZÆÇØß
12345678900@.,!?')]§*""»«/–½©€$£¥&→

অ আ ই ঈ উ ঊ ঋ ৠ ঌ ৡ এ ঐ ও ঔ ক খ গ ঘ ঙ চ ছ জ ঝ
ঞ ট ঠ ড ঢ ণ ত থ দ ধ ন প ফ ব ভ ম য র ল শ ষ স হ ড় ঢ়
য় ৰ ৱ ৎ ◌া ি◌ ◌ী ◌ৗ ে◌ ৈ◌ ো ৌ ০১২৩৪৫৬৭৮৯

Noort Bengali is a typeface of five weights: Regular, Book, **Semi Bold, Bold, and Extra Bold**

→ P. 457

X

**Wut,**
**Angst,**
**Freude,**
Ekel,
Kummer.

Nouvelle Grotesk

→ P. 452

Seventy years after the start of the success story of grotesque typefaces, we are ready to make a contribution to this genre. It took us some time to find a perfect form that fills the gap between simplicity and neutrality. We didn't want to design yet another "neutral" typeface. We have searched for shapes that are simple and which encourage the designer to create amazing things—and by the way, make other people smile.

**Design:** 2020, Anton Studer → p. 483

**Foundry:** Nouvelle Noire Type Foundry, Switzerland, nouvellenoire.ch → p. 490

**Language support:** Latin Extended

**OpenType features:** Tabular Lining, Standard Ligatures, Superscript, Subscript, Contextual Ligatures, Fractions, Numerator, Denominator, Arrows, Stylistic Alternates, Slashed Zero

**Test version available:** Yes

**Web font format available:** Yes

abcdefghijklmnopqrstuvwxyzæflåçéñöûß
ABCDEFGHIJKLMNOPQRSTUVWXYZÆÇØ
12345678900@.,!?')]§*“”»«/–½©€$£¥&↗∅

Nouvelle Grotesk is a typeface of seven weights plus *Diagonals:* Thin, *Thin Diagonal,* Light, *Light Diagonal,* Regular, *Diagonal,* **Medium,** ***Medium Diagonal,*** **Bold,** ***Bold Diagonal,*** **Black,** ***Black Diagonal,*** **Fat,** ***and Fat Diagonal***

# Neo-Tokyo

hi-tech

## the Capsules versus the Clowns. 1988

Nuova Volte

The Nuova Volte typeface was inspired by the fitting of puzzle pieces. The terminals of the lowercase forms have been cut diagonally which fits the form of rounded or barred letterforms. This typeface performs well on posters, signage, logos, or titles given its characteristics as a Display font.

**Design:** 2021, Alfredo Marco Pradil, → p. 481

**Foundry:** Hanken Design Co., Philippines, hanken.co → p. 489

**Language support:** Latin Extended

**OpenType features:** Tabular Lining, Proportional Lining, Standard Ligatures, Discretionary Ligatures, Superscript, Subscript, Ordinals, Fractions, Numerator, Denominator, Localized Forms, Case Sensitive Forms

**Test version available:** Yes

**Web font format available:** Yes

→ P. 452

abcdefghijklmnopqrstuvwxyzæfjåçéñöûß
ABCDEFGHIJKLMNOPQRSTUVWXYZÆÇØß
1234567890⓪@.,!?')]§*“”»«/–½©€$£¥&→♻

Nuova Volte is a typeface of five weights: Light, Regular, **Medium, Semi Bold, and Bold**

# Man of Steel

Henry Cavill.
Amy Adams.
Michael Shannon.
Kevin Costner.

Diane Lane.
Laurence Fishburne.
Russel Crowe.
—

# 2013

Nure

Nure is the evolution of the known custom font designed for Abitare Magazine. It is a variable font family designed in three axes (Weight, Optical, Width) to cover all graphic design needs. Based on 1,350 glyphs per weight it can be customized widely. Thanks to alternative letters available via nine OpenType Stylistic Set features, you can for example setup an *a* in a *Helvetica* or *Futura* mood, a *g* in a *Franklin Gothic* mood, and much more.

**Design:** 2021, Fabrizio Schiavi → p. 482

**Foundry:** FSD, Italy, fsd.it → p. 489

**Language support:** Latin Extended, Cyrillic

**OpenType features:** Tabular Lining, Proportional Lining, Standard Ligatures, All Caps, Small Caps, Capitals to Small Caps, Superscript, Subscript, Ordinals, Fractions, Numerator, Denominator, Ornaments Arrows, Stylistic Alternates, Stylistic Sets, Historical Forms, Slashed Zero, Optical size, Font Variations

**Test version available:** Yes

**Web font format available:** Yes

→ P. 452, 463

abcdefghijklmnopqrstuvwxyzæfjåçéñöûß
ABCDEFGHIJKLMNOPQRSTUVWXYZÆÇØẞ
12345678900@.,!?')]§*""»«/–½©€$£¥&⇱

абвгдеёжзийклмнопрстуфхцчшщъыьэюя
АБВГДЕЁЖЗИЙКЛМНОПРСТУФХЦЧШЩЪЫЬЭ
12345678900@.,!?')]§*""»«/–½©€$£¥&↪

Nure is a family of two styles: Text and Display, each in three widths: Condensed, Normal, and Expanded, each in nine weights: Text Condensed Thin, Text Condensed Extra Light, Text Condensed Light, Text Regular, Text Medium, **Text Semi Bold, Text Expanded Bold, Text Expanded Extra Bold, and Text Expanded Black.** Display Condensed Thin, Display Condensed Extra Light, Display Condensed Light, Display Regular, Display Medium, **Display Semi Bold, Display Expanded Bold, Display Expanded Extra Bold, and Display Expanded Black**

School of Rock!

No1 × 2003

↘ WE DON'T NEED NO EDUCATION!

Oakley

Oakley is an homage to the expressive, soft, and rounded old-style serif typefaces from the sixties and seventies. Its gentle and juicy serifs give the typeface the right amount of warmth and nostalgia. While hinting at the classic *Cooper*-like style, the reinterpretation features several unconventional letterforms which make both the roman and italic styles remarkably dynamic.

**Design:** 2022, Mark van Leeuwen
→ p. 478

**Foundry:** Mark van Leeuwen, Germany, markvanleeuwen.co
→ p. 490

**Language support:** Latin Extended

**OpenType features:** Proportional Oldstyle, Proportional Lining, Standard Ligatures, Discretionary Ligatures, Swashes, Contextual Swashes, Contextual Alternates, Contextual Ligatures, Arrows, Stylistic Alternates, Stylistic Sets

**Test version available:** No

**Web font format available:** Yes

→ P. 463

**abcdefghijklmnopqrstuvwxyzæåçéñöûß**
**ABCDEFGHIJKLMNOPQRSTUVWXYZÆÇØß**
**1234567890@.,!?')]§*“”»«/–©€$£¥&↕**

**Oakley is a typeface of two weights plus *Italics:* Bold, *Bold Italic,* Black, *and Black Italic***

⁂

MIRROR,
ЗЕРКАЛО ON
THE WALL,
***is this not the
most perfect
Βασίλειο of
them all!?***

→ P. 457

Occupant Oldstyle is a 21st century text face from Cyrus Highsmith, assisted by June Shin. The rounded triangular endings are the result of a long fermentation process that combines ingredients from Japanese Mincho style typefaces, rounded Sans Serifs, electronic music, and toys. Highsmith calls them "child-safe serifs."

**Design:** 2021, Cyrus Highsmith → p. 476

**Foundry:** Occupant Fonts, United States of America, occupantfonts.com → p. 490

**Language support:** Latin Extended, Cyrillic, Greek

**OpenType features:** Tabular Lining, Proportional Lining, Standard Ligatures, Small Caps, Capitals to Small Caps, Ordinals, Fractions, Numerator, Denominator, Localized Forms

**Test version available:** Yes

**Web font format available:** Yes

abcdefghijklmnopqrstuvwxyzæfiåçéñöûß
ABCDEFGHIJKLMNOPQRSTUVWXYZÆß
1234567890@.,!?')]§*‘“”»«/–½©€$£¥&☛✽

абвгдеёжзийклмнопрстуфхцчшщъыьэюя
АБВГДЕЁЖЗИЙКЛМНОПРСТУФХЦЧШЩЪЫ
1234567890@.,!?')]§*‘“”»«/–½©€$£¥&↖✭

Occupant Oldstyle is a typeface of five weights plus *Italics:* Extra Light, *Extra Light Italic,* **Light,** ***Light Italic,*** **Medium,** ***Medium Italic,*** **Semi Bold,** ***Semi Bold Italic,*** **Bold,** ***and Bold Italic***

asav-
age
ταξίδι
сер to the
ще
/of the/
AMERICAN
DREAM

Okay! Serif

Okay! Serif is a loud Display Serif that comes in a single weight with a matching italic style but appears to have many different sub-tones. It has a personality that bursts with a strong attitude, tropical warmth, and sweet aftertaste. Okay! Serif is pretty fluent in Cyrillic and Greek, too. Whether you're a print nostalgic or digital freak, you will be definitely *Okay!* with it.

**Design:** 2021, Milos Mitrovic
→ p. 479

**Foundry:** Gradient Type, Norway, wearegradient.net → p. 489

**Language support:** Latin Extended, Cyrillic, Greek

**OpenType features:** Tabular Lining, Discretionary Ligatures, Superscript, Subscript, Ordinals, Fractions, Numerator, Denominator, Arrows, Stylistic Sets, Slashed Zero, Case Sensitive Forms

**Test version available:** Yes

**Web font format available:** Yes

→ P. 463

***abcdefghijklmnopqrstuvwxyzœfjåçéñöûß***
***ABCDEFGHIJKLMNOPQRSTUVWXYZÆÇØ***
***12345678900@.,!?')]§*“”»«/–½©€$£¥₿↗***

**αβγδεζηθικλμνξοπρσςτυφχψωάέήίόώϊϋΰ**
**ΑΒΓΔΕΖΗΘΙΚΛΜΝΞΟΠΡΣΤΥΦΧΨΩΆΈΉΊΌΏΪΫ**
**12345678900@.,!?')]§*“”»«/–½©€$£¥₿←**

# Okay! Serif is a typeface of one Bold weight plus *Italics*

STYLE WARS
HIP HOP—MARIJUANA
new york city
1983

graffiti
×bboying
& rapping

Oldschool Grotesk

Oldschool Grotesk is a look behind the facade of Victorian sans serif inscriptions. Inheriting some of the distinct aspects of early British Grotesques and lettering from that period, it peels away the top layers of apparent quirkiness and eccentric detail. A reflection of Modernist roots through the lens of modern typography.

**Design:** 2019, William Montrose → p. 480

**Foundry:** Kilotype, Germany, kilotype.de → p. 489

**Language support:** Latin Extended

**OpenType features:** Proportional Oldstyle, Tabular Lining, Proportional Lining, Tabular Oldstyle, Standard Ligatures, Discretionary Ligatures, All Caps, Superscript, Subscript, Ordinals, All Alternates, Fractions, Numerator, Denominator, Arrows, Stylistic Sets, Slashed Zero, Localized Forms, Case Sensitive Forms, Mark Positioning, Font Variations

**Test version available:** Yes

**Web font format available:** Yes

→ P. 452

abcdefghijklmnopqrstuvwxyzæffåçéñöûß
ABCDEFGHIJKLMNOPQRSTUVWXYZÆÇØẞ
1234567890@.,!?')]§*""»«/–½©€$£¥&↖❤

Oldschool Grotesk is a family of four widths: Compressed, Condensed, Compact, and Normal, each in ten weights: Compressed Air, Compressed Thin, Condensed Extra Light, Condensed Light, Condensed Book, **Compact Regular, Compact Medium, Compact Bold, Extra Bold, and Heavy**

{KYOTO}
THE
LAST
SAMURAI

/2003/&
Tom
Cruise

Onamura

Onamura has all of the organic meandering lines and push-pull vitality of Art Nouveau lettering, but rather than being a dogmatic revival of some forgotten specimen, it's a sort of archaeological unearthing and exciting blend of Nouveau's Japanese and Medieval influences. The designers have given it what they'd call a "deep bench"—tons of stylistic alternates and a breadth of weights that will allow designers to paint with type—basking in the revelry of a plethora of new typographic expressions.

**Design:** 2021, Wayan Bill Natih
→ p. 480

**Foundry:** Balibilly Design, Indonesia, balibillydesign.com → p. 488

**Language support:** Latin Extended

**OpenType features:** Standard Ligatures, Discretionary Ligatures, Small Caps, Capitals to Small Caps, Ordinals, All Alternates, Fractions, Numerator, Denominator, Arrows, Stylistic Alternates, Stylistic Sets, Localized Forms, Case Sensitive Forms

**Test version available:** Yes

**Web font format available:** Yes

abcdefghijklmnopqrstuvwxyzæàåçéñöûß
ABCDEFGHIJKLMNOPQRSTUVWXYZÆÇØß
1234567890@.,!?']]§*“”»«/–½©€$£¥&

Onamura is a typeface of ten weights: Light, Normal, Regular, Medium, **Demi Bold, Semi Bold, Bold, Extra Bold, Ultra Bold, and Black**

→ P. 457, 463

I'M CAPABLE OF MUCH UNPLEASANTNESS →

# THE FAVOURITE

© 2018

№ 4

Palast

Palast is a type system of three size-specific optical sub-families: Palast Poster, Palast Display, and Palast Text. Palast Poster is intended for use in extra large sizes, at which the extreme contrast between thick and thin strokes looks spot on. Palast Display is designed for headlines, medium sizes, and short text. Palast Text has the lowest contrast of the three optical sizes, making it perfect for long texts in small sizes.

**Design:** 2021, Hannes von Döhren → p. 475

**Foundry:** HvD Fonts, Germany, hvdfonts.com → p. 489

**Language support:** Latin Extended

**OpenType features:** Proportional Oldstyle, Tabular Lining, Proportional Lining, Tabular Oldstyle, Standard Ligatures, Discretionary Ligatures, All Caps, Superscript, Subscript, Contextual Alternates, Fractions, Numerator, Denominator, Ornaments, Arrows, Stylistic Alternates, Stylistic Sets, Case Sensitive Forms Optical size

**Test version available:** Yes

**Web font format available:** Yes

abcdefghijklmnopqrstuvwxyzæfjåçéñöûß
ABCDEFGHIJKLMNOPQRSTUVWXYZÆÇØẞ
1234567890@.,!?')]§*“”»«/–½©€$£¥&↕✡

Palast is a family of three styles: Text, Display, and Poster, each in six weights plus *Italics:* Text Thin, *Text Thin Italic,* Text Light, *Text Light Italic,* Text Regular, *Text Italic,* Text Medium, *Text Medium Italic,* **Text Bold,** ***Text Bold Italic,*** **Text Black,** ***Text Black Italic,*** Display Thin, *Display Thin Italic,* Display Light, *Display Light Italic,* Display Regular, *Display Italic,* Display Medium, *Display Medium Italic,* **Display Bold,** ***Display Bold Italic,*** **Display Black,** ***Display Black Italic,*** Poster Thin, *Poster Thin Italic,* Poster Light, *Poster Light Italic,* Poster Regular, *Poster Italic,* Poster Medium, *Poster Medium Italic,* **Poster Bold,** ***Poster Bold Italic,*** **Poster Black,** ***and Poster Black Italic***

→ P. 457, 463

# QUANTUM **LEAP** ↙

March 26th, 1989 — **May 5th, 1993**

Paranorma

Paranorma is a font for all things fast. Inspired by the iconic *Eurostile Bold Extended*–which played a significant role in defining the future of the collective imagination–we created a typeface to set a new futuristic standard for the supermodern world. As we developed Paranorma, we observed significant interest in extended grotesque-style fonts. We took this on board and adopted a less radical approach, in order to deliver typography suitable for a wider range of industries.

**Design:** 2021, Mattia Bonanomi
→ p. 473

**Foundry:** TYPE FIRM, Italy, type.firm.gs→ p. 492

**Language support:** Latin Extended

**OpenType features:** Standard Ligatures, Discretionary Ligatures, Superscript, Ordinals, All Alternates, Fractions, Numerator, Denominator, Localized Forms, Case Sensitive Forms

**Test version available:** Yes

**Web font format available:** Yes

abcdefghijklmnopqrstuvwxyzæfjåçéñöûß
ABCDEFGHIJKLMNOPQRSTUVWXYZ
1234567890@.,!?')]§⁺""»«/—½©€$£¥&↖

Paranorma is a family of three styles: Mid, Rnd, and Sq, each in seven weights: Thin Mid, Light Mid, Regular Mid, Medium Mid, **Bold Mid, Ultra Mid, Black Mid,** Thin Rnd, Light Rnd, Regular Rnd, Medium Rnd, **Bold Rnd, Ultra Rnd, Black Rnd,** Thin Sq, Light Sq, Regular Sq, Medium Sq, **Bold Sq, Ultra Sq, and Black Sq**

→ P. 452, 463

WALT DISNEY'S

# Snow & White
# The Seven Dwarfs

**Grumpy**

*Doc*

**Happy**

*Sleepy*

Bashful

***Sneezy***

Dopey

**Patufet**

Patufet is a type family intended to be readable for text purposes. The design is based on Patufet, the main character of one of the most famous folktales of Catalan tradition. The family comes with basic weighted strokes: Finet (Ultra Light) is a touch of delicacy and elegance. Prim (Light) is somehow respectable and humble while the Mig (Regular) weight is quiet and unpretentious. A more rustic text appearance is provided with its Gras (Bold) weight, in order to speak a bit louder and naively.

**Design:** 2020, Andreu Balius → p. 472, Ricard Garcia → p. 475

**Foundry:** Typerepublic, Spain, typerepublic.com → p. 492

**Language support:** Latin Extended

**OpenType features:** Proportional Oldstyle, Proportional Lining, Standard Ligatures, Discretionary Ligatures, Historical Ligatures, Superscript, Subscript, Ordinals, All Alternates, Contextual Alternates, Fractions, Numerator, Denominator, Ornaments, Stylistic Alternates, Stylistic Sets, Historical Forms, Slashed Zero, Localized Forms, Case Sensitive Forms, Required Ligatures

**Test version available:** Yes

**Web font format available:** Yes

→ P. 458

abcdefghijklmnopqrstuvwxyzæfjåçéñöûß
ABCDEFGHIJKLMNOPQRSTUVWXYZÆÇØß
12345678900@.,!?')]§*“”»«/–½©€$£¥&

Patufet is a typeface of five weights plus *Italics:* Finet, *Finet Italic,* Prim, *Prim Italic,* Mig, *Mig Italic,* **Gras,** ***Gras Italic,*** **Obès, *and Obès Italic***

[let's ↓]

# *Netflix & Chill*

Sometimes, all we need is a Pausa. This is the story of a typeface that was started in 2015 in New York. In an intense experience of more than twelve hours per day, Eduilson delved into the history, typography practice, and hand-drawing techniques in the Type@Cooper program. Born freely, it began to show its forms. After the program, over the course of six years, it received new features and refinements. Its horizontal design values space. Just as its process, Pausa is a typeface that asks for calm.

**Design:** 2022, Eduilson Coan
→ p. 474

**Foundry:** Fabio Haag Type, Brazil, fabiohaagtype.com/en → p. 488

**Language support:** Latin

**OpenType features:** Proportional Oldstyle, Tabular Lining, Proportional Lining, Tabular Oldstyle, Standard Ligatures, Discretionary Ligatures, All Caps, Small Caps, Superscript, Subscript, Ordinals, Swashes, All Alternates, Fractions, Numerator, Denominator, Ornaments

**Test version available:** Yes

**Web font format available:** Yes

→ P. 457

abcdefghijklmnopqrstuvwxyzæfjåçéñöûß
ABCDEFGHIJKLMNOPQRSTUVWXYZÆÇØß
1234567890@.,!?’)]§*“”»«/–½©€$£¥&↓❦

Pausa is a typeface of three weights plus *Italics:* Regular, *Italic,* **Semi Bold,** ***Semi Bold Italic,*** **Bold,** ***and Bold Italic***

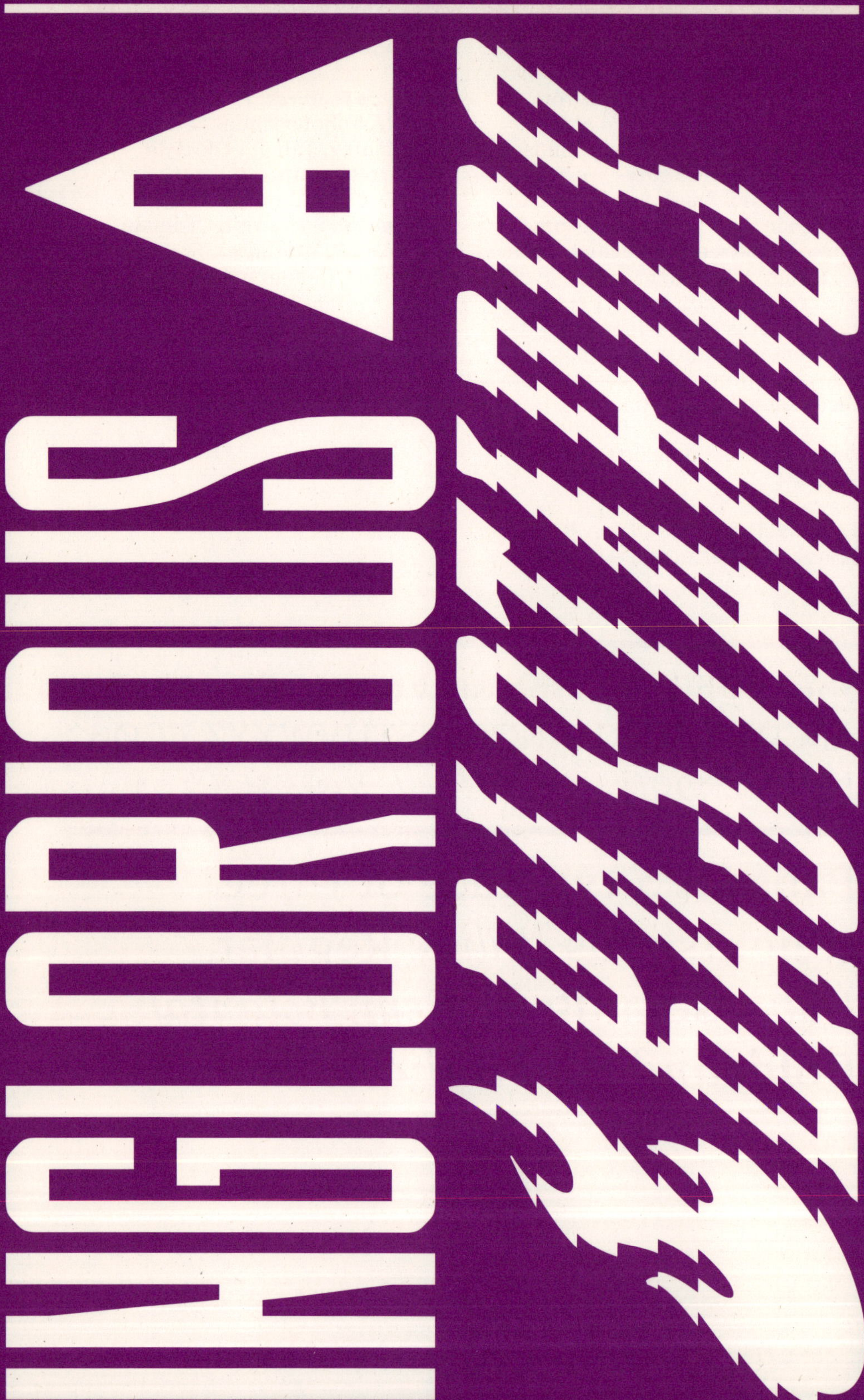


Penitente BT

Penitente BT was designed from the headline of a newspaper of the same name in the city of Cartagena de Indias in 1907. Penitente was born as a typographical revival exercise, however, it evolved in the search to generate a variability of distortion and modular complexity. It is important to note that the variability of distortion was born from the need to have a custom design version of Penitente BT for a reggaeton club in Medellin. So it has been a project that has gone from researching the historical background to a search of technological possibilities to display music.

**Design:** 2022, Bastarda Type → p. 488

**Foundry:** Bastarda Type, Colombia, bastardatype.com → p. 488

**Language support:** Latin

**OpenType features:** All Caps, Unicase

**Test version available:** Yes

**Web font format available:** Yes

→ P. 463

ABCDEFGHIJKLMNOPQRSTUVWXYZÆÅÇÉÑÖÜß
1234567890@.,!?’]]*“‘/-$&

PENITENTE BT IS A FAMILY OF TWO STYLES: SANS AND SERIF, EACH IN VARIABLE DEGREES OF *SLANT AND DISTORTION:* SANS, *SANS SLANTED, SANS SLANTED,* SANS DISTORTED 1, *SANS DISTORTED 1, SANS DISTORTED 1,* SANS DISTORTED 2, *SANS SLANTED DISTORTED 2, SANS SLANTED DISTORTED 2,* SERIF, *SERIF SLANTED, SERIF SLANTED,* SERIF 1, *SERIF 1 SLANTED DISTORTED, SERIF SLANTED DISTORTED,* SERIF DISTORTED 2, *SERIF SLANTED DISTORTED 2, AND SERIF SLANTED DISTORTED 2*

"Dyin' ain't much of a living, boy."

♡

—CLINT EAST-WOOD

THE OUTLAW JOSEY WALES {1976}

Pensum Stencil

Pensum Stencil exaggerates. Inspired by *Pensum Display,* it turns up the contrast: breaking letters into individual shapes to create a fusion of brushy elements and spiky details. A high contrast design, Pensum Stencil brings expression to editorial headlines, confident branding, artisanal packaging, or anywhere its sharp stencil cuts can work their magic.

**Design:** 2021, Nils Thomsen → p. 483

**Foundry:** TypeMates, Germany, typemates.com → p. 492

**Language support:** Latin Extended

**OpenType features:** Proportional Oldstyle, Tabular Lining, Proportional Lining, Tabular Oldstyle, Standard Ligatures, Discretionary Ligatures, Historical Ligatures, All Caps, Small Caps, Capitals to Small Caps, Superscript, Subscript, Ordinals, Contextual Alternates, Fractions, Numerator, Denominator, Arrows, Slashed Zero, Localized Forms, Case Sensitive Forms

**Test version available:** Yes

**Web font format available:** Yes

→ P. 467

abcdefghijklmnopqrstuvwxyzæfjåçéñöûß
ABCDEFGHIJKLMNOPQRSTUVWXYZÆÇØ
1234567890ø@.,!?')]§*“”»«/–½©€$£¥&➢❤

Pensum Stencil is a typeface of nine weights: Thin, Extra Light, Light, Regular, Book, Medium, Bold, Extra Bold, and Black

*До сих пор вы никогда по-настоящему не видели мир, в котором живете.*

In Pentameter, Marie Otsuka explores the polyrhythmic potential usually dormant within the limitations of monospaced typefaces. As an "upright italic," the letterforms create a lively pattern while their uniform metrics remain steady. The result is an inventive design on a syncopated beat that resonates with the poetics beyond code.

**Design:** 2021, Marie Otsuka
→ p. 480

**Foundry:** Occupant Fonts, United States of America, occupantfonts.com → p. 490

**Language support:** Latin Extended, Cyrillic, Greek

**OpenType features:** Tabular Oldstyle, Ordinals, Fractions, Numerator, Denominator, Localized Forms

**Test version available:** Yes

**Web font format available:** Yes

→ P. 466

abcdefghijklmnopqrstuvwxyzæfjåçéß
ABCDEFGHIJKLMNOPQRSTUVWXYZÆÇØẞ
1234567890@.,!?')]§*""»«/-½©€$£¥&↓

αβγδεζηθικλμνξοπρσςτυφχψωάέήίόώϊϋΰ
ΑΒΓΔΕΖΗΘΙΚΛΜΝΞΟΠΡΣΤΥΦΧΨΩΆΈΉΊΌΏΪΫ
1234567890@.,!?')]§*""»«/-½©€$£¥&→

Pentameter is a family of three widths: Condensed, Normal, and Wide, each in seven weights plus *Italics:* Thin Condensed, *Thin Italic Condensed,* Extra Light Condensed, *Extra Light Italic Condensed,* Light, *Light Italic,* Regular, *Italic,* Medium, *Medium Italic,* **Semi Bold Wide,** ***Semi Bold Wide Italic,*** **Bold Wide,** ***and Bold Wide Italic***

* *Mr.* {**Mister**} *Robot*

# @cyber- *security*, hacking, & social *anxiety*

PolySans Mono

PolySans Mono is a monospaced cut of *PolySans,* with the same set of properties as its cousin and with the same recognizable soft-edge Inktrap feature. The roman styles embrace conservative proportions and dynamics, while the Italics have exaggerated forms that break all genre rules to the point where its concept almost takes the shape to the utmost degree of quirkiness, but still calmly rolls back to its non-italic interlocutor.

**Design:** 2021, Milos Mitrovic
→ p. 479

**Foundry:** Gradient Type, Norway, wearegradient.net → p. 489

**Language support:** Latin Extended

**OpenType features:** Tabular Lining, Discretionary Ligatures, Superscript, Subscript, Ordinals, Fractions, Numerator, Denominator, Arrows, Stylistic Alternates, Stylistic Sets, Slashed Zero, Case Sensitive Forms

**Test version available:** Yes

**Web font format available:** Yes

→ P. 466

abcdefghijklmnopqrstuvwxyzæåçéñöûß
ABCDEFGHIJKLMNOPQRSTUVWXYZÆÇØ
12345678900@.,!?')]§*“”»«/–½©€$£¥&↓

PolySans Mono is a typeface of four weights plus *Italics:* Slim Mono, *Slim Mono Italic,* Neutral Mono, *Neutral Mono Italic,* **Median Mono,** ***Median Mono Italic,*** **Bulky Mono,** ***and Bulky Mono Italic***

بيروت الغربية

مدغشقر

جاذبية الارض

العصب

مسلسلات طويلة

مدرسة قديمة

Portada Arabic

Designed for superlative performance in long-form reading on screens, in UI, and in apps, Portada Arabic is a modern font family and icon set that's clear and readable in restrictive digital environments and warm in print. Portada Arabic's text and display styles were engineered from the Naskh style for superlative performance to make great use of balanced letterforms, ample character height, clear interior negative space, and its subservient personality.

**Design:** 2021, Sahar Afshar → p. 472, Veronika Burian → p. 473, José Scaglione → p. 482

**Foundry:** TypeTogether, Czech Republic, type-together.com → p. 492

**Language support:** Latin, Arabic, Farsi

**OpenType features:** Proportional Oldstyle, Tabular Lining, Proportional Lining, Tabular Oldstyle, Standard Ligatures, All Caps, Small Caps, Capitals to Small Caps, Superscript, Subscript, Ordinals, Contextual Alternates, Fractions, Alternative Fractions, Numerator, Denominator, Ornaments, Arrows, Stylistic Alternates, Stylistic Sets, Historical Forms, Slashed Zero, Localized Forms, Case Sensitive Forms, Required Ligatures, Mark Positioning, Terminal Form, Initial Form, Isolated Form, Medial Form, Optical size, Font Variations

**Test version available:** Yes

**Web font format available:** Yes

abcdefghijklmnopqrstuvwxyzæﬀåçéñöûß
ABCDEFGHIJKLMNOPQRSTUVWXYZÆÇØẞ
1234567890@.,!?')]§*“”»«/–½©€$£¥&

ء اا أأ إإ آآ ٱٱ ب ببب ت تتت ث ثثث ج ججج ح ححح خ خخخ
د ـد ذ ـذ ر ـر ز ـز س سسس ش ششش ص صصص ض ضضض
ط ططط ظ ظظظ ع ععع غ غغغ ف ففف ق ققق
ك ككك ل للل م ممم ن ننن ه ههه ة ـة و ـو ؤ ـؤ ي ييي
ئ ئئئ ى ـى لا ـلا لأ ـلأ لإ ـلإ لآ ـلآ لٱ ـلٱ ٠١٢٣٤٥٦٧٨٩ .،؛؟

Portada Arabic is a family of two styles: Normal and **Icons.** Normal in six weights: Thin, Light, Regular, **Semi Bold, Bold, and Extra Bold**

→ P. 452, 457

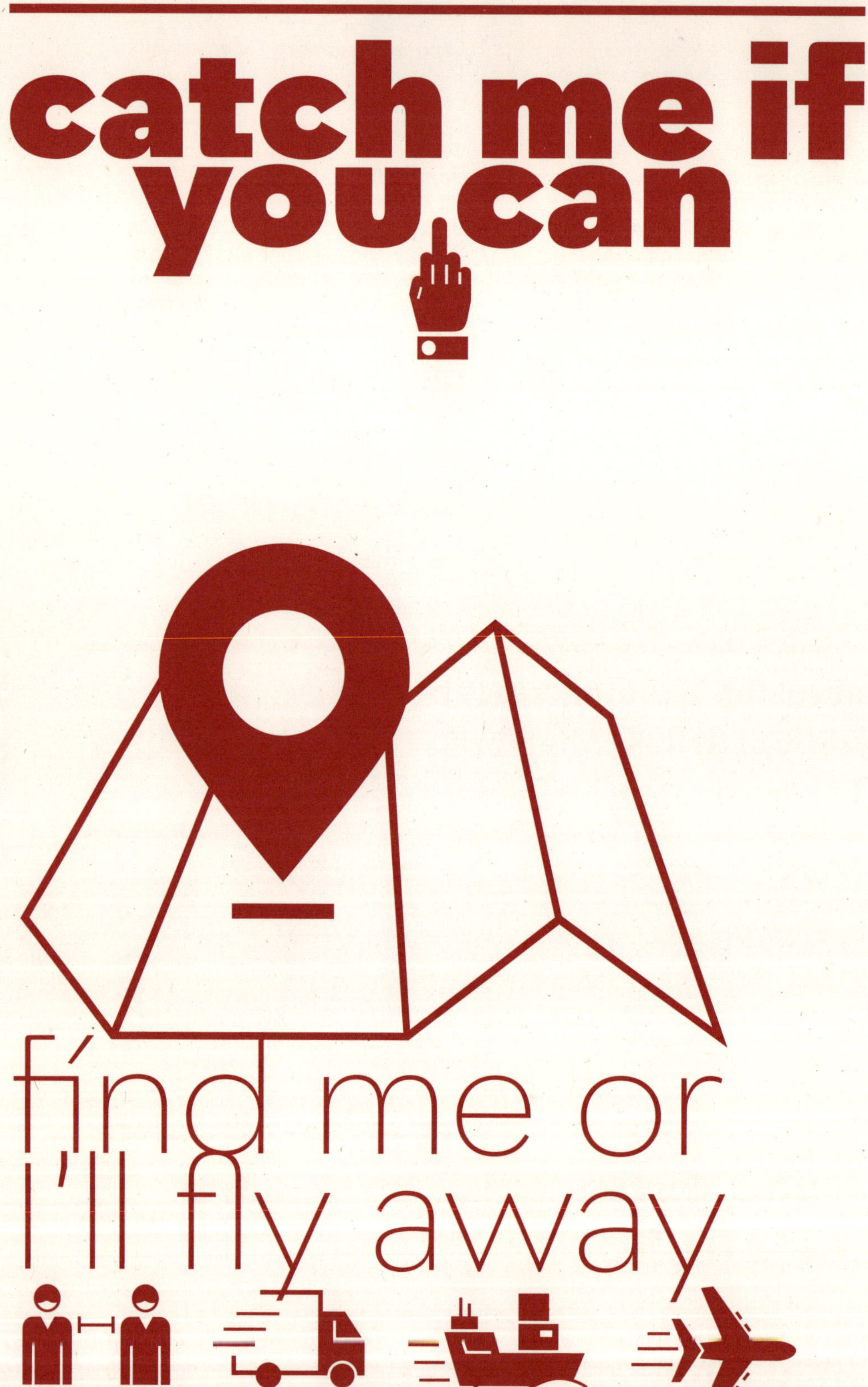


Postea

Beginning with midcentury virtues, Postea is the rational response for pixel or paper text—a lyrical take on geometric Sans Serifs. Classic curves and purposeful details make it ideal for branding, signage, corporate typefaces, and magazines.

**Design:** 2021, Veronika Burian → p. 473, José Scaglione → p. 481

**Foundry:** TypeTogether, Czech Republic, type-together.com → p. 492

**Language support:** Latin

**OpenType features:** Proportional Oldstyle, Tabular Lining, Proportional Lining, Tabular Oldstyle, Standard Ligatures, Discretionary Ligatures, All Caps, Small Caps, Superscript, Subscript, Ordinals, Contextual Alternates, Fractions, Alternative Fractions, Numerator, Denominator, Ornaments, Arrows, Stylistic Alternates, Stylistic Sets, Historical Forms, Slashed Zero, Localized Forms, Case Sensitive Forms, Font Variations

**Test version available:** Yes

**Web font format available:** Yes

→ P. 452

abcdefghijklmnopqrstuvwxyzæflåçéñöûß
ABCDEFGHIJKLMNOPQRSTUVWXYZÆÇØẞ
12345678900@.,!?')]§*""»«/-½©€$£¥&↙◉

Postea is a typeface of seven weights plus *Italics:* Hairline, *Hairline Italic,* Thin, *Thin Italic,* Light, *Light Italic,* Regular, *Italic,* **Semi Bold, *Semi Bold Italic,* Bold, *Bold Italic,* Extra Bold, *and Extra Bold Italic***

AGATHA CHRISTIE'S

# /EVIL UNDER THE SUN*

When Hercule Poirot arrived on Daphne's Glamorous Island Resort, he found Murder, Mystery, and Evil Under the Sun

**Povetarac Display**

The Povetarac Display font family is part of *Povetarac Superfamily.* Available in six weights and one variable font file, Povetarac Display relays on lively uppercase proportions that took inspiration from vintage typefaces. It is well balanced, elegant, and fully recognizable high contrasted sans serif family. Some of its characteristics are straight and wide terminals. With sharp overhang, Povetarac Display works pretty well in all situations—from editorial use to branding, websites, or just titles.

**Design:** 2022, Dušan Jelesijević
→ p. 477

**Foundry:** Tour de Force Font Foundry, Serbia, tourdefonts.com
→ p. 492

**Language support:** Latin Extended

**OpenType features:** Small Caps, Fractions, Stylistic Sets, Font Varaitions

**Test version available:** Yes

**Web font format available:** Yes

abcdefghijklmnopqrstuvwxyzæflåçéñöûß
ABCDEFGHIJKLMNOPQRSTUVWXYZÆÇØß
1234567890@.,!?')]§*""»«/–½©€$£¥&

Povetarac Display is a typeface of six weights: Regular, Medium, **Semi Bold, Bold, Heavy, and Black**



→ P. 452, 463

# #10 Things I *Hate* About You:

Pragmatic, as its name implies, is focused on function. Initiated for Michael Worthington (Counterspace Design), the typeface was further developed for the publication *Inside Out & Upside Down: Posters from CalArts 1970–2019*, published by Worthington. References were directed towards the goal of creating an optimal typeface that performs well from captions to large display settings.

**Design:** 2022, Greg Lindy → p. 478

**Foundry:** LuxTypo, United States of America, luxtypo.com → p. 490

**Language support:** Latin Extended

**OpenType features:** Tabular Lining, Proportional Lining, Discretionary Ligatures, All Caps, Superscript, Subscript, Ordinals, Titling Alternates, Fractions, Numerator, Denominator, Ornaments, Arrows, Stylistic Sets, Slashed Zero, Localized Forms

**Test version available:** Yes

**Web font format available:** Yes

abcdefghijklmnopqrstuvwxyzæfjåçéñöûß
ABCDEFGHIJKLMNOPQRSTUVWXYZÆÇØ
12345678900@.,!?')]§*“”»«/–½©€$£¥&↗★

Pragmatic is a typeface of six weights plus *Italics:* Thin, *Thin Italic,* Light, *Light Italic,* Regular, *Italic,* **Medium,** ***Medium Italic,*** **Bold,** ***Bold Italic,*** **Black,** ***and Black Italic***


→ P. 452

Yeah!

I will not sleep
through my education.

I will not sleep
through my education.

I will not sleep
through my education.

I will not sleep
through my education.

* Bravo!!!

Prima

Prima was commissioned by the Wiener Bildungsserver to be used as a new model for teaching reading and writing. Its two styles are closely related in order to aid learners to progress seamlessly from one set of letterforms to the other. Owing to the innovative use of joints between letters as a distinct set of shapes, the type efficiently provides flexible, and therefore ergonomic connections. This model offers a sound foundation for the acquisition of individual handwriting.

**Design:** 2022, Titus Nemeth → p. 480, Martin Tiefenthaler → p. 483

**Foundry:** Wiener Schriften, Austria, wienerschriften.at → p. 492

**Language support:** Latin Extended

**OpenType features:** Proportional Oldstyle, Tabular Lining, Proportional Lining, Discretionary Ligatures, Contextual Alternates, Localized Forms, Case Sensitive Forms

**Test version available:** Yes

**Web font format available:** Yes

abcdefghijklmnopqrstuvwxyzœåçéñöûß
ABCDEFGHIJKLMNOPQRSTUVWXYZÆÇØẞ
1234567890@.,!?')]§*“”»«/–€$£&§

Prima is a typeface of one Regular weight plus *Italics*



→ P. 468, 469

# Beltracchi

2014

## *THE ART OF FORGERY*

Proxima Sera

Proxima Sera is the Serif companion to *Proxima Nova.* It is a hybrid design, combining characteristics of old-style and modern serif typefaces into something new that is clean and highly readable. Its even color and large x-height make it a logical choice for text settings, but Proxima Sera still has enough warmth for display use—especially Thin and Black.

**Design:** 2022, Mark Simonson → p. 482

**Foundry:** Mark Simonson Studio, United States of America, marksimonson.com → p. 490

**Language support:** Latin Extended

**OpenType features:** Proportional Oldstyle, Tabular Lining, Proportional Lining, Tabular Oldstyle, Standard Ligatures, All Caps, Small Caps, Capitals to Small Caps, Superscript, Subscript, Ordinals, All Alternates, Fractions, Numerator, Denominator, Stylistic Alternates, Stylistic Sets, Slashed Zero, Localized Forms, Case Sensitive Forms, Mark Positioning

**Test version available:** Yes

**Web font format available:** Yes



abcdefghijklmnopqrstuvwxyzæfjåçéñöûß
ABCDEFGHIJKLMNOPQRSTUVWXYZÆÇØẞ
12345678900@.,!?')]§*“”»«/–½©€$£¥&↓★

→ P. 457

Proxima Sera is a typeface of nine weights plus *Italics:* Thin, *Thin Italic,* Extra Light, *Extra Light Italic,* Light, *Light Italic,* Regular, *Italic,* **Medium,** ***Medium Italic,*** **Semi Bold,** ***Semi Bold Italic,*** **Bold,** ***Bold Italic,*** **Extra Bold,** ***Extra Bold Italic,*** **Black,** ***and Black Italic***

You were the only thing in my life that was real.

{BLUE IS THE WARMEST COLOR}

Pure Energy was inspired by artwork found on memorabilia such as record covers, VHS tapes, and cassettes. It is expressively handwritten with marker rooted from 80s nostalgia. Due to the personal and signature feel in which it was crafted, Pure Energy allows for universal usage with a timeless essence that can be conveyed through both print and digital applications.

**Design:** 2022, Derek Campbell → p. 473, Justin Graefer → p. 476

**Foundry:** BLKBK Inc., Canada, blkbk.ink → p. 488

**Language support:** Latin Extended

**OpenType features:** Standard Ligatures, Swashes, All Alternates

**Test version available:** Yes

**Web font format available:** Yes

→ P. 468

abcdefghijklmnopqrstuvwxyzæfjåçéñöûß

ABCDEFGHIJKLMNOPQRSTUVWXYZÆÇØ

1234567890@.,!?')]§*""»«/-½©€$£¥&

*Pure Energy is a typeface of one Regular weight*

# TOY STORY 1, 2, & 3

→ 1995, 1999, 2010

@ ANDY & WOODY *

Q

The Q Project is a game-like type system that enables users to create a nearly infinite number of variations. Inspired by toys like Lego or Meccano, Q invites you to explore its vast creative space and discover not only new solutions but also new problems.

**Design:** 2020, Peter Biľak → p. 472

**Foundry:** Typotheque, The Netherlands, typotheque.com → p. 492

**Language support:** Latin Extended

**OpenType features:** Contextual Alternates, Font Variations

**Test version available:** Yes

**Web font format available:** Yes

ABCDEFGHIJKLMNOPQRSTUVWXYZÆFJÅÇÉÑÖÛß
1234567890@.,!?')]§*""»«/–©€$£¥&←

Q IS A FAMILY OF SIX BASE MODELS: BASE DOTS, BASE THIN, BASE STENCIL, BASE SQUARES, BASE NORMAL, **BASE HEAVY, AND 36 ATTACHEMENT MODELS:**

MECHANIC NORMAL, MECHANIC ZERO GRAVITY,

→ P. 464

# RO-
# ZPU-
# STE-
# NÝ

A VYPUS-
TENÝ
{1985}

Quartier

Quartier Solo is a seriffed geometric deco typeface influenced by art nouveau. The very first letters were inspired by the Purple Diary lettering and served as a style template for the rest of the alphabet. All curves and curvatures are simulated by polygonal edges and any of the letterforms have been aligned individually on a grid. The complete character set contains over eight hundred characters and serves almost all Latin languages.

**Design:** 2020, Martin Aleith
→ p. 472

**Foundry:** PFA Typefaces, Germany, pfa-typefaces.com → p. 491

**Language support:** Latin Extended

**OpenType features:** Proportional Oldstyle, Tabular Lining, Tabular Oldstyle, Standard Ligatures, Discretionary Ligatures, All Caps, Small Caps, Superscript, Subscript, Ordinals, Fractions, Numerator, Denominator, Stylistic Alternates, Stylistic Sets, Slashed Zero

**Test version available:** Yes

**Web font format available:** Yes

abcdefghijklmnopqrstuvwxyzæfjåçéñöûß
ABCDEFGHIJKLMNOPQRSTUVWXYZÆÇØß
1234567890Ø@.,!?')]*“”»«/–½©€$£¥&»→

Quartier is a typeface of two weights: Solo *and Solo Italic*



→ P. 464

**Cate Blanchett**
QUEEN ELIZABETH I.
*in* ***Elizabeth***
(1998)

**Dame Helen Mirren**
QUEEN ELIZABETH II.
*in* ***The Queen***
(2006)

**Helena Bonham Carter**
THE QUEEN MOTHER
*in* ***The King's Speech***
(2010)

Generous, confident, adaptive. Such is the realm of Queens and its many different faces. As the layout gets narrower, Queens commands the letters to follow. And they obey, for they are flexible and ready to serve. Not relying on a particular historical reference point, Queens' lineage can be traced back to the *Bodonis* and *Didots*—inheriting some of the classical elegance but renouncing the rigid mannerist construction in favor of playfulness.

**Design:** 2019, Sebastian Losch → p. 479

**Foundry:** Kilotype, Germany, kilotype.de → p. 489

**Language support:** Latin Extended

**OpenType features:** Proportional Oldstyle, Tabular Lining, Proportional Lining, Tabular Oldstyle, Standard Ligatures, All Caps, Small Caps, Capitals to Small Caps, Superscript, Subscript, Ordinals, Swashes, All Alternates, Contextual Alternates, Fractions, Numerator, Denominator, Arrows, Stylistic Sets, Localized Forms, Case Sensitive Forms, Mark Positioning, Font Variations

**Test version available:** Yes

**Web font format available:** Yes

abcdefghijklmnopqrstuvwxyzæfiåçéñöûß
ABCDEFGHIJKLMNOPQRSTUVWXYZÆÇØß
1234567890@.,!?')]§*“”»«/–½©€$£¥&

→ P. 457, 464

Queens is a family of three widths: Compressed, Condensed, and Normal, each in seven weights plus *Italics:* Compressed Air, *Compressed Air Italic,* Compressed Thin, *Compressed Thin Italic,* Compressed Light, *Condensed Light Italic,* Condensed Regular, Condensed Italic, Condensed Medium, *Medium Italic,* **Bold,** ***Bold Italic,*** **Extra Bold,** ***and Extra Bold Italic***

# BULLY'S MASTERPIECE

# 20 Nº1 01

# Der Schuh des MANITU

Quirkwood

Robby Woodard revisits the classic Egyptienne / Italienne / French Clarendon aesthetic and makes it his very own with two extra spoons of fun and a generous dollop of cheer. By reconfiguring a classic archetype's DNA and introducing new quirks to it, Robby presents a uniquely sunny and wholesome character with this typeface. The common reverse-stress-slab treatment goes a long way for sure, but there are also plenty of unusual elements working hard in the background.

**Design:** 2021, Robby Woodard
→ p. 484

**Foundry:** Canada Type, Canada, canadatype.com → p. 488

**Language support:** Latin Extended

**OpenType features:** Standard Ligatures, Discretionary Ligatures, Small Caps, Capitals to Small Caps, Ordinals, All Alternates, Contextual Alternates, Stylistic Alternates, Stylistic Sets, Localized Forms

**Test version available:** No

**Web font format available:** Yes

abcdefghijklmnopqrstuvwxyzæfjåçéñöû
ABCDEFGHIJKLMNOPQRSTUVWXYZÆÇØ
1234567890@.,!?')]§*"""»«/-©€$£¥&

Quirkwood is a family of three styles: Normal, Text, AND CHUNKY. Normal in four weights: Regular, Bright, Highlight, and Shadow. Text in five weights: Regular, Bright, Medium, Bold Bright, and Bold. CHUNKY IN FOUR WEIGHTS: REGULAR, BRIGHT, BOLD BRIGHT, AND BOLD



→ P. 458, 464

انظر إلى ما
وراء
ما تراه

Quiverleaf Arabic CF

Quiverleaf Arabic CF brings the flowing movement and subtlety of the original *Quiverleaf CF* to the Arabic script—a perfect pairing. Designed for visual unity across both Latin and Arabic scripts.

**Design:** 2022, Connary Fagen → p. 475

**Foundry:** Connary Fagen, Inc., United States of America, connary.com → p. 488

**Language support:** Latin, Arabic

**OpenType features:** Fractions, Stylistic Alternates, Initial Form, Isolated Form, Medial Form

**Test version available:** Yes

**Web font format available:** Yes

→ P. 468, 452

ء ا ـا أ ـأ إ ـإ آ ـآ ٱ ـٱ ب ببب ت تتت ث ثثث ج ججج ح ححح خ خخخ
د ـد ذ ـذ ر ـر ز ـز س سسس ش ششش ص صصص ض ضضض
ط ططط ظ ظظظ ع ععع غ غغغ ف ففف ق ققق
ك ككك ل للل م ممم ن ننن ه ههه ة ـة و ـو ؤ ـؤ ي ييي
ئ ئئئ ى ـى لا ـلا لأ ـلأ لإ ـلإ لآ ـلآ لٱ ـلٱ ٠١٢٣٤٥٦٧٨٩ ـ،؛؟

كويفرليف عربية CF هو عائلة الخط في خمسة
أنماط: خفيف, عادٍ, شبه جريئة, جريئة,
جريئة جدا

THE
LION
KING

Quiverleaf CF

Designed with the graceful movement of a ribbon in mind, Quiverleaf CF moves smoothly from letter to letter. A simple construction masks a longing and aching imbued into the typeface.

**Design:** 2022, Connary Fagen → p. 475

**Foundry:** Connary Fagen, Inc., United States of America, connary.com → p. 488

**Language support:** Latin Extended

**OpenType features:** Discretionary Ligatures, Fractions, Numerator, Denominator, Stylistic Alternates

**Test version available:** Yes

**Web font format available:** Yes

abcdefghijklmnopqrstuvwxyzæijåçéñöûß
ABCDEFGHIJKLMNOPQRSTUVWXYZÆÇØẞ
1234567890@.,!?')]§*“”»«/–½©€$£¥&

Quiverleaf CF is a typeface of five weights plus *Italics:* Light, *Light Italic*, Regular, *Italic*, Semi Bold, *Semi Bold Italic*, Bold, *Bold Italic*, Extra Bold, *and Extra Bold Italic*

→ P. 452, 464

# JOHN WAYNE

The Man who shot Liberty Valance

1962

Ranchstyle

# Ranchstyle

Based on the designer's interest and research into the visual language of livestock branding in Nevada from the 19th century, Ranchstyle takes the vernacular of cattle ranchers brands of the old west, digitizes it, and brings it into the contemporary world as a vivacious spunky typeface. The letterforms mimic bent metal and have the fluidity that follows such a material.

**Design:** 2021, Monica Maccaux → p. 479, Rod Cavazos → p. 473

**Foundry:** PSY/OPS, United States of America, psyops.com → p. 491

**Language support:** Latin Extended

**OpenType features:** Contextual Alternates, Ornaments, Arrows, Stylistic Sets

**Test version available:** No

**Web font format available:** No

→ P. 464, 469

abcdefghijklmnopqrstuvwxyzæåçéñöûß
ABCDEFGHIJKLMNOPQRSTUVWXYZÆÇØ
12345678900@.,!?')]§*“”»«/-©€$£¥&→

Ranchstyle is a typeface of two styles: Normal and

Morton DaCosta

# "The Music Man"

Music by

Meredith Willson & Ray Heindorf

Ravals

With a funky approach, Ravals is a script typeface intended for display purposes. Initially inspired by brush lettering models from the fifties and sixties, it's a perfect fit for music from that era. The spontaneous design of Ravals is mainly a homage to the vitality and rhythm of one of the most important neighborhoods in Barcelona. All characters have been carefully designed to connect fluidly, even in some specific combinations with alternative constructions.

**Design:** 2020, Ricard Garcia
→ p. 475

**Foundry:** Typerepublic, Spain, typerepublic.com → p. 492

**Language support:** Latin Extended

**OpenType features:** Proportional Lining, Standard Ligatures, Discretionary Ligatures, Ordinals, Swashes, Contextual Swashes, All Alternates, Contextual Alternates, Contextual Ligatures, Historical Forms, Localized Forms, Case Sensitive Forms

**Test version available:** Yes

**Web font format available:** Yes

→ P. 464, 468

abcdefghijklmnopqrstuvwxyzæĳåçéñöûß
ABCDEFGHIJKLMNOPQRSTUVWXYZÆÇØß
1234567890@.,!?')]§*“”»«/-©€$£¥&↑

Ravals is a typeface of one
Regular weight

just keep swimming

{Finding Nemo}

[В поисках Немо]

Rebrand

Rebrand is all about geometry—a typography that boosts confidence. However, contrary to pure, cold mathematics, this font seeks a more jovial and friendly face. The goal with Rebrand is to offer a geometric sans serif font that can work in various instances, from symbols and titles, to text and everything in between. It also creates a whole lot of personality, ideal for branding.

**Design:** 2021, Latinotype Team → p. 490

**Foundry:** Latinotype, Chile, latinotype.com → p. 490

**Language support:** Latin Extended, Cyrillic

**OpenType features:** Tabular Lining, Standard Ligatures, Small Caps, Capitals to Small Caps, Superscript, Ordinals, Fractions, Stylistic Alternates, Stylistic Sets, Localized Forms

**Test version available:** No

**Web font format available:** Yes

→ P. 452, 464

abcdefghijklmnopqrstuvwxyzæfiåçéñöûß
ABCDEFGHIJKLMNOPQRSTUVWXYZÆÇØ
1234567890@.,!?')]§*“”»«/–½©€$£¥&→

абвгдеёжзийклмнопрстуфхцчшщъыьэюя
АБВГДЕЁЖЗИЙКЛМНОПРСТУФХЦЧШЩЪЫЬ
1234567890@.,!?')]§*“”»«/–½©€$£¥&↕

Rebrand is a family of three styles: Text, Display, and . Text in in seven weights plus *Italics:* Extra Light, *Extra Light Italic,* Light, *Light Italic,* Regular, *Italic,* Medium, *Medium Italic,* **Semi Bold,** ***Semi Bold Italic,*** **Bold,** ***Bold Italic,*** **Black, and *Black Italic.*** Display in nine weights plus *Italics:* Thin, *Thin Italic,* Extra Light, *Extra Light Italic,* Light, *Light Italic,* Regular, *Italic,* Medium, *Medium Italic,* **Semi Bold,** ***Semi Bold Italic,*** **Bold,** ***Bold Italic,*** **Extra Bold,** ***Extra Bold Italic,*** **Heavy, *and Heavy Italic***

BRAD PITT — ANTHONY HOPKINS

# RENDEZ VOUS mit [MEET] JOE BLACK

*[Sooner or Later Everyone Does]*

Resonay

Resonay is a vivacious layer font that takes classical lettering somewhere new. Combining elegant details from stone carving with the flow of calligraphy, a sharp attitude with exuberant bézier curves, Resonay is suitable for logotypes and refined display setting. Enriched with swashes, titling alternates, and a broad range of decorative ligatures, Resonay brings expression and poetry to headlines.

**Design:** 2022, Andrej Dieneš
→ p. 474

**Foundry:** TypeMates, Germany, typemates.com → p. 492

**Language support:** Latin Extended

**OpenType features:** Proportional Oldstyle, Tabular Lining, Proportional Lining, Tabular Oldstyle, Standard Ligatures, Discretionary Ligatures, Historical Ligatures, All Caps, Small Caps, Capitals to Small Caps, Superscript, Subscript, Ordinals, Titling Alternates, Swashes, Contextual Swashes, Contextual Alternates, Contextual Ligatures, Fractions, Numerator, Denominator, Ornaments, Arrows, Stylistic Alternates, Stylistic Sets, Slashed Zero, Localized Forms, Case Sensitive Forms

**Test version available:** Yes

**Web font format available:** Yes

abcdefghijklmnopqrstuvwxyzæfjåçéñöûß
ABCDEFGHIJKLMNOPQRSTUVWXYZÆÇØẞ
1234567890ø@.,!?')]§*“”»«/–½©€$£¥&↕×

Resonay is a family of three styles: Cover, Base, and Solid, each in five weights plus *Italics:* Cover Thin, *Cover Thin Italic,* Cover Light, *Cover Light Italic,* Cover Regular, *Cover Italic,* Cover Medium, *Cover Medium Italic,* Cover Bold, *Cover Bold Italic,* Base Thin, *Base Thin Italic,* Base Light, *Base Light Italic,* Base Regular, *Base Italic,* **Base Medium,** ***Base Medium Italic,*** **Base Bold,** ***Base Bold Italic,*** Solid Thin, *Solid Thin Italic,* Solid Light, *Solid Light Italic,* Solid Regular, *Solid Italic,* **Solid Medium,** ***Solid Medium Italic,*** **Solid Bold,** ***and Solid Bold Italic***

→ P. 457, 464

SEDUCTIVE

RED

SPARROW

DECEPTIVE

{2018}

»Я знаю твои секреты!«

DEADLY

Right Sans

Right Sans is just a tiny bit fancier than your favorite Serif fonts, except it keeps it sans. This huge variable family comes at you in a variety of weights, widths, and italic angles, in both classic and variable formats. It is a high-contrast sibling of previously released Right Grotesk and Right Gothic. The three of them give you over 300 fonts perfect for pairing in big and small sizes.

**Design:** 2022, Alexander Slobzheninov → p. 482

**Foundry:** Pangram Pangram, Canada, pangrampangram.com → p. 491

**Language support:** Latin Extended, Cyrillic

**OpenType features:** Tabular Lining, Proportional Lining, Discretionary Ligatures, Contextual Alternates, Fractions, Numerator, Denominator, Arrows, Stylistic Alternates, Stylistic Sets, Slashed Zero, Case Sensitive Forms

**Test version available:** Yes

**Web font format available:** Yes

→ P. 452, 464

abcdefghijklmnopqrstuvwxyzæftåçéñöûß
ABCDEFGHIJKLMNOPQRSTUVWXYZÆÇØß
12345678900@.,!?')]§*“”»«/–½©€$£¥&⇔

абвгдеёжзийклмнопрстуфхцчшщъыьэюя
АБВГДЕЁЖЗИЙКЛМНОПРСТУФХЦЧШЩЪЫЬЭЮЯ
12345678900@.,!?')]§*“”»«/–½©€$£¥&↖

Right Sans is a family of seven widths: Tall, Tight, Narrow, Compact, Normal, Wide, and Spatial, each in seven weights plus *Italics:* Tall Fine, *Tall Fine Italic,* Tight Light, *Tight Light Italic,* Narrow Regular, *Narrow Regular Italic,* Compact Medium, *Compact Medium Italic,* **Bold,** ***Bold Italic,*** **Wide Dark,** ***Wide Dark Italic,*** **Spatial Black,** ***and Spatial Black Italic***

# who gets to call it Art ☛ ?

The New York
art scene
of the 60's
@nd the man
who made it
(2006) ☮
POP!

Rike Mono

Rike Mono was drawn to be used in a publication about artists in the German Democratic Republic. The design is based on a few letters which were typed on the back of photographs from the 1970s. This low-contrast monospace typeface doesn't deny its roots and its relationship to the *Bullit* typeface of the Italian typewriter manufacturer Olivetti, but has developed its own personality: Rike Mono offers bold and classical typewriter letters in a contemporary typeface design.

**Design:** 2021, Felix Link → p. 478

**Foundry:** Gregorij, Germany, gregorij.com → p. 489

**Language support:** Latin

**OpenType features:** Tabular Lining, Tabular Oldstyle, Arrows, Stylistic Alternates, Stylistic Sets, Slashed Zero

**Test version available:** Yes

**Web font format available:** Yes

→ P. 466

abcdefghijklmnopqrstuvwxyzfjåçéñöûß
ABCDEFGHIJKLMNOPQRSTUVWXYZÇ
1234567890Ø@.,!?')]§*“”»«/-©€$£¥&

Rike Mono is a typeface of one Regular weight

Roadhouse

The
ASSASSINATION
OF JESSE JAMES
BY THE COWARD
ROBERT FORD

Roadhouse is a layering typeface family that is part of the greater *Evanston* type collection, which is inspired by American typefaces commonly used at the turn of the century leading up to Prohibition. Roadhouse reflects the style of lettering used on tavern signage and printed ephemera during the early 20th century.

**Design:** 2020, Kimmy Kirkwood
→ p. 477

**Foundry:** Kimmy Design, United States of America, kimmydesign.com → p. 489

**Language support:** Latin Extended

**OpenType features:** Standard Ligatures, All Caps

**Test version available:** Yes

**Web font format available:** Yes

ABCDEFGHIJKLMNOPQRSTUVWXYZÆFJÅÇÉÑÖÛß
1234567890@.,!?')]*""/-©€$£¥&

ROADHOUSE IS A FAMILY OF TWELVE STYLES: OUTLINE, EXTRUDE, STRIPES, LIGHT, HALF FILL, INLINE, *Script*, MEDIUM, DROP, BASE, AND BOLD. OUTLINE IN TWO WEIGHTS: LIGHT AND BOLD. EXTRUDE IN FIVE WEIGHTS: A, B, C, FULL, AND SHADOW. STRIPES IN TWO WEIGHTS: REGULAR AND OUTLINE. INLINE IN A REGULAR WEIGHT. *Script in two weights: Upright and Oblique.* LIGHT, MEDIUM, AND BOLD IN THREE WEIGHTS: LIGHT No1, LIGHT No2, LIGHT No3, MEDIUM No1, MEDIUM No2, MEDIUM No3, BOLD No1, BOLD No2, BOLD No3. HALF FILL IN THREE WEIGHTS: REGULAR, OUTLINE, AND STRIPES. DROP IN FOUR WEIGHTS: EXTRUDE, EXTRUDE 2, LINE, AND LINE 2. BASE IN 13 WEIGHTS: REGULAR, HIGHLIGHT, 1A, 1B, 2A, 2B, 2C, 2D, HIGHLIGHT, LINE ALT, LINE BD, LINE FILL, AND LINE LT





→ P. 464

# INTO THE WILD 2007

Rockhopper

Two typefaces in one. Firstly, Rockhopper is a rounded Sans with a softness designed to function well on the high resolution screens used today. Its extended character set handles all manner of text with ease whether this is on-screen or off. Secondly, Rockhopper explores the potential of cumulative swashes—from single to overkill. A single swash can be used to enhance a word, or many swashes added to visually push the bounds of legibility and expression.

**Design:** 2022, Jeremy Tankard → p. 483

**Foundry:** Jeremy Tankard Typography, United Kingdom, typography.net → p. 489

**Language support:** Latin Extended

**OpenType features:** Proportional Oldstyle, Tabular Lining, Proportional Lining, Tabular Oldstyle, All Caps, Small Caps, Capitals to Small Caps, Superscript, Subscript, Ordinals, Swashes, All Alternates, Fractions, Alternative Fractions, Numerator, Denominator, Stylistic Alternates, Stylistic Sets, Case Sensitive Forms

**Test version available:** Yes

**Web font format available:** Yes

→ P. 453, 464

abcdefghijklmnopqrstuvwxyzæflåçéñöûß
ABCDEFGHIJKLMNOPQRSTUVWXYZÆÇØẞ
1234567890@.,!?')]§*“”»«/–½©€$£¥&

Rockhopper is a typeface of seven weights plus *Italics:* Extra Light, *Extra Light Italic,* Light, *Light Italic,* Regular, *Italic,* **Medium,** ***Medium Italic,*** **Bold,** ***Bold Italic,*** **Extra Bold,** ***Extra Bold Italic,*** **Black,** ***and Black Italic***

# *THE ODYSSEY*

# TROY

# MCMXCVII

Romis

Romis is a roman capital typeface, renaissance style. Individually shaped serifs and the absence of any geometrically straight lines signify this humanist interpretation of the *Capitalis Monumentalis*. It is characterized by exceptional quality of shape and utmost attention to detail. Curved shafts and delicate transitions bring Romis to life. Its unique details give this typeface a humanity seldom found in the age of digital type. Perfect for authentic exhibition design or your next movie poster

**Design:** 2019, Prof. Hans R. Heitmann → p. 476, Johannes Ammon → p. 472

**Foundry:** Finaltype, Germany, finaltype.de → p. 489

**Language support:** Latin Extended

**OpenType features:** Proportional Oldstyle, Tabular Lining, Proportional Lining, Tabular Oldstyle, Standard Ligatures, Discretionary Ligatures, Small Caps, Capitals to Small Caps, Superscript, Ordinals, All Alternates, Contextual Alternates, Fractions, Stylistic Alternates, Stylistic Sets, Localized Forms, Case Sensitive Forms

**Test version available:** Yes

**Web font format available:** Yes

→ P. 457

ABCDEFGHIJKLMNOPQRSTUVWXYZÆFTÅÇÉÑÖÛß
ABCDEFGHIJKLMNOPQRSTUVWXYZÆÇØß
12345678900@.,!?')]§*“”»«/-½©€$£¥&→

ROMIS IS A TYPEFACE OF SIX WEIGHTS PLUS *ITALICS:* ULTRA LIGHT, *ULTRA LIGHT ITALIC,* LIGHT, *LIGHT ITALIC,* REGULAR, *ITALIC,* MEDIUM, *MEDIUM ITALIC,* SEMI BOLD, *SEMI BOLD ITALIC,* BOLD, *AND BOLD ITALIC*

“ ”

# Might a gent steal *a* KIẞ?”

POSSESSED ft. *Clarke Gable*

Ronaldson Pro

Ronaldson Pro is Patrick Griffin's take on *Ronaldson Old Style,* the Alexander Kay design widely viewed as the New World's first original text face, published in 1884 by the MacKellar, Smiths and Jordan Company in Philadelphia. The metal face enjoyed tremendous popularity for more than five decades leading up to the Second World War.

**Design:** 2021, Patrick Griffin → p. 476

**Foundry:** Canada Type, Canada, canadatype.com → p. 488

**Language support:** Latin Extended

**OpenType features:** Proportional Oldstyle, Tabular Lining, Proportional Lining, Standard Ligatures, Discretionary Ligatures, Historical Ligatures, Small Caps, Capitals to Small Caps, Superscript, Subscript, Ordinals, All Alternates, Fractions, Numerator, Denominator, Stylistic Alternates, Stylistic Sets, Historical Forms, Localized Forms, Case Sensitive Forms, Font Variations

**Test version available:** No

**Web font format available:** Yes

→ P. 457

abcdefghijklmnopqrstuvwxyzæſjåçéñöûß
ABCDEFGHIJKLMNOPQRSTUVWXYZÆÇØß
1234567890@.,!?')]§*"”»«/–½©€$£¥&

Ronaldson Pro is a typeface of four weights plus *Italics:* Regular, *Italic,* Medium, *Medium Italic,* **Semi Bold,** ***Semi Bold Italic,*** **Bold,** ***and Bold Italic***

»
æeev.v
eryyø
onnne
!!?!!«
— Stan-
field

Saes Grotesk

Saes Grotesk is inspired by the first sans serif typefaces from the 19th century. In America, these sorts of fonts were called Gothics, in Britain Grotesques, and Grotesks in Germany. Despite these different labels, they pointed out two things: the lack of refinement and the change of type paradigm. In general, the main idea of this project was to combine the beautiful imperfections of the first Sans Serifs with the trend and standards of this new and weird century.

**Design:** 2021, Diego Aravena → p. 472

**Foundry:** W Type Foundry, Chile, wtypefoundry.com → p. 492

**Language support:** Latin

**OpenType features:** Tabular Lining, Proportional Lining, Tabular Oldstyle, Standard Ligatures, Superscript, Subscript, Ordinals, Fractions, Numerator, Denominator, Arrows, Stylistic Alternates, Slashed Zero, Case Sensitive Forms, Required Ligatures, Font Variations

**Test version available:** Yes

**Web font format available:** Yes

→ P. 453

abcdefghijklmnopqrstuvwxyzæfiåçéñöûß
ABCDEFGHIJKLMNOPQRSTUVWXYZÆÇØ
1234567890O@.,!?')]§*“”»«/–½©€$£¥&→

Saes Grotesk is a typeface of nine weights plus *Italics:* Thin, *Thin Italic,* Ultra Light, *Ultra Light Italic,* Light, *Light Italic,* Book, *Book Italic,* Regular, *Italic,* **Bold,** ***Bold Italic,*** **Extra Bold,** ***Extra Bold Italic,*** **Black,** ***Black Italic,*** **Heavy,** ***and Heavy Italic***

# HE'S DYING TO BECOME A CHEF!!

# RATATOUILLE

(rat·a·too·ee)

à PARIS

Salad

Salad provides extreme versatility through its range of five weights, its extended character set, and its set of OpenType features. While the roman family with its italic counterpart provides a good workhorse tool for informal branding, packaging, and editorial projects, the interlocking, and the inline weights add additional possibilities for display purposes. This is enriched by the inclusion of a set of hand-drawn decorative dingbats in the typeface that further complement the sign painting vibe of the family.

**Design:** 2021, Francesco Canovaro → p. 473

**Foundry:** Zetafonts Foundry, Italy, zetafonts.com → p. 492

**Language support:** Latin Extended, Cyrillic

**OpenType features:** Proportional Oldstyle, Tabular Lining, Proportional Lining, Tabular Oldstyle, Standard Ligatures, Discretionary, Ligatures, Small Caps, Superscript, Subscript, Ordinals, Fractions, Numerator, Denominator, Ornaments, Stylistic Sets, Slashed Zero, Alternate Annotation, Case Sensitive Forms

**Test version available:** Yes

**Web font format available:** Yes

→ P. 453, 464

abcdefghijklmnopqrstuvwxyzæflåçéñöûß
ABCDEFGHIJKLMNOPQRSTUVWXYZÆÇØß
1234567890O@.,!?')]§*""»«/–½©€$£¥&

абвгдеёжзийклмнопрстуфхцчшщъыьэюя
АБВГДЕЁЖЗИЙКЛМНОПРСТУФХЦЧШЩЪЫЬЭЮЯ
12345678900@.,!?')]§*""»«/–½©€$£¥&

Salad is a family of two styles: Normal and Interlock. Normal in six weights plus *Italics:* Extra Light, *Extra Light Italic,* Light, *Light Italic,* Regular, *Italic,* **Bold,** ***Bold Italic,*** **Extra Bold,** ***Extra Bold Italic,*** **and Inline.** Interlock in five weights: Extra Light, Light, Regular, **Bold,** **and Extra Bold**

Hum
phrey de
Forest
Bogart

—

December 25th,
1899 – January
14th, 1957

Salter

Salter is an exploration of 20th century book jacket calligraphy by Lucas Sharp. The typeface is inspired by various designs attributed to Oscar Ogg and George Salter, two masters of this period. While Salter Roman draws its construction methodology from the work of Ogg, Salter's lowercase italic construction is based on a piece of lettering penned by Salter in 1941. The contrast of blunt, chiseled edges and smooth, inky terminals echo dynamic moments in history that Salter inhabited.

**Design:** 2021, Lucas Sharp → p. 482, My-Lan Thuong → p. 483

**Foundry:** Sharp Type, United States of America, sharptype.co → p. 491

**Language support:** Latin Extended

**OpenType features:** Proportional Oldstyle, Tabular Lining, Proportional Lining, Tabular Oldstyle, Standard Ligatures, All Caps, Superscript, Subscript, Contextual Alternates, Contextual Ligatures, Fractions, Numerator, Denominator, Localized Forms, Case Sensitive Forms

**Test version available:** Yes

**Web font format available:** Yes

abcdefghijklmnopqrstuvwxyzæfjåçéñöûß
ABCDEFGHIJKLMNOPQRSTUVWXYZÆÇØẞ
1234567890@.,!?')]§*""»«/-½©€$£¥&♥

Salter is a typeface of one Regular weight plus *Italics*



→ P. 457, 464

humanity&technology

*humanity&technology*

humanity&technology

*humanity&technology*

humanity&technology

*humanity&technology*

humanity&technology

*humanity&technology*

humanity&technology

*humanity&technology*

**humanity&technology**

***humanity&technology***

**humanity&technology**

***humanity&technology***

**humanity&technology**

***humanity&technology***

**Salva**

Idealized for a briefing aiming at a mixture between "humanity" and "technology," we filtered the best characteristics and removed the impurities–less "technology," and more room for "humanity." Thus, we have the contrast modulation increasing when the curves meet the stems, or the slanted bar of the letter *e*, inherited from calligraphy and the human hand. We brought a subtle charm to the number eight, and designed an inventive letter *g* that doesn't conform to the standard.

**Design:** 2021, Eduilson Coan
→ p. 474

**Foundry:** Fabio Haag Type, Brazil, fabiohaagtype.com/en → p. 488

**Language support:** Latin

**OpenType features:** Tabular Lining, Proportional Lining, Standard Ligatures, All Caps, Superscript, Subscript, All Alternates, Fractions, Numerator, Denominator, Stylistic Sets, Localized Forms, Font Variations

**Test version available:** Yes

**Web font format available:** Yes

→ P. 453

abcdefghijklmnopqrstuvwxyzæffåçéñöûß
ABCDEFGHIJKLMNOPQRSTUVWXYZÆÇØẞ
1234567890@.,!?')]§*""»«/–½©€$£¥&

Salva is a typeface of nine weights plus *Italics:* Thin, *Thin Italic,* Extra Light, *Extra Light Italic,* Light, *Light Italic,* Regular, *Italic,* Medium, *Medium Italic,* **Semi Bold,** ***Semi Bold Italic,*** **Bold,** ***Bold Italic,*** **Extra Bold,** ***Extra Bold Italic,*** **Black,** ***and Black Italic***

# THE GREAT GATSBY

FRANCIS SCOTT FITZGERALD

Scootchy

Scootchy is a high contrast, narrow typeface destined for use in both large and small point sizes. Blending an industrial and humanist approach, this typeface includes four weights ranging from a slender, regular style to a dark and contrasted black weight. With an Extended Latin character set and a wide range of OpenType features, Scootchy aims to provide a versatile solution that can be applied to a wide range of layouts.

**Design:** 2021, Michael Parson
→ p. 481

**Foundry:** Typogama, Switzerland, typogama.com → p. 492

**Language support:** Latin Extended

**OpenType features:** Proportional Oldstyle, Tabular Lining, Proportional Lining, Standard Ligatures, Discretionary Ligatures, Superscript, Subscript, Ordinals, Fractions, Ornaments, Arrows, Font Variations

**Test version available:** No

**Web font format available:** Yes

abcdefghijklmnopqrstuvwxyzæfjåçéñöûß
ABCDEFGHIJKLMNOPQRSTUVWXYZÆÇØ
1234567890@.,!?')]§*“”»«/–½©€$£¥&→

Scootchy is a typeface of four weights plus *Italics:* Regular, *Italic,* Medium, ***Medium Italic,*** **Bold, *Bold Italic,* Black, *and Black Italic***

→ P. 453, 464

The Devil Wears Prada

{2006}

After many years of seeing their fonts take starring roles in leading fashion magazines including *Vogue, ELLE,* and *GQ,* the designers of Moshik Nadav Typography came up with a new and exciting recipe. They call it Segol Typeface—a beautiful and innovative way to take fashion typography to the next level. Segol Typeface is a leap forward. It's an exponential evolution in typeface design packed with all the innovative features Moshik Nadav Typography is known for.

**Design:** 2020, Moshik Nadav → p. 480

**Foundry:** Moshik Nadav Typography, United States of America, moshik.net → p. 490

**Language support:** Latin Extended

**OpenType features:** Standard Ligatures, Swashes, Contextual Swashes, All Alternates, Contextual Alternates, Contextual Ligatures, Custom Ready-Made Words, Custom Alternate Ligatures, Custom Alternate Number Ligatures, Alternate Numbers, Year Ligatures, Custom Ready-Made Names, Custom Ready-Made Words

**Test version available:** No

**Web font format available:** Yes

→ P. 465

abcdefghijklmnopqrstuvwxyzæﬁåçéñöûß
ABCDEFGHIJKLMNOPQRSTUVWXYZÆÇØ
1234567890@.,!?')]§*“”»«/–½©€$£¥&

Segol Typeface is a family of two styles: Calligraphic and Dreamline

*1974{✻}«
April
28th

# Pené
# lope
# Cruz
# *Sánchez*

Seiva

Transformation in its essence. From Seiva's modern roots only the high contrast of *Bodoni* or *Didot* remains as it grew up defying tradition. As the letters grow, the expressiveness blossoms with delicate lines, contrasting with voluminous organic forms. Seiva adapts using variable font technology: the exuberance of large letters is pruned as the size decreases, in favor of legibility. Delicate details gain the vitality needed to work at text sizes. Italics grew vivid with stylistic alternates.

**Design:** 2021, Ana Laydner
→ p. 478

**Foundry:** Fabio Haag Type, Brazil, fabiohaagtype.com/en → p. 488

**Language support:** Latin

**OpenType features:** Proportional Oldstyle, Tabular Lining, Proportional Lining, All Caps, Superscript, Subscript, Ordinals, Swashes, All Alternates, Fractions, Numerator, Denominator, Stylistic Alternates, Stylistic Sets, Localized Forms

**Test version available:** Yes

**Web font format available:** Yes

abcdefghijklmnopqrstuvwxyzæftåçéñöûß
ABCDEFGHIJKLMNOPQRSTUVWXYZÆÇØß
1234567890@.,!?')]§*""»«/–½©€$£¥&

Seiva is a family of three styles: Normal, Display, and Poster, each in six weights plus *Italics:* Thin, *Thin Italic,* Light, *Light Italic,* Regular, *Italic,* **Medium, *Medium Italic,*** **Bold, *Bold Italic,*** **Extra Bold, *Extra Bold Italic,*** Display Thin, *Display Thin Italic,* Display Light, *Display Light Italic,* Display Regular, *Display Italic,* **Display Medium, *Display Medium Italic,*** **Display Bold, *Display Bold Italic,*** **Display Extra Bold, *Display Extra Bold Italic,*** Poster Thin, *Poster Thin Italic,* Poster Light, *Poster Light Italic,* Poster Regular, *Poster Italic,* **Poster Medium, *Poster Medium Italic,*** **Poster Bold, *Poster Bold Italic,*** **Poster Extra Bold, *and Poster Extra Bold Italic***


→ P. 453, 465

SPEED

СКОРОСТЬ

get ready

FOR {RUSH}

HØUR®

Seriguela

Seriguela is an ultra condensed sans serif typeface with a unique personality. A very distinctive recipe to design its alphabet was followed, starting with a grotesque base and applying movement in a very original way. The unconventional relationship between thick and thin lines in Seriguela, as it does not strictly follow any historical model of contrast construction, makes it noticeable. The blacker and more contrasted, the tastier. Its high contrast is not present in every single character and is often in the “wrong” places.

**Design:** 2022, Sofia Mohr → p. 479

**Foundry:** Latinotype, Chile, latinotype.com → p. 490

**Language support:** Latin Extended, Cyrillic

**OpenType features:** Standard Ligatures, Superscript, Ordinals, Fractions, Stylistic Alternates, Stylistic Sets, Localized Forms, Case Sensitive Forms

**Test version available:** No

**Web font format available:** Yes

→ P. 453, 465

abcdefghijklmnopqrstuvwxyzæåçéñöûß
ABCDEFGHIJKLMNOPQRSTUVWXYZÆÇØẞ
1234567890@.,!?')]§*“”»«/-½©€$£¥&

абвгдеёжзийклмнопрстуфхцчшщъыьэюя
АБВГДЕЁЖЗИЙКЛМНОПРСТУФХЦЧШЩЪЫЬЭЮЯ
1234567890@.,!?')]§*“”»«/-½©€$£¥&

Seriguela is a family of two styles: Normal and Display, each in nine weights plus *Italics and Reverse Italics:* Extra Light, *Extra Light Italic,* Extra Light Reverse Italic, Regular, *Italic,* Reverse Italic, **Semi Bold,** ***Semi Bold Italic,*** **Semi Bold Reverse Italic, Black, *Black Italic,* Black Reverse Italic,** Display Thin, *Display Thin Italic,* Display Thin Reverse Italic, Display Light, *Display Light Italic,* Display Light Reverse Italic, **Display Medium,** ***Display Medium Italic,*** **Display Medium Reverse Italic, Display Bold, *Display Bold Italic,* Display Bold Reverse Italic, Display Poster, *Display Poster Italic,* and Display Poster Reverse Italic**

“UGH!
~~As
if!”

Sharoa Pro

Sharoa Pro is a humanist sans serif type characterized by clear elements and slightly wider counters. It comes in ten weights with a wealth of OpenType features, including Small Caps and Numerals, making it suitable for setting long texts. Since the Latin alphabet of *Aoto Gothic* is based on Sharoa Pro, both typefaces work well together in bilingual typesetting.

**Design:** 2021, Sakura Taruno → p. 483

**Foundry:** Morisawa.Inc, Japan, morisawa.co.jp → p. 490

**Language support:** Latin Extended

**OpenType features:** Proportional Oldstyle, Tabular Lining, Standard Ligatures, Small Caps, Superscript, Subscript, Ordinals, Contextual Alternates, Fractions, Numerator, Denominator, Historical Forms, Slashed Zero, Localized Forms, Case Sensitive Forms

**Test version available:** No

**Web font format available:** Yes

abcdefghijklmnopqrstuvwxyzæfiåçéñöûß
ABCDEFGHIJKLMNOPQRSTUVWXYZÆÇØẞ
1234567890o@.,!?')]§*""»«/–½©€$£¥&

→ P. 453

Sharoa Pro is a typeface of ten weights plus *Italics:* Ultra Light, *Ultra Light Italic,* Extra Light, *Extra Light Italic,* Light, *Light Italic,* Regular, *Italic,* Medium, *Medium Italic,* Demi Bold, *Demi Bold Italic,* Bold, *Bold Italic,* Extra Bold, *Extra Bold Italic,* Heavy, *Heavy Italic,* Ultra, ***and Ultra Italic***

かもめ

KAMOME
DINER →

2006

食堂

Shorai Sans

Shorai Sans was designed as a companion typeface to *Avenir Next,* built to work harmoniously in modern global designs, while preserving the essence of Japanese handwriting. Shorai goes beyond existing Japanese Sans Serifs to provide a wide spectrum of expression and personality for designers to play with. Shorai Sans is opening new horizons in Japanese typography.

**Design:** 2022, Akira Kobayashi → p. 478, Ryota Doi → p. 475, Yukihiro Nakamura → p. 480

**Foundry:** Monotype, United Kingdom, monotype.com → p. 490

**Language support:** Latin Extended, Cyrillic, Greek, Japanese, Hanzi/Kanji

**OpenType features:** Standard Ligatures, Discretionary Ligatures, All Alternates, Slashed Zero, Vertical Alternates and Rotation, Proportional Alternate Vertical Metrics, Expert forms, Full Widths, Half Widths, JIS78 forms, JIS90 forms, NLC Kanji Forms, Proportional Alternate Widths, Proportional Widths, Traditional Forms, Vertical Writing, Vertical Kerning

**Test version available:** Yes

**Web font format available:** Yes

abcdefghijklmnopqrstuvwxyzæffåçéñöûß
ABCDEFGHIJKLMNOPQRSTUVWXYZÆÇØ
12345678900@.,!?')]§*“”»«/–½©€$£¥&⇔☎

あいうえおかきくけこサシスセソタチツテト
永東愛国大見今糸力北心南西女分文父母子衣花
12345678900@.,!?')]§*“”»«/–½©€$£¥&↓↑☃

Shorai Sans is a typeface of ten weights: Ultra Light, Thin, Light, Regular, **Medium, Semi Bold, Bold, Extra Bold, Black, and Heavy**

→ P. 453, 465

#LIVE.

DIE.

REPEAT.

Tom Cruise ≈ 2 0 14 ∞ Emily Blunt

# EDGE OF TOMMOROW

Slussen

Slussen is a neo-grotesque typeface well suited to tech and industrial companies. Slussen's inspiration comes from the rhythm and organization of construction sites. When compared to more conventional neo-grotesque typefaces, Slussen's design structure is based on a linear evolution through angular outlines. Combined with flat endings and a slight contrast in letterforms, this font family has been designed to cover a very large range of uses, from small captions to huge titles.

**Design:** 2022, Hugo Jourdan → p. 477

**Foundry:** Blaze Type, France, blazetype.eu → p. 488

**Language support:** Latin Extended

**OpenType features:** Proportional Oldstyle, Tabular Lining, Proportional Lining, Tabular Oldstyle, All Caps, Small Caps, Capitals to Small Caps, Petite Caps, Capitals to Petite Caps, Superscript, Subscript, Ordinals, All Alternates, Contextual Alternates, Fractions, Alternative Fractions, Numerator, Denominator, Arrows, Stylistic Alternates, Stylistic Sets, Slashed Zero, Localized Forms, Case Sensitive Forms, Mark Positioning, Font Variations

**Test version available:** Yes

**Web font format available:** Yes

abcdefghijklmnopqrstuvwxyzæijåçéñöûß
ABCDEFGHIJKLMNOPQRSTUVWXYZÆÇØẞ
12345678900@.,!?')]§*“”»«/–½©€$£¥&↗

Slussen is a family of three styles: Normal, Mono, and Stencil. Normal in five widths: Compressed, Condensed, Normal, Extended, and Expanded, each in eight weights plus *Italics:* Compressed Thin, *Compressed Thin Italic*, Compressed Extra Light, *Condensed Extra Light Italic*, Condensed Light, *Condensed Light Italic*, Regular, *Italic*, Medium, ***Medium Italic***, **Extended Semi Bold**, ***Extended Semi Bold Italic***, **Expanded Black**, ***and Expanded Black Italic.*** Mono in eight weights plus *Italics:* Thin, *Thin Italic*, Extra Light, *Extra Light Italic*, Light, *Light Italic*, Regular, *Italic*, Medium, ***Medium Italic***, **Semi Bold**, ***Semi Bold Italic***, **Bold**, ***Bold Italic***, **Black**, ***and Black Italic.*** Stencil in eight weights: Thin, Extra Light, Light, Regular, Medium, **Semi Bold**, **Bold, and Black**

→ P. 453, 466, 467

Snare

# Whipl*ash

# WHIPLASH

# Snare

→ P. 465, 467

Snare is a jazzy little display type that presents like a stencil but behaves in its own way. Featuring angled section breaks and variable heights, Snare keeps each character's footprint steady as its heights change, revealing unique crossbars, periscoping capitals, and deep-sinking descenders. Because each character follows its own rules, the more each word grows, the more it shows the beautiful rhythm of variety. Or stretch individual characters to shape the contours of your words.

**Design:** 2021, Michu Benaim → p. 472, Alexander Wright → p. 484, Rodrigo Fuenzalida → p. 475

**Foundry:** In-House International, United States of America / Spain, weareinhouse.com/types → p. 489

**Language support:** Latin

**OpenType features:** Proportional Lining, All Caps, Stylistic Alternates, Unicase

**Test version available:** Yes

**Web font format available:** Yes

abcdefghijklmnopqrstuvwxyzéñ
ABCDEFGHIJKLMNOPQRSTUVWXYZ
12345678900(.,!?')]§*“”»«/-θ€$£¥&

Snare is a family of two styles: Normal and Unicase, each in ten heights: 100, 200, 300, 400, 500, 600, 700, 800, 900, 1000, unicase 100, unicase 200, unicase 300, unicase 400, unicase 500, unicase 600, unicase 700, unicase 800, unicase 900, and unicase 1000

COMMANDER *CLIFF*
*ALLISTER MCLANE* &
BESATZUNG IM SICH
ENTWICKELNDEN
KRIEG GEGEN
DIE FREMDARTIGEN
*FROGS*

↖↘*()

***Raumpatrouille***
***ORION***

**CA Spotnik**

The initial inspiration for CA Spotnik was the opening title of an early Andrei Tarkovsky movie. There was this very unconventional hand drawn s which drew the attention of the designer, and which eventually led him to the design of a full type family. Although CA Spotnik looks best in larger sizes, it's fine for medium size texts as well. In case you find the swirly s somehow uncomfortable, there is a standard s included.

**Design:** 2022, Stefan Claudius → p. 474

**Foundry:** Cape Arcona Type Foundry, Germany, cape-arcona.com → p. 488

**Language support:** Latin Extended

**OpenType features:** Tabular Lining, Proportional Lining, Superscript, Subscript, Contextual Alternates, Fractions, Numerator, Denominator, Arrows, Stylistic Alternates, Stylistic Sets, Slashed Zero, Localized Forms

**Test version available:** Yes

**Web font format available:** Yes



abcdefghijklmnopqrstuvwxyzæåçéñöûß
ABCDEFGHIJKLMNOPQRSTUVWXYZÆÇØẞ
12345678900@.,!?')]§*“”»«/–©€$£¥&↘

→ P. 453

CA Spotnik is a typeface of twelve weights plus *Italics:* Thin, *Thin Italic*, Light, *Light Italic*, **Regular**, ***Italic***, **Medium**, ***Medium Italic***, **Bold**, ***Bold Italic***, **Extra Bold**, ***and Extra Bold Italic***

This is

# Harold

&

नासमझ

बेतुका

1970

This is

# Maude

Stadio Now

Stadio Now is the revival of an original design by Aldo Novarese for the dry transfer brand R41, published in 1974. The original typeface is an extra bold grotesque Sans Serif that is notable for its reverse contrast. Stadio Now expands the original design into a versatile multi-weight family, with text and display variants and a variable version to fully explore its reverse contrast design space. In 2021 the family was expanded with the inclusion of Stadio Deva, a Devanagari version.

**Design:** 2021, Cosimo Lorenzo Pancini → p. 480

**Foundry:** Zetafonts Foundry, Italy, zetafonts.com → p. 492

**Language support:** Latin Extended, Cyrillic, Devanagari

**OpenType features:** Proportional Oldstyle, Tabular Lining, Proportional Lining, Tabular Oldstyle, Standard Ligatures, Discretionary Ligatures, Small Caps, Superscript, Subscript, Ordinals, Fractions, Numerator, Denominator, Stylistic Sets, Slashed Zero, Case Sensitive Forms, Unicase, Font Variations

**Test version available:** Yes

**Web font format available:** Yes

abcdefghijklmnopqrstuvwxyzæfjåçéñöûß
ABCDEFGHIJKLMNOPQRSTUVWXYZÆÇØß
1234567890Ø@.,!?')]§*“”»«/–½©€$£¥&↔

अ आ इ ई उ ऊ ऋ ॠ ऌ ॡ ऍ ऎ ए ऐ ऑ ऒ ओ औ अं अः
क ख ग घ ङ च छ ज झ ञ ट ठ ड ढ ण त थ द ध न प
फ ब भ म य र ल व श ष स ह ळ क्ष ज्ञ १२३४५६७८९०

Stadio Now is a family of six styles: Monolinea, Sottile, **Text, Display, Weirdo, Poster, Nero, and Banner.** Display and Text each in two weights plus *Italics:* Display Regular, *Display Italic,* **Display Bold, *Display Bold Italic,*** Text Regular, *Text Italic,* **Text Bold, *and Text Bold Italic.*** Sottile, Monolinea, **Poster, Banner, Nero, and** Weirdo each in one Regular weight plus *Italics:* Monolinea Regular, *Monolinea Italic,* Sottile Regular, *Sottile Italic,* **Poster Regular, *Poster Italic,* Banner Regular, *Banner Italic,* Nero Regular, *Nero Italic,*** Weirdo Regular, *and Weirdo Italic*





→ P. 453, 465

Back↙ to the *future!*

gal@ctic ~
~ ADVENTURES

"GREAT SCOTT!"

Striated

Striated was designed with display purposes in mind. It is a mixture of grotesque and geometric typefaces, with a pinch of heavily formalized elements. The typeface uses letterforms that are often seen—and more or less registered—since the beginning of the 19th century and it is also clearly rooted in the experiments of Bauhaus. It tries to strike a balance in negotiating the past and future by evoking a feeling of being an old companion and being visionary at the same time.

**Design:** 2022, René Rieger
→ p. 481

**Foundry:** Road to Venice Type, Germany, r-vtype.com → p. 491

**Language support:** Latin

**OpenType features:** Proportional Lining, Standard Ligatures, Discretionary Ligatures, Arrows, Stylistic Alternates, Stylistic Sets, Case Sensitive Forms

**Test version available:** Yes

**Web font format available:** Yes

→ P. 465

abcdefghijklmnopqrstuvwxyzæfjåçéñöûß
ABCDEFGHIJKLMNOPQRSTUVWXYZÆÇØ
1234567890@.,!?')]§*“”»«/–©€$£¥&→

Striated is a typeface of three weights plus *Italics:* Medium, *Medium Italic*, Bold, ***Bold Italic***, **Heavy**, ***and Heavy Italic***

# THE TWILIGHT ZONE

Af Stuce

The Stuce typeface was created in 2004 for the visual identity of a contemporary art exhibition about Humor and Art that took place in Lille, France. The alphabet was optimized and expanded in 2022 to be published and distributed online by the digital type foundry AinsiFont. Stuce is a fantasy, minimalist, and geometric typeface designed for titling and short text. The lowercase and uppercase letters are not aligned, giving the typographic compositions a playful and musical look.

**Design:** 2022, Sébastien Delobel → p. 474

**Foundry:** AinsiFont, France, ainsifont.com → p. 488

**Language support:** Latin

**OpenType features:** Standard Ligatures, Petite Caps, Stylistic Alternates, Fractions

**Test version available:** No

**Web font format available:** Yes

→ P. 465

abcdefghijklmnopqrstuvwxyzÆfiAçÉñöûB
ABCDEFGHIJKLMNOPQRSTUVWXYZÆÇø
1234567890@.,!?)]§*“”»«/-½©€$£¥&

AF stuce is a typeface of one bold weight

*Verschollen.*
Náufrago.
*Seul au monde.*
**Yeni Hayat.**
***Cast Away.***

→

**FedEx.**
**Offtrack.**
**Wilson!!**

**Subtil Grotesk**

Functional, low contrast, sans serif–Subtil Grotesk is a Neogrotesque that stands out: true to the classical notion of a Grotesque, yet infused with a masterly understated warmth and elegance. Subtil comes forward with a set of cool and characterful design advantages–it concedes neutrality to sensitivity and brings serious play to an otherwise strict design construction. Add to it remarkable legibility, a generous x-height, and a ton of typographic features for the die-hard design aficionados.

**Design:** 2020, Thomas Thiemich → p. 483

**Foundry:** TYPE BY, Belgium, typeby.com → p. 492

**Language support:** Latin Extended

**OpenType features:** Proportional Oldstyle, Tabular Lining, Proportional Lining, Tabular Oldstyle, Standard Ligatures, Discretionary Ligatures, All Caps, Small Caps, Capitals to Small Caps, Petite Caps, Capitals to Petite Caps, Superscript, Subscript, Ordinals, All Alternates, Contextual Alternates, Fractions, Numerator, Denominator, Ornaments, Arrows, Stylistic Alternates, Stylistic Sets, Historical Forms, Slashed Zero, Localized Forms, Case Sensitive Forms, Required Ligatures

**Test version available:** No

**Web font format available:** Yes

→ P. 453

abcdefghijklmnopqrstuvwxyzæfjåçéñöûß
ABCDEFGHIJKLMNOPQRSTUVWXYZÆÇØẞ
1234567890 0@.,!?')]§*“”»«/–½©€$£¥&↙★

Subtil Grotesk is a typeface of eight weights plus *Italics:* Thin, *Thin Italic,* Light, *Light Italic,* Blond, *Blond Italic,* Normal, *Normal Italic,* Medium, *Medium Italic,* **Semi Bold,** ***Semi Bold Italic,*** **Bold,** ***Bold Italic,*** **Extra Bold, and** ***Extra Bold Italic***

# A ROOM WITH A VIEW

&

# O Mio Babbino Caro

Swanstone

Mario De Libero designed Swanstone while investigating 19th-century old-style typefaces—designs like Theophile Beaudoire's *Romana* (1860) or Miller & Richard's *Modernized Old Style*, that re-imagined the classical Venetian letterforms adding flared serifs and early Art Nouveau influences. In Italy, one of these fonts was Raffaello Bertieri's Raffaello, which De Libero used as the starting point of his research in a contemporary retelling of these exuberant and sexily unsettling letterforms.

**Design:** 2021, Mario De Libero
→ p. 478

**Foundry:** Zetafonts Foundry, Italy, zetafonts.com → p. 492

**Language support:** Latin Extended

**OpenType features:** Standard Ligatures, Discretionary Ligatures, Historical Ligatures, Ordinals, Contextual Alternates, Stylistic Sets

**Test version available:** Yes

**Web font format available:** Yes

abcdefghijklmnopqrstuvwxyzæfjåçéñöûß
ABCDEFGHIJKLMNOPQRSTUVWXYZÆÇOẞ
1234567890@.,!?')]§*“”»«/–©€$£¥&

# Swanstone is a typeface of one Regular weight


→ P. 457, 465

“SAY
HELLO
**TO MY**
little”
**FRIEND!**
*ALPACINO*
***SCARFACE***
↘ Directed
BY
BRIAN de PALMA

With its eye-grabbing proportions and friendly feel, Marc Rouault designed Tarnac bearing in mind a particularly French style of slanted Égyptienne. Its roots can be traced to a variety of 20th century French Egyptian models, as featured in posters, newspaper headlines, and French road sign plaques, which have become an intractable aesthetic element of French culture. Tarnac's wonky proportions and flat-interior bowl shapes are only further accentuated by its rotated italic design.

**Design:** 2021, Marc Rouault
→ p. 482

**Foundry:** Sharp Type, United States of America, sharptype.co → p. 491

**Language support:** Latin Extended

**OpenType features:** Proportional Oldstyle, Tabular Lining, Proportional Lining, Tabular Oldstyle, Standard Ligatures, All Caps, Superscript, Subscript, Ordinals, Fractions, Numerator, Denominator, Arrows, Stylistic Alternates, Stylistic Sets, Slashed Zero, Localized Forms, Case Sensitive Forms

**Test version available:** Yes

**Web font format available:** Yes

→ P. 458

abcdefghijklmnopqrstuvwxyzæåçéñß
ABCDEFGHIJKLMNOPQRSTUVWXZ
12345678900@.,!?')]§*“”»«/–½©€$£¥&←

Tarnac is a typeface of five weights plus *Italics:* Thin, *Thin Italic,* Light, *Light Italic,* Regular, *Italic,* **Bold,** ***Bold Italic,*** **Black,** ***and Black Italic***

# The W0L₣

# o–f ②0❶④

# ₩A₺ℓ

# $T₹€e₮

Tarnac Sans

The development of a sans serif version of Tarnac became evident as soon as the Slab's contrast disappeared: Rouault sliced off the Slabs, revealing the beginnings for a viable sans serif family. The result is a refreshingly wonky monolinear Sans, true to the origin of the genre. Telltale formulations like the excessively wide *T* and oversized tittles indicate its origin, and harken back to the methodology employed for the very first sans serif typeface cast by the Caslon foundry in London, 1816.

**Design:** 2021, Marc Rouault → p. 482

**Foundry:** Sharp Type, United States of America, sharptype.co → p. 491

**Language support:** Latin Extended

**OpenType features:** Proportional Oldstyle, Tabular Lining, Proportional Lining, Tabular Oldstyle, Standard Ligatures, All Caps, Superscript, Subscript, Ordinals, Fractions, Numerator, Denominator, Arrows, Stylistic Alternates, Stylistic Sets, Slashed Zero, Localized Forms, Case Sensitive Forms

**Test version available:** Yes

**Web font format available:** Yes

→ P. 453

abcdefghijklmnopqrstuvwxyzæfjåçéñöûß
ABCDEFGHIJKLMNOPQRSTUVWXYZÆÇØ
1234567890Ø@.,!?')]§*“”»«/–½©€$£¥&→♧

Tarnac Sans is a typeface of five weights plus *Italics:* Thin, *Thin Italic*, Light, *Light Italic*, **Regular**, ***Italic***, **Bold**, ***Bold Italic***, **Black**, ***and Black Italic***

# LE TARTUFFE OU L'IMPOSTEUR

## *COMEDIE*

PAR I.B.P. DE MOLIÈRE.

À PARIS
la Porte de l'Église de
la Sainte Chapelle

Tartuffo is a fresh typeface, inspired by many characters from various literature pieces. Its name comes from a famous character called Tartuffe, from *Tartuffe or the impersonator* by the French playwright, actor, and poet Molière. Also, the font was influenced by the Tartufo di Pizzo, a traditional Italian dessert with a chocolate base.

**Design:** 2021, Bouk Ra → p. 481

**Foundry:** Lifttype, France, lift-type.fr → p. 490

**Language support:** Latin Extended

**OpenType features:** Proportional Oldstyle, Tabular Lining, Proportional Lining, Tabular Oldstyle, Standard Ligatures, Discretionary Ligatures, Superscript, Ordinals, All Alternates, Contextual Alternates, Fractions, Numerator, Denominator, Arrows, Stylistic Alternates, Stylistic Sets, Localized Forms, Case Sensitive Forms

**Test version available:** Yes

**Web font format available:** Yes

abcdefghijklmnopqrstuvwxyzæfjåçéñöûß
ABCDEFGHIJKLMNOPQRSTUVWXYZÆÇØ
1234567890ø@.,!?')]§*“”»«/–½©€$£¥&↗

Tartuffo is a typeface of five weights plus *Italics:* Thin, *Thin Italic,* Light, *Light Italic,* **Regular,** ***Italic,*** **Medium,** ***Medium Italic,*** **Bold,** ***and Bold Italic***

→ P. 457, 465

Where's the money, Lebowski?

Where's the füking money, s h *!head?

Tempus Futurum

Tempus Futurum is not a typeface! It is a tribute to the Werkstatt Rixdorfer Drucke, a German artists' collective. Play, typesetting, and printing have shaped the forms and subtleties of this type in the Buchdruck Museum Hannover. Printed and played in lead, then digitized, this typeface was realized and implemented together with typesetter Peter Thiel.

**Design:** 2022, Sebastian Moock
→ p. 480

**Foundry:** Bureau Sebastian Moock, Germany, sebastianmoock.de
→ p. 488

**Language support:** Latin

**OpenType features:** Stylistic Alternates

**Test version available:** Yes

**Web font format available:** Yes



abcdefghijklmnopqrstuvwxyzæåçéñöûß
ABCDEFGHIJKLMNOPQRSTUVWXYZÇØß
1234567890@.,!?')]§*"""»«–©€&

→ P. 465, 469

Tempus Futurum is a typeface of one Regular weight

Written & Directed by

*Woody Allen*

× with Owen Wilson

*Carla Bruni* ↖

Rachel McAdams ✓

↘ *Marion Cotillard*

**Tom Hiddleston** ↑

***Alison Pill*** ►

Ⓤ **Adrien Brody**

***Corey Stoll*** ✠

**Michael Sheen** ☑

& ***Kathy Bates***‽

Tremolo Sans

Nikola Djurek's *Tremolo,* a popular font that was awarded a TDC Certificate of Typographic Excellence in 2016, now has a new companion typeface, Tremolo Sans. Quirky and engaging, Tremolo Sans is a low-contrast typeface with humanist features, a very large x-height, narrow proportions, and unorthodox cursive details, such as the handwriting-inspired *k, g,* and *y,* that lend a remarkable warmth to shorter texts and headlines.

**Design:** 2020, Nikola Djurek
→ p. 474

**Foundry:** Typotheque, The Netherlands, typotheque.com
→ p. 492

**Language support:** Latin

**OpenType features:** Proportional Oldstyle, Tabular Lining, Proportional Lining, Tabular Oldstyle, Standard Ligatures, All Caps, Small Caps, Capitals to Small Caps, Superscript, Subscript, Fractions, Numerator, Denominator

**Test version available:** Yes

**Web font format available:** Yes

→ P. 453

abcdefghijklmnopqrstuvwxyzæfjåçéñöûß
ABCDEFGHIJKLMNOPQRSTUVWXYZÆÇØẞ
1234567890@.,!?')]§*""»«/–½©€$£¥&↗☞

Tremolo Sans is a typeface of six weights plus *Italics:* Thin, *Thin Italic,* Light, *Light Italic,* Regular, *Italic,* **Text,** ***Text Italic,*** **Medium,** ***Medium Italic,*** **Bold,** ***and Bold Italic***

# HE'S JUST **NOT** THAT INTO YOU!

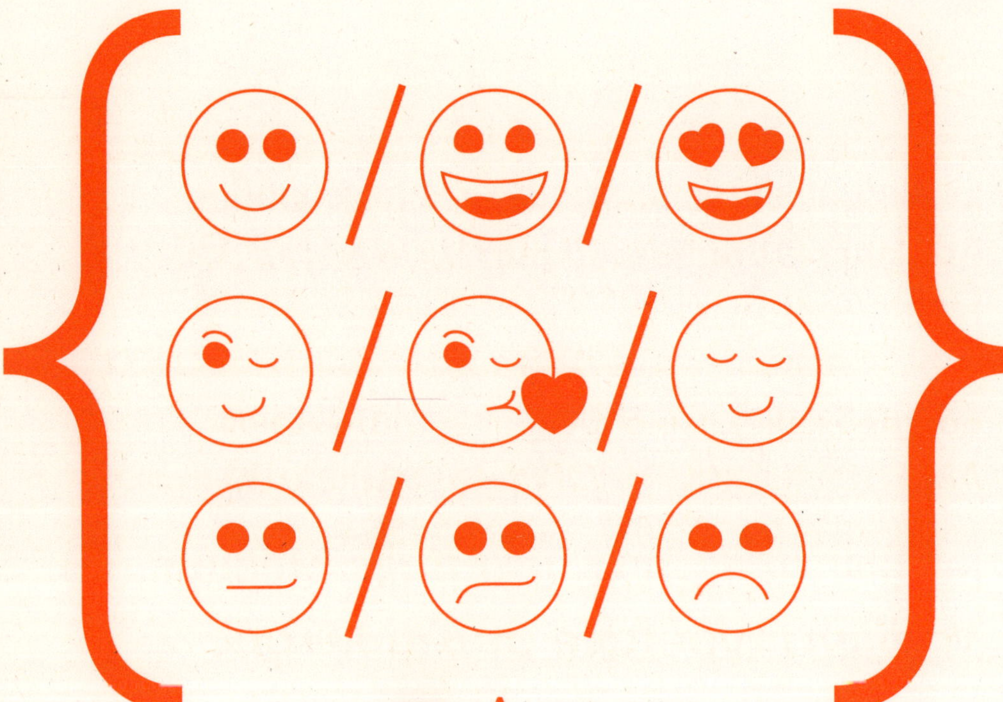

♥ Да

☒ **нет**—

☐ Maybe

Vary

Vary is fun and adaptable and was built with three feelings (variations): classic, modern, and loopy, offering an opportunity for designers to be playful in their creations.

**Design:** 2021, Olli Meier → p. 479

**Foundry:** Monotype, United Kingdom, monotype.com → p. 490

**Language support:** Latin Extended, Cyrillic

**OpenType features:** Standard Ligatures, Discretionary Ligatures, Superscript, Subscript, Ordinals, All Alternates, Contextual Alternates, Fractions, Alternative Fractions, Numerator, Denominator, Ornaments, Stylistic Alternates, Localized Forms, Case Sensitive Forms, Mark Positioning, Scientific Inferiors, Glyph Composition/Decomposition

**Test version available:** Yes

**Web font format available:** Yes

abcdefghijklmnopqrstuvwxyzæfiåçéñöûß
ABCDEFGHIJKLMNOPQRSTUVWXYZÆÇØẞ
1234567890@.,!?')]§*“”»«/–½©€$£¥&↕☻

абвгдеёжзийклмнопрстуфхцчшщъыьэюя
АБВГДЕЁЖЗИЙКЛМНОПРСТУФХЦЧШЩЪЫЬЭЮЯ
1234567890@.,!?')]§*“”»«/–½©€$£¥&

Vary is a typeface of ten weights:
Hairline, Thin, Extra Light, Light,
Regular, Medium, Bold, Extra Bold,
Black, and Extra Black

→ P. 454, 465

§ A GRAPHIC ¶

1993 A film
by Peter
SAVAGE
Grenaway
The Baby
Of Mâcon

¶ BEAUTIFUL §

Vivala bl has a high black ratio that supports a compact typographic style. It is particularly suitable for decorative typesetting, for example, for posters, logos, and book illustrations. Complementing the ornamental style, Black Letter has a narrow style that works well for smaller type sizes. And it is equipped with various contextual alternates and ligatures.

**Design:** 2019, Johannes Hoffmann → p. 476

**Foundry:** VivalaType, Germany, vivalatype.com → p. 492

**Language support:** Latin Extended

**OpenType features:** Standard Ligatures, Contextual Alternates, Contextual Ligatures, Arrows, Stylistic Alternates, Localized Forms, Terminal Form

**Test version available:** No

**Web font format available:** Yes

→ P. 468

abcdefghijklmnopqrstuvwxyzæſlåçéñöûß
ABCDEFGHIJJKLMNOPQRSTUVWXYZÆÇØ
1234567890@.,!?')]§*“ ” »«/–½©€$£¥&↖

Vivala bl is a typeface of six weights: Regular, Medium, Demi Bold, Semi Bold, Bold, and Bold Ornament

# THE ALPHABET OF YOU.

ALL FOUR SYMBOLS.

<{ATGC}&{01}>

I'M ONLY

# TWO:

ØNE & ZERØ.+

ZAP is an all-caps monospaced and (almost) monoline typeface family. ZAP comes along in square and round shapes, two widths (ZAP 360 and ZAP 500), and eight weights. Slanted and backslanted styles are available, too.

**Design:** 2019, Ekke Wolf → p. 484

**Foundry:** Wannatype, Austria, wannatype.com → p. 492

**Language support:** Latin Extended, Greek

**OpenType features:** Tabular Lining, All Caps, Small Caps, Petite Caps, Superscript, Subscript, Stylistic Alternates, Stylistic Sets, Mark Positioning

**Test version available:** No

**Web font format available:** Yes

→ P. 465, 466

ABCDEFGHIJKLMNOPQRSTUVWXYZÆÅÇÉß

ABCDEFGHIJKLMNOPQRSTUVWXYZÆÇØ

1234567890@.,!?'›]§*“”»«/–@€$£¥₺

ΑΒΓΔΕΖΗΘΙΚΛΜΝΞΟΠΡΣΤΥΦΧΨΩΆΈΉΊΌΏΪΫ

ΑΒΓΔΕΖΗΘΙΚΛΜΝΞΟΠΡΣΤΥΦΧΨΩΆΈΉΊΌΏΪΫ

01234567890@.,!?'›]§*“”»«/–@€$£¥₺

ZAP is a family of two styles: Normal and Round, each in two widths: 360 and 500, each in eight weights plus Slanteds and Backslanteds: Light 360, *Light 360 Slanted*, Light 360 Backslanted, **Heavy 360**, ***Heavy 360 Slanted***, **Heavy 360 Backslanted**, Light 500, *Light 500 Slanted*, Light 500 Backslanted, **Heavy 500**, ***Heavy 500 Slanted***, **Heavy 500 Backslanted**, Round Light 360, *Round Light 360 Slanted*, Round Light 360 Backslanted, **Round Heavy 360**, ***Round Heavy 360 Slanted***, **Round Heavy 360 Backslanted**, Round Light 500, *Round Light 500 Slanted*, Round Light 500 Backslanted, **Round Heavy 500**, ***Round Heavy 500 Slanted***, and **Round Heavy 500 Backslanted**

# *2009)→ [ENTER the{VOID} GASPAR NOE→***

*

Zimula

Zimula is a classic and friendly take on contemporary geometric typefaces. Besides the normal styles, suitable for everyday design tasks, the family comes in InkTrap and InkSpot styles. They simulate the leaving out and filling of joints in an exaggerated way, creating interesting textures on the more extreme weights while adding extra functionality to the rest. The result is a workhorse family that can take up any task from small body copy to huge titles with a strong impact.

**Design:** 2021, Fabian Dornhecker → p. 475

**Foundry:** LA BOLDE VITA, Germany, laboldevita.com → p. 489

**Language support:** Latin Extended

**OpenType features:** Tabular Lining, Proportional Lining, Standard Ligatures, Discretionary Ligatures, Superscript, Subscript, All Alternates, Contextual Alternates, Fractions, Numerator, Denominator, Arrows, Stylistic Alternates, Stylistic Sets, Slashed Zero, Localized Forms, Case Sensitive Forms

**Test version available:** Yes

**Web font format available:** Yes

→ P. 454

abcdefghijklmnopqrstuvwxyzæijåçéñöûß
ABCDEFGHIJKLMNOPQRSTUVWXYZÆÇØẞ
12345678900@.,!?')]§*“”»«/–½©€$£¥&→*

Zimula is a family of three styles: Normal, InkTrap, and InkSpot, each in nine weights: Thin, Extra Light, Light, Regular, **Medium, Semi Bold, Bold, Extra Bold, Black,** Thin InkTrap, Extra Light InkTrap, Light InkTrap, Regular InkTrap, **Medium InkTrap, Semi Bold InkTrap, Bold InkTrap, Extra Bold InkTrap, Black InkTrap,** Thin InkSpot, Extra Light InkSpot, Light InkSpot, Regular InkSpot, **Medium InkSpot, Semi Bold InkSpot, Bold InkSpot, Extra Bold InkSpot, and Black InkSpot**

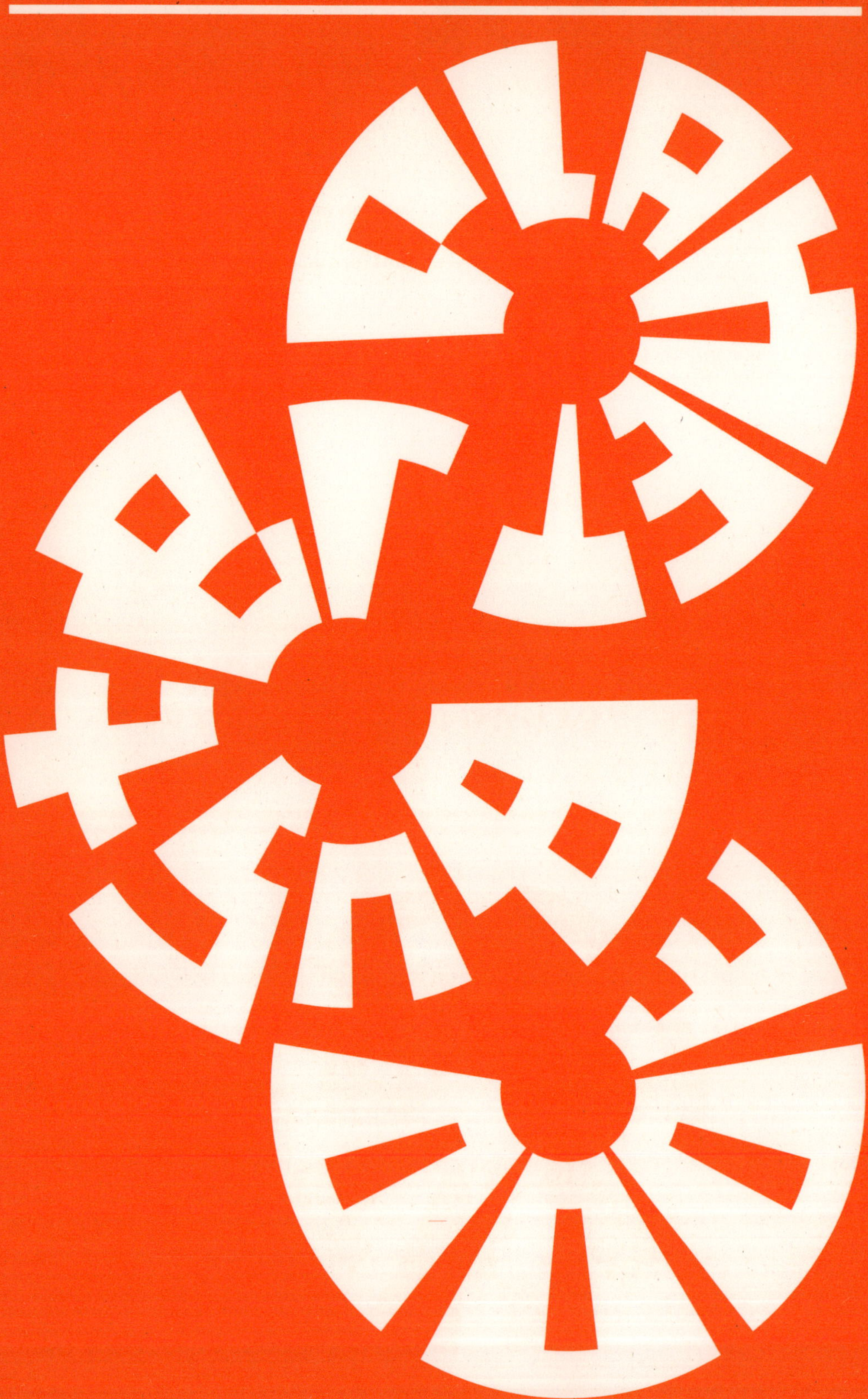

Zyrkles

This font will make you dizzy. It spins around in circles and is a mind-curving challenge in legibility. Whether you want to make recursive labels for your LPs or make posters fighting climate change, Zyrkles does it all. Let us know if you can't figure out how to use it.

**Design:** 2022, Alexander Branczyk
→ p. 473

**Foundry:** Face2Face, Germany, czyk.de → p. 489

**Language support:** Latin

**OpenType features:** Proportional Oldstyle, Tabular Lining, Proportional Lining, Stylistic Sets, Case Sensitive Forms

**Test version available:** Yes

**Web font format available:** No

→ P. 465

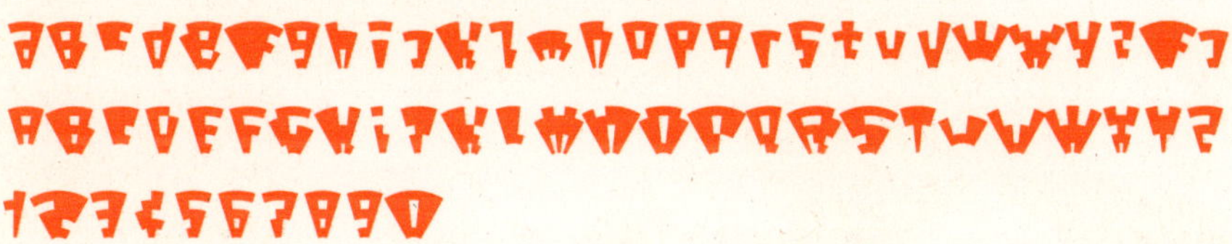

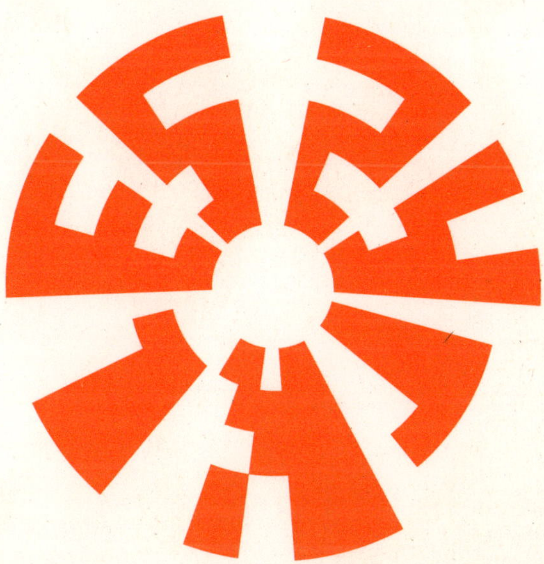

See all typefaces online at *yearbookoftype.com,* sorted by categories and linked to the foundries' websites

Enter the code: *YOT6MOVIES*

**Acherus Grotesque**
→ p. 32/33

Aa

R13&gKdsH

**Adapter PE**
→ p. 34/35

Aa

R13&gKdsH

**Adelle Sans Georgian**
→ p. 36/37

ა

ზნვჴტჭჯთც

**Adelle Sans Hebrew**
→ p. 38/39

א

ב13&טלפצש

**Adelle Sans Lao**
→ p. 40/41

ກ

ງສຕຍຜ₭ໝ໒ຐ

**Adelphi PE**
→ p. 42/43

Aa

R13&gKdsH

**Albula Pro**
→ p. 52/53

Aa

R13&gKdsH

**Album**
→ p. 54/55

Aa

R13&gKdsH

**Aoto Gothic**
→ p. 60/61

Aa

R13&gKdsH

**Asgard**
→ p. 66/67

Aa

R13&gKdsH

**ATBT**
→ p. 70/71

Aa

R13&gKdsH

**Babetta**
→ p. 74/75

Aa

R13&gKdsH

**Bajazzo**
→ p. 80/81

Aa

R13&gKdsH

**Bakemono**
→ p. 82/83

Aa

R13&gKdsH

**Bakewell**
→ p. 86/87

Aa

R13&gKdsH

**Bartok**
→ p. 88/89

Aa
R13&gKdsH

**Berlin Type**
→ p. 92/93

Aa
R13&gKdsH

**Bourton Text**
→ p. 100/101

Aa
R13&gKdsH

**Bree Arabic**
→ p. 102/103

ات
ضعمۺ٥ع

**Bree Thai**
→ p. 104/105

ก
ขฅฆ๕ญฐหฟ๘

**Brutalista**
→ p. 108/109

Aa
R13&gKdsH

**Chesna Grotesk**
→ p. 124/125

Aa
R13&gKdsH

**AG Choijeongho Minburi Std.** → p. 126/127

Aa
R13&gKdsH

**Claymore**
→ p. 128/129

Aa
R13&gKdsH

**Cobertura**
→ p. 130/131

Aa
R13&gKdsH

**Contralto**
→ p. 136/137

Aa
R13&gKdsH

**Fizz**
→ p. 174/175

Aa
R13&gKdsH

**Fontanella**
→ p. 178/179

Aa
R13&gKdsH

**PP Fragment**
→ p. 182/183

Aa
R13&gKdsH

**Franzi**
→ p. 184/185

Aa
R13&gKdsH

| | | |
|---|---|---|
| **Futura Now**<br>→ p. 186/187<br>Aa<br>R13&gKdsH | **BF Garant Pro**<br>→ p. 188/189<br>Aa<br>R13&gKdsH | **Garino**<br>→ p. 190/191<br>Aa<br>R13&gKdsH |
| **Geóso**<br>→ p. 196/197<br>Aa<br>R13&gKdsH | **Ghost**<br>→ p. 198/199<br>Aa<br>R13&gKdsH | **Gineto**<br>→ p. 200/201<br>Aa<br>R13&gKdsH |
| **Goldplay**<br>→ p. 202/203<br>Aa<br>R13&gKdsH | **Happiness Sans**<br>→ p. 218/219<br>Aa<br>R13&gKdsH | **Heading Now**<br>→ p. 222/223<br>Aa<br>R13&gKdsH |
| **Heliuum**<br>→ p. 224/225<br>Aa<br>R13&gKdsH | **MNKY Jane**<br>→ p. 234/235<br>Aa<br>R13&gKdsH | **Kaybuts**<br>→ p. 236/237<br>Aa<br>R13&gKdsH |
| **Klub**<br>→ p. 242/243<br>Aa<br>R13&gKdsH | **FT Kunst Grotesk**<br>→ p. 244/245<br>Aa<br>R13&gKdsH | **Legit Superfamily**<br>→ p. 246/247<br>Aa<br>R13&gKdsH |

***yearbookoftype.com*, code: YOT6MOVIES**

**TR Lox Compressed**
→ p. 256/257

Aa

R13&gKdsH

**Lucius**
→ p. 258/259

Aa

R13&gKdsH

**Margit**
→ p. 266/267

Aa

R13&gKdsH

**Marlon Pro**
→ p. 270/271

Aa

R13&gKdsH

**MNKY Maurice**
→ p. 276/277

Aa

R13&gKdsH

**Mersey**
→ p. 282/283

Aa

R13&gKdsH

**Miasma**
→ p. 286/287

Aa

R13&gKdsH

**Milligram**
→ p. 288/289

Aa

R13&gKdsH

**Muoto**
→ p. 292/293

Aa

R13&gKdsH

**Murtaugh & Riggs**
→ p. 294/295

Aa

R13&gKdsH

**Natom Pro**
→ p. 296/297

Aa

R13&gKdsH

**Neptun**
→ p. 298/299

Aa

R13&gKdsH

**Neue Rational**
→ p. 300/301

Aa

R13&gKdsH

**MD Nichrome**
→ p. 302/303

Aa

R13&gKdsH

**OPS Noise Abroad**
→ p. 304/305

Aa

R13&gKdsH

**Non Natural**
→ p. 306/307
Aa
R13&gKdsH

**Non Sans**
→ p. 308/309
Aa
R13&gKdsH

**Nouvelle Grotesk**
→ p. 312/313
Aa
R13&gKdsH

**Nuova Volte**
→ p. 314/315
Aa
R13&gKdsH

**Nure**
→ p. 316/317
Aa
R13&gKdsH

**Oldschool Grotesk**
→ p. 324/325
Aa
R13&gKdsH

**Paranorma**
→ p. 330/331
Aa
R13&gKdsH

**Portada Arabic**
→ p. 344/345
ات
ضعمشںهج

**Postea**
→ p. 346/347
Aa
R13&gKdsH

**Povetarac Display**
→ p. 348/349
Aa
R13&gKdsH

**Pragmatic**
→ p. 350/351
Aa
R13&gKdsH

**Quiverleaf Arabic CF**
→ p. 366/367
ات
ضعمشںهج

**Quiverleaf CF**
→ p. 368/369
Aa
R13&gKdsH

**Rebrand**
→ p. 374/375
Aa
R13&gKdsH

**Right Sans**
→ p. 378/379
Aa
R13&gKdsH

**Rockhopper**
→ p. 384/385

Aa

R13&gKdsH

**Saes Grotesk**
→ p. 390/391

Aa

R13&gKdsH

**Salad**
→ p. 392/393

Aa

R13&gKdsH

**Salva**
→ p. 396/397

Aa

R13&gKdsH

**Scootchy**
→ p. 398/399

Aa

R13&gKdsH

**Seiva**
→ p. 402/403

Aa

R13&gKdsH

**Seriguela**
→ p. 404/405

Aa

R13&gKdsH

**Sharoa Pro**
→ p. 406/407

Aa

R13&gKdsH

**Shorai Sans**
→ p. 408/409

Aa

R13&gKdsH

**Slussen**
→ p. 410/411

Aa

R13&gKdsH

**CA Spotnik**
→ p. 414/415

Aa

R13&gKdsH

**Stadio Now**
→ p. 416/417

Aa

R13&gKdsH

**Subtil Grotesk**
→ p. 422/423

Aa

R13&gKdsH

**Tarnac Sans**
→ p. 428/429

Aa

R13&gKdsH

**Tremolo Sans**
→ p. 434/435

Aa

R13&gKdsH

**Vary**
→ p. 436/437

Aa
R13&gKdsH

**Zimula**
→ p. 442/443

Aa
R13&gKdsH

## Serif

**Abstract**
→ p. 30/31

Aa
R13&gKdsH

**Aktuell**
→ p. 50/51

Aa
R13&gKdsH

**Aloma**
→ p. 56/57

Aa
R13&gKdsH

**Antonia**
→ p. 58/59

Aa
R13&gKdsH

**Arsenica**
→ p. 64/65

Aa
R13&gKdsH

**Astronomer**
→ p. 68/69

Aa
R13&gKdsH

**Avona Serif**
→ p. 72/73

Aa
R13&gKdsH

**Bartok**
→ p. 88/89

Aa
R13&gKdsH

**Benedikt**
→ p. 90/91

Aa
R13&gKdsH

**Borax**
→ p. 98/99

Aa
R13&gKdsH

**Calvino**
→ p. 110/111

Aa
R13&gKdsH

**Capricho**
→ p. 112/113

Aa
R13&gKdsH

**Cardone**
→ p. 114/115

Aa
R13&gKdsH

**Chassi**
→ p. 120/121

Aa
R13&gKdsH

**Contane**
→ p. 134/135

Aa
R13&gKdsH

**Convey**
→ p. 138/139

Aa
R13&gKdsH

**Cotford**
→ p. 140/141

Aa
R13&gKdsH

**Delvard Serif**
→ p. 142/143

Aa
R13&gKdsH

**Denton**
→ p. 144/145

Aa
R13&gKdsH

**Didot Modern**
→ p. 146/147

Aa
R13&gKdsH

**LD Elsnac**
→ p. 158/159

Aa
R13&gKdsH

**Ereganto Serif**
→ p. 162/163

Aa
R13&gKdsH

**Exposure**
→ p. 166/167

Aa
R13&gKdsH

**Flecha**
→ p. 176/177

Aa
R13&gKdsH

**PP Fragment**
→ p. 182/183
Aa
R13&gKdsH

**Granit Display**
→ p. 208/209
Aa
R13&gKdsH

**Greenstone**
→ p. 112/113
Aa
R13&gKdsH

**Grunt**
→ p. 214/215
Aa
R13&gKdsH

**Haultin**
→ p. 220/221
Aa
R13&gKdsH

**Helsa Display**
→ p. 226/227
Aa
R13&gKdsH

**Hernandez Bros**
→ p. 228/229
Aa
R13&gKdsH

**Immortel**
→ p. 232/233
Aa
R13&gKdsH

**Kaybuts**
→ p. 236/237
Aa
R13&gKdsH

**Legit Superfamily**
→ p. 246/247
Aa
R13&gKdsH

**Loretta**
→ p. 254/255
Aa
R13&gKdsH

**Lucius**
→ p. 258/259
Aa
R13&gKdsH

**Mantar**
→ p. 264/265
Aa
R13&gKdsH

**Marlide Display**
→ p. 268/269
Aa
R13&gKdsH

**Maru Buri**
→ p. 274/275
Aa
R13&gKdsH

**Miasma**
→ p. 286/287

Aa
R13&gKdsH

**Noort Bengali**
→ p. 310/311

Aa
R13&gKdsH

**Occupant Oldstyle**
→ p. 320/321

Aa
R13&gKdsH

**Onamura**
→ p. 326/327

Aa
R13&gKdsH

**Palast**
→ p. 328/329

Aa
R13&gKdsH

**Pausa**
→ p. 334/335

Aa
R13&gKdsH

**Portada Arabic**
→ p. 344/345

Aa
R13&gKdsH

**Proxima Sera**
→ p. 354/355

Aa
R13&gKdsH

**Queens**
→ p. 362/363

Aa
R13&gKdsH

**Resonay**
→ p. 376/377

Aa
R13&gKdsH

**Romis**
→ p. 386/387

AA
R13&GKDSH

**Ronaldson Pro**
→ p. 388/389

Aa
R13&gKdsH

**Salter**
→ p. 394/395

Aa
R13&gKdsH

**Swanstone**
→ p. 324/325

Aa
R13&gKdsH

**Tartuffo**
→ p. 430/431

Aa
R13&gKdsH

**Album**
→ p. 54/55

Aa
R13&gKdsH

**Blatt**
→ p. 96/97

Aa
R13&gKdsH

**Chatham Slab**
→ p. 122/123

A
R13&GKDSH

**Edge**
→ p. 154/155

Aa
R13&gKdsH

**Firelli**
→ p. 172/173

Aa
R13&gKdsH

**Fizz**
→ p. 174/175

Aa
R13&gKdsH

**Geometrico Slab**
→ p. 194/195

Aa
R13&gKdsH

**Legit Superfamily**
→ p. 246/247

Aa
R13&gKdsH

**Madley**
→ p. 262/263

Aa
R13&gKdsH

**Marlon Pro**
→ p. 270/271

Aa
R13&gKdsH

**Patufet**
→ p. 332/333

Aa
R13&gKdsH

**Quirkwood**
→ p. 364/365

Aa
R13&gKdsH

**Tarnac**
→ p. 426/427

Aa
R13&gKdsH



***yearbookoftype.com*, code: YOT6MOVIES**

**Abstract**
→ p. 30/31

Aa
R13&gKdsH

**Acherus Grotesque**
→ p. 32/33

Aa
R13&gKdsH

**Adapter PE**
→ p. 34/35

Aa
R13&gKdsH

**Adelphi PE**
→ p. 42/43

Aa
R13&gKdsH

**ADS Display**
→ p. 44/45

Aa
R13&gKdsH

**Aerobik**
→ p. 46/47

Aa
R13&gKdsH

**Afronaut & Yalla**
→ p. 48/49

Aa
R13&gKdsH

**Aloma**
→ p. 56/57

Aa
R13&gKdsH

**Apice**
→ p. 62/63

Aa
R13&gKdsH

**Arsenica**
→ p. 64/65

Aa
R13&gKdsH

**Asgard**
→ p. 66/67

Aa
R13&gKdsH

**Babetta**
→ p. 74/75

Aa
R13&gKdsH

**Bacalar**
→ p. 76/77

Aa
R13&gKdsH

**Bagatelle**
→ p. 78/79

Aa
R13&gKdsH

**Bakerie**
→ p. 84/85

AA
R13&GKDSH

**Bakewell**
→ p. 86/87

Aa
R13&gKdsH

**Bartok**
→ p. 88/89

Aa
R13&gKdsH

**Blak**
→ p. 94/95

Aa
R13&gKdsH

**Bourton Text**
→ p. 100/101

Aa
R13&gKdsH

**Broker**
→ p. 106/107

Aa
R13&gKdsH

**Chassi**
→ p. 120/121

Aa
R13&gKdsH

**Cobertura**
→ p. 130/131

Aa
R13&gKdsH

**Compass Point**
→ p. 132/133

Aa
R13&gKdsH

**Contralto**
→ p. 136/137

Aa
R13&gKdsH

**Cotford**
→ p. 140/141

Aa
R13&gKdsH

**Delvard Serif**
→ p. 142/143

Aa
R13&gKdsH

**Denton**
→ p. 144/145

Aa
R13&gKdsH

**Distel**
→ p. 148/149

Aa
R13&gKdsH

**Division**
→ p. 150/151

Aa
R13&gKdsH

**Edge**
→ p. 154/155

Aa
R13&gKdsH

**Ender**
→ p. 160/161

Aa

R13&gKdsH

**Exposure**
→ p. 166/167

Aa

R13&gKdsH

**Felka**
→ p. 168/169

Aa

R13&gKdsH

**Fernhout**
→ p. 170/171

a

r13&gkdsh

**Flecha**
→ p. 176/177

Aa

R13&gKdsH

**Fontanella**
→ p. 178/179

Aa

R13&gKdsH

**Formulate**
→ p. 180/181

Aa

R13&gKdsH

**Futura Now**
→ p. 186/187

Aa

R13&gKdsH

**Genie**
→ p. 192/193

Aa

R13&gKdsH

**Goldplay**
→ p. 202/203

Aa

R13&gKdsH

**Good2Type**
→ p. 204/205

A

R13&GKDSH

**Gosna**
→ p. 206/207

Aa

R13&gKdsH

**Granit Display**
→ p. 208/209

Aa

R13&gKdsH

**Gustella**
→ p. 216/217

Aa

R13&gKdsH

**Happiness Sans**
→ p. 218/219

Aa

R13&gKdsH

**Heading Now**
→ p. 222/223
Aa
R13&gKdsH

**Helsa Display**
→ p. 226/227
Aa
R13&gKdsH

**Hernandez Bros**
→ p. 228/229
Aa
R13&gKdsH

---

**Hubble**
→ p. 230/231
Aa
R13&gKdsH

**Kaybuts**
→ p. 236/237
Aa
R13&gKdsH

**Keratine**
→ p. 238/239
Aa
R13&gKdsH

---

**Kjell**
→ p. 240/241
Aa
R13&gKdsH

**Klub**
→ p. 242/243
Aa
R13&gKdsH

**Lingerie Wild Pro**
→ p. 248/249
Aa
R13&gKdsH

---

**Lingerie XO**
→ p. 250/251
Aa
R13&gKdsH

**LONGINUS**
→ p. 252/253
A
R13&GKDSH

**TR Lox Compressed**
→ p. 256/257
Aa
R13&gKdsH

---

**Maax Unicase**
→ p. 260/261
a
r13&GKDSH

**Mantar**
→ p. 264/265
Aa
R13&gKdsH

**Margit**
→ p. 266/267
Aa
R13&gKdsH

**Marlide Display**
→ p. 268/269

Aa
R13&gKdsH

**Maro**
→ p. 272/273

Aa
R13&gKdsH

**MBI DCMNT-15**
→ p. 278/279

Aa
R13&GKDSH

**Mersey**
→ p. 282/283

Aa
R13&gKdsH

**Murtaugh & Riggs**
→ p. 294/295

Aa
R13&gKdsH

**Natom Pro**
→ p. 296/297

A
R13&gKdsH

**MD Nichrome**
→ p. 302/303

Aa
R13&gKdsH

**Nure**
→ p. 316/317

Aa
R13&gKdsH

**Oakley**
→ p. 318/319

Aa
R13&gKdsH

**Okay! Serif**
→ p. 322/323

Aa
R13&gKdsH

**Onamura**
→ p. 326/327

Aa
R13&gKdsH

**Palast**
→ p. 328/329

Aa
R13&gKdsH

**Paranorma**
→ p. 330/331

Aa
R13&gKdsH

**Penitente BT**
→ p. 336/337

A
R13&GKDSH

**Povetarac Display**
→ p. 348/349

Aa
R13&gKdsH

| | | |
|---|---|---|
| **Q**<br>→ p. 358/359<br>AA<br>R13&GKDSH | **Quartier**<br>→ p. 360/361<br>Aa<br>R13&gKdsH | **Queens**<br>→ p. 362/363<br>Aa<br>R13&gKdsH |
| **Quirkwood**<br>→ p. 364/365<br>Aa<br>R13&gKdsH | **Quiverleaf CF**<br>→ p. 368/369<br>Aa<br>R13&gKdsH | **Ranchstyle**<br>→ p. 370/371<br>Aa<br>R13&gKdsH |
| **Ravals**<br>→ p. 372/373<br>Aa<br>R13&gKdsH | **Rebrand**<br>→ p. 374/375<br>Aa<br>R13&gKdsH | **Resonay**<br>→ p. 376/377<br>Aa<br>R13&gKdsH |
| **Right Sans**<br>→ p. 378/379<br>Aa<br>R13&gKdsH | **Roadhouse**<br>→ p. 382/383<br>A<br>R13&GKDSH | **Rockhopper**<br>→ p. 384/385<br>Aa<br>R13&gKdsH |
| **Salad**<br>→ p. 392/393<br>Aa<br>R13&gKdsH | **Salter**<br>→ p. 394/395<br>Aa<br>R13&gKdsH | **Scootchy**<br>→ p. 398/399<br>Aa<br>R13&gKdsH |

**Segol Typeface**
→ p. 400/401

Aa

R13&gKdsH

**Seiva**
→ p. 402/403

Aa

R13&gKdsH

**Seriguela**
→ p. 404/405

Aa

R13&gKdsH

**Shorai Sans**
→ p. 408/409

Aa

R13&gKdsH

**Snare**
→ p. 412/413

Aa

R13&gKdsH

**Stadio Now**
→ p. 416/417

Aa

R13&gKdsH

**Striated**
→ p. 418/419

Aa

R13&gKdsH

**Af Stuce**
→ p. 420/421

Aa

R13&gKdsH

**Swanstone**
→ p. 424/425

Aa

R13&gKdsH

**Tartuffo**
→ p. 430/431

Aa

R13&gKdsH

**Tempus Futurum**
→ p. 432/433

Aa

R13&gKdsH

**Vary**
→ p. 436/437

Aa

R13&gKdsH

**ZAP**
→ p. 440/441

Aa

R13&gKdsH

**Zyrkles**
→ p. 444/444

Aa

R13&gKdsH

**Bakemono**
→ p. 82/83

Aa
R13&gKdsH

**Centra Mono**
→ p. 116/117

Aa
R13&gKdsH

**Charte Mono**
→ p. 118/119

Aa
R13&gKdsH

**Drafting Mono**
→ p. 152/153

Aa
R13&gKdsH

**Ellograph CF**
→ p. 156/157

Aa
R13&gKdsH

**Method Mono**
→ p. 284/285

Aa
R13&gKdsH

**Monoflow**
→ p. 290/291

Aa
R13&gKdsH

**Neue Rational**
→ p. 300/301

Aa
R13&gKdsH

**Non Natural**
→ p. 306/307

Aa
R13&gKdsH

**Pentameter**
→ p. 340/341

Aa
R13&gKdsH

**PolySans Mono**
→ p. 342/343

Aa
R13&gKdsH

**Rike Mono**
→ p. 380/381

Aa
R13&gKdsH

**Slussen**
→ p. 410/411

Aa
R13&gKdsH

**ZAP**
→ p. 440/441

Aa
R13&gKdsH

**Futura Now**
→ p. 186/187

Aa
R13&gKdsH

**Maro**
→ p. 272/273

Aa
R13&gKdsH

**Pensum Stencil**
→ p. 338/339

Aa
R13&gKdsH

**Slussen**
→ p. 410/411

Aa
R13&gKdsH

**Snare**
→ p. 412/413

Aa
R13&gKdsH

## Script

**Apice**
→ p. 62/63

Aa
R13&gKdsH

**Compass Point**
→ p. 132/133

Aa
R13&gKdsH

**Division**
→ p. 150/151

Aa
R13&gKdsH

**Eugenia**
→ p. 164/165

Aa
R13&gKdsH

**Formulate**
→ p. 180/181

Aa
R13&gKdsH

**Futura Now**
→ p. 186/187

Aa
R13&gKdsH

**Genie**
→ p. 192/193

Aa

R13&gKdsH

**Gosna**
→ p. 206/207

Aa

R13&gKdsH

**Grato Marker**
→ p. 210/211

Aa

R13&gKdsH

**Hubble**
→ p. 230/231

Aa

R13&gKdsH

**Prima**
→ p. 352/353

Aa

R13&gKdsH

**Pure Energy**
→ p. 356/357

Aa

R13&gKdsH

**Quiverleaf Arabic CF**
→ p. 366/367

ات

ضعمشهج

**Ravals**
→ p. 372/373

Aa

R13&gKdsH

## Blackletter

**Blak**
→ p. 94/95

Aa

R13&gKdsH

**Vivala bl**
→ p. 438/439

Aa

R13&gKdsH

**ADS Display**
→ p. 44/45

Aa

R13&gKdsH

**Berlin Type**
→ p. 92/93

Aa

R13&gKdsH

**Chatham Slab**
→ p. 122/123

A

R13&GKDSH

**Fernhout**
→ p. 170/171

a

r13&gkdsh

**Good2Type**
→ p. 204/205

A

R13&GKDSH

**Grunt**
→ p. 214/215

Aa

R13&gKdsH

**Happiness Sans**
→ p. 218/219

Aa

R13&gKdsH

**Maru Buri**
→ p. 274/275

Aa

R13&gKdsH

**MBI DCMNT-15**
→ p. 278/279

Aa

R13&GKDSH

**Merantix NUM**
→ p. 280/282

12

345890

**Prima**
→ p. 352/353

Aa

R13&gKdsH

**Ranchstyle**
→ p. 370/371

Aa

R13&gKdsH

**Tempus Futurum**
→ p. 432/433

Aa

R13&gKdsH

Index Designers

D

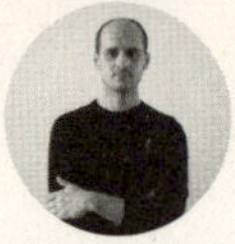



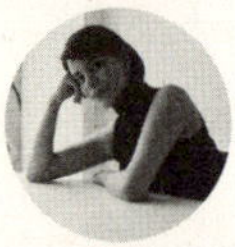



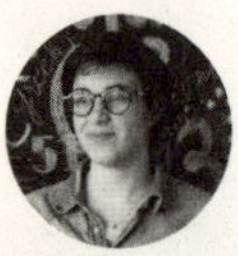



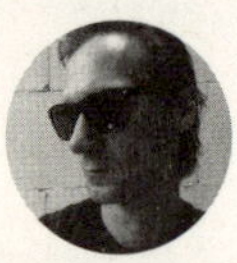



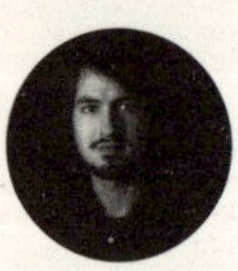



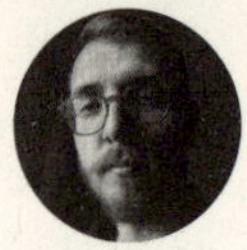



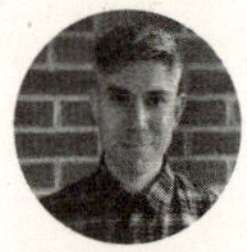



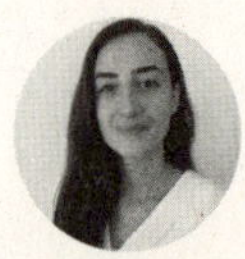



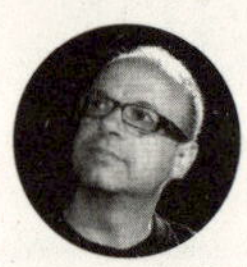



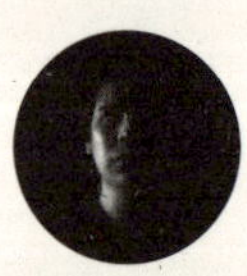



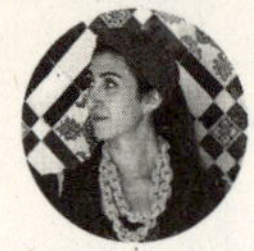





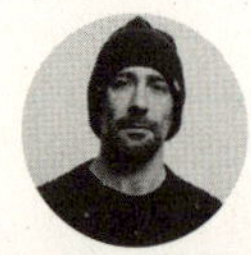



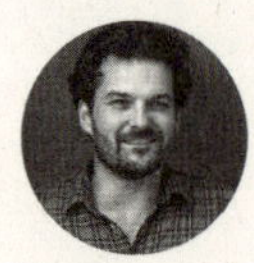



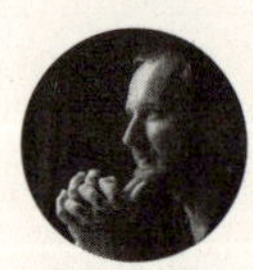



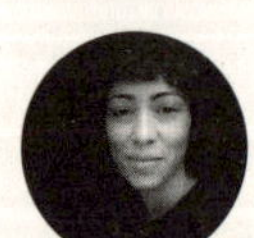

# Index Designers

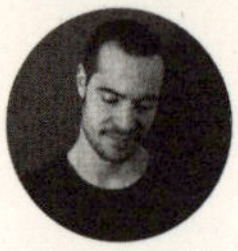

**Chavot, Alex**
**alexchavot.fr**
**Granit Display**
→ p. 208/209

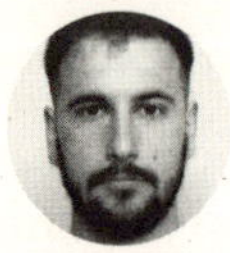

**Chemin, Arnaud**
**arnaudchemin.com**
**Didot Modern**
→ p. 146/147

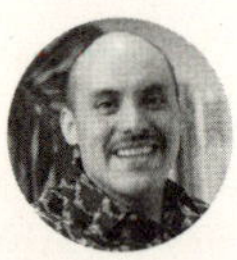

**Cisterna, Jorge**
**latinotype.com**
**Brutalista**
→ p. 108/109

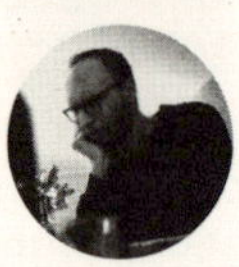

**Claudius, Stefan**
**cape-arcona.com**
**CA Spotnik**
→ p. 414/415

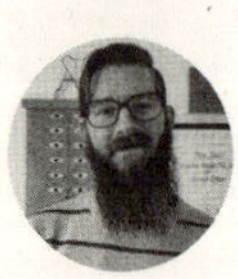

**Coan, Eduilson**
**fabiohaagtype.com/en/**
**Pausa** → p. 334/335
**Salva** → p. 396/397

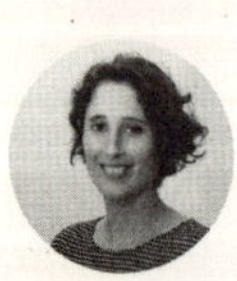

**Correia, Joana**
**novatypefoundry.com**
**Loretta** → p. 254/255

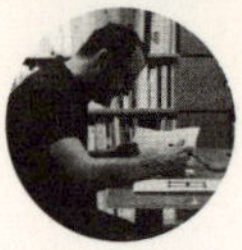

**Cortat, Matthieu**
**www.205.tf**
**Muoto** → p. 292/293

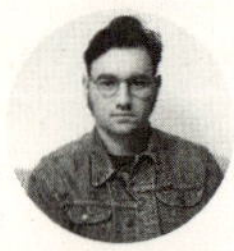

**Coupas, Fabien**
**fabiencoupas.com**
**Method Mono**
→ p. 284/285

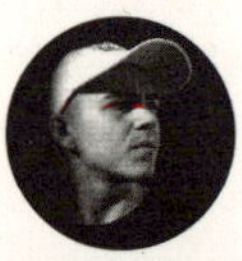

**Craze, Rutherford**
**mass-driver.com**
**MD Nichrome**
→ p. 302/303

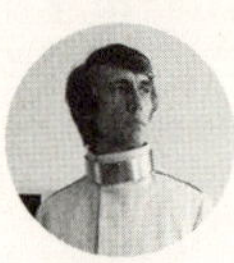

**Crouwel, Wim**
**Fernhout** → p. 170/171

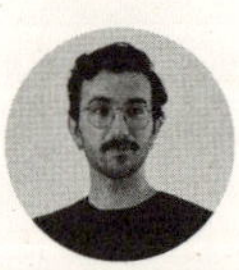

**Davenport, Connor**
**sharptype.co**
**Greenstone**
→ p. 212/213

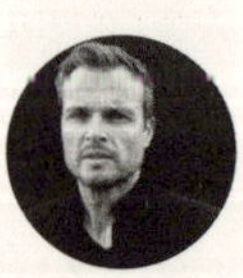

**Delobel, Sébastien**
**ateliertelescopique.com**
**Af Stuce** → p. 420/421

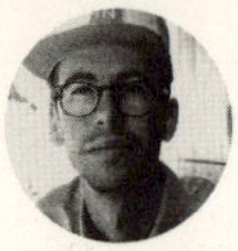

**Derkert, Teddy**
**teddyderkert.se**
**Firelli** → p. 172/173

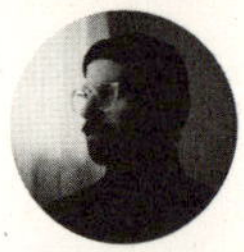

**Desjardins, Mathieu**
**pangrampangram.com**
**PP Fragment**
→ p. 182/183

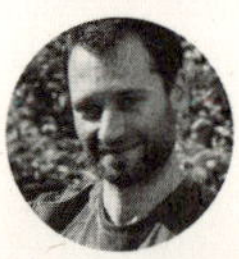

**Dieneš, Andrej**
**adtypo.com**
**Resonay** → p. 376/377

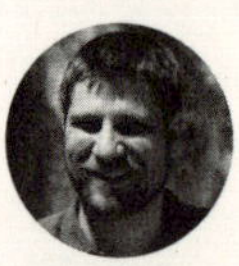

**Dimitrijević, Lazar**
**behance.net/**
**LazarDimitrijevic**
**Hubble** → p. 230/231

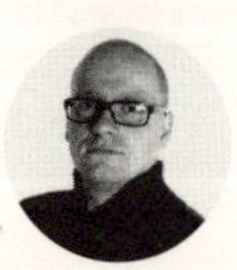

**Djurek, Nikola**
**typotheque.com**
**Delvard Serif**
→ p. 142/143
**Maro** → p. 272/273
**Murtaugh & Riggs**
→ p. 294/295
**Tremolo Sans**
→ p. 434/435

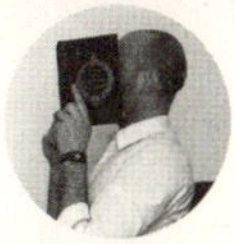

**Huot-Marchand, Thomas**
**205.tf**
**Album** → p. 54/55

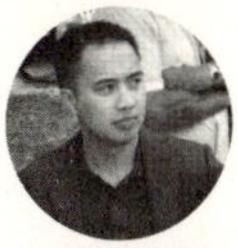

**Inosanto, Nico**
**nootype.com**
**Charte Mono**
→ p. 118/119

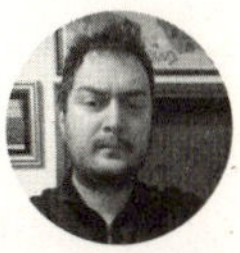

**Jelesijević, Dušan**
**dusanjelesijevic.com**
**Povetarac Display**
→ p. 348/349

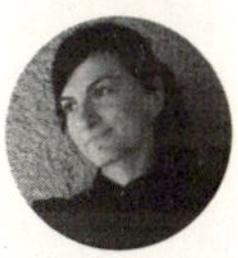

**Jevčinová, Sláva**
**instagram.com/intothetype**
**Adapter PE**
→ p. 34/35

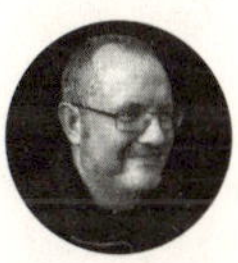

**Job, Nick**
**nickjob.co.uk**
**Adelphi PE**
→ p. 42/43

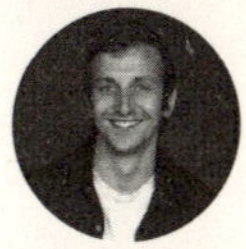

**John, Markus**
**a-second-place.com**
**Kjell** → p. 240/241

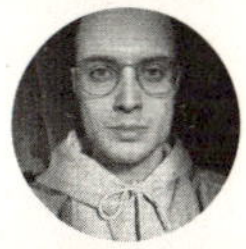

**Jourdan, Hugo**
**blazetype.eu**
**Slussen** → p. 410/411

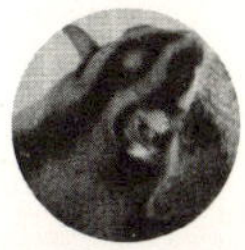

**Kikuchi, Shuji**
**sugargliderz.com**
**Kaybuts**
→ p. 236/237

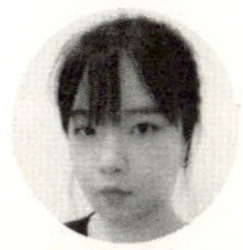

**Kim, Jookyeong**
**agfont.com/en**
**Happiness Sans**
→ p. 218/219

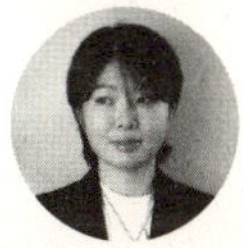

**Kim, Hyunjin**
**instagram.com/pot_works**
**AG Choijeongho Minburi Std.**
→ p. 126/127

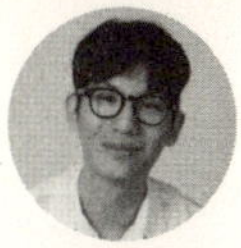

**Kim, Seunghwan**
**agfont.com/en**
**AG Choijeongho Minburi Std.**
→ p. 126/127
**Happiness Sans**
→ p. 218/219

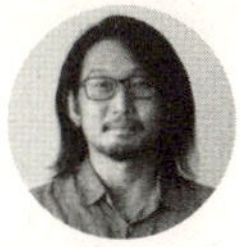

**Kimura, Masaru**
**morisawa.co.jp**
**Aoto Gothic** → p. 60/61

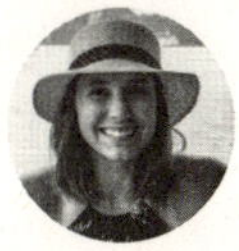

**Kirkwood, Kimmy**
**kimmydesign.com**
**Bakewell**
→ p. 86/87
**Bourton Text**
→ p. 100/101
**Madley** → p. 262/263
**Roadhouse**
→ p. 382/383

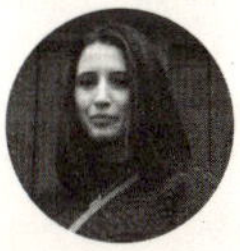

**Klaebe, Emily**
**order.design**
**Chatham Slab**
→ p. 122/123

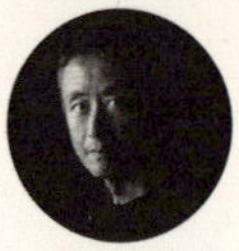



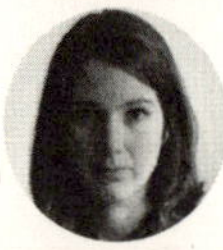



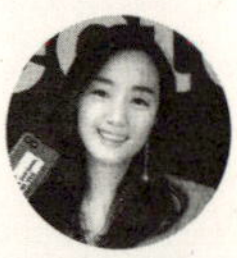



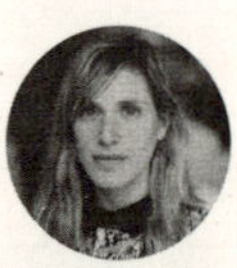



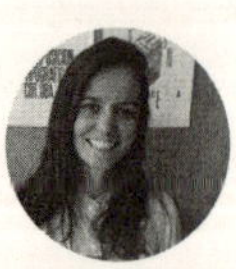



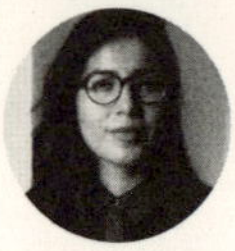



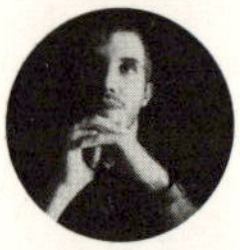



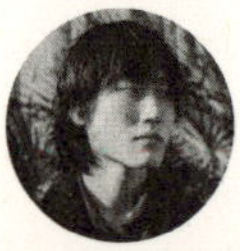



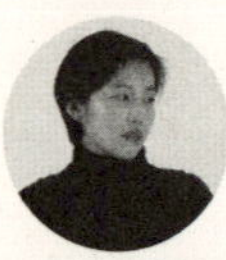



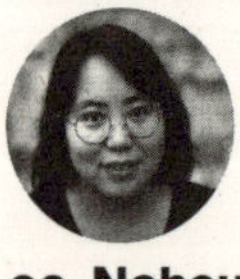



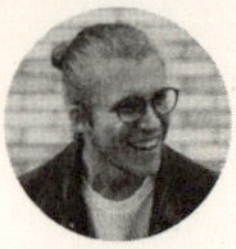



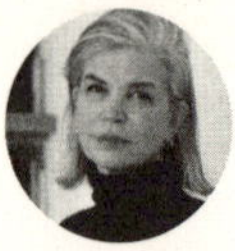



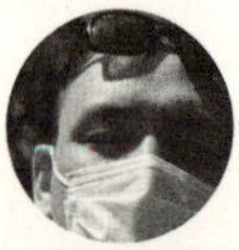



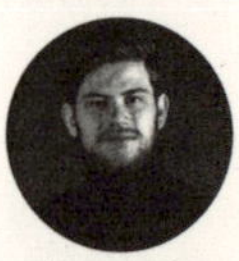



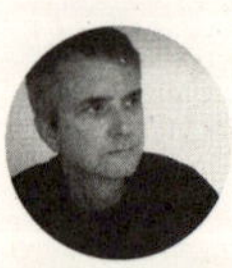



FL

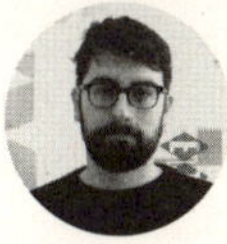



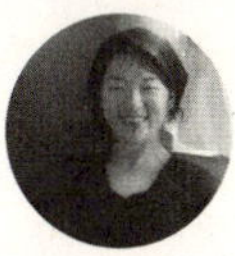



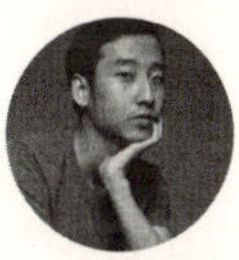



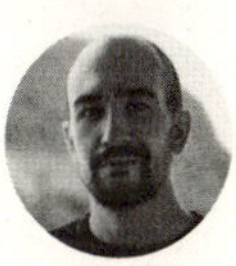



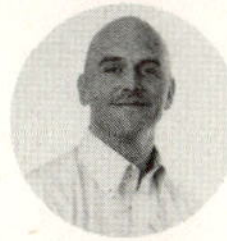



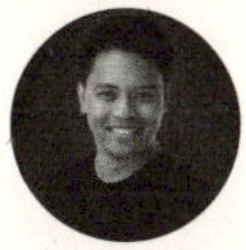



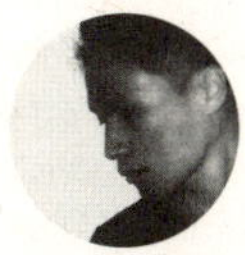



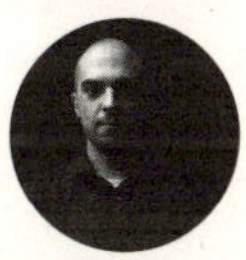



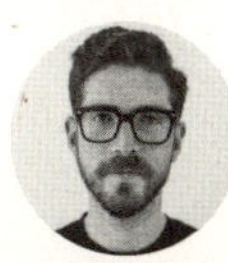



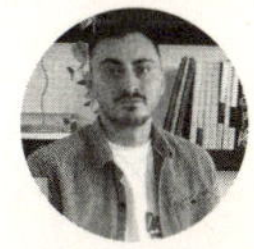



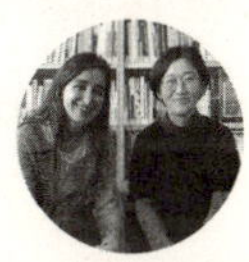



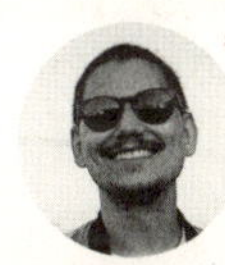



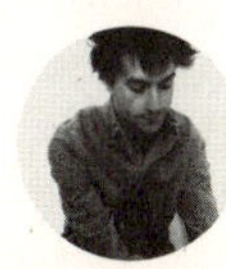

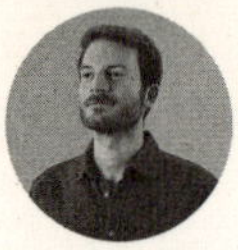





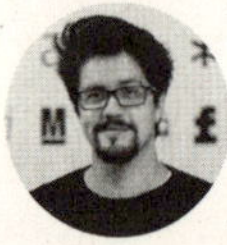



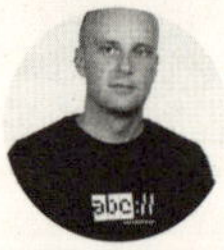



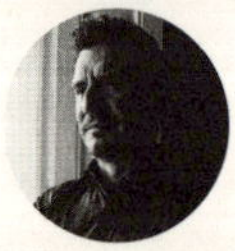



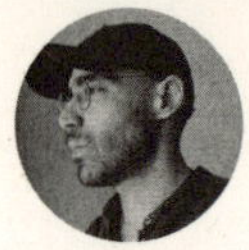



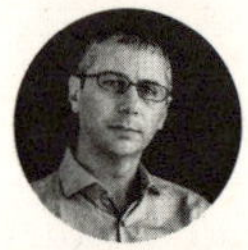



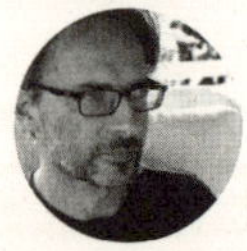





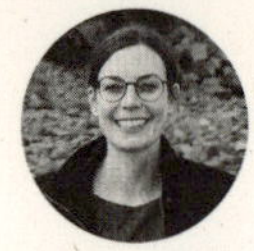



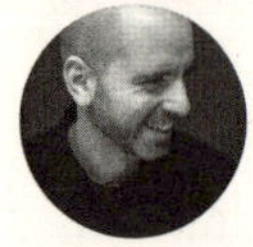



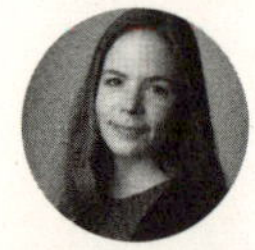



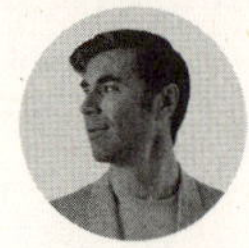



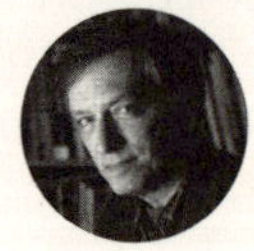



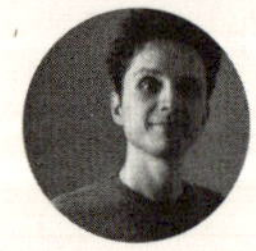

Index Foundries

E

Yearbook of Type 2022 / 23

# F Index OpenType Features

**Proportional Oldstyle**
Oldstyle numerals are typeset with varying heights, based on the line of running text. This allows them to integrate more smoothly with mixed uppercase and lowercase letters and small capitals. Proportional figures have variable spacing between each letter.

**Tabular Oldstyle**
Oldstyle numerals are typeset with varying heights, based on the line of running text. They integrate better into mixed uppercase and lowercase letters and small capitals. Tabular figures each have the same width and are preferably used when numerals will be read in columns.

**Proportional Lining**
The height of lining numerals is usually based on the height of the capital letters and uniform throughout. The figures are positioned on the baseline and align with the capital height of the typeface. Proportional lining figures have variable spacing between each letter.

**Tabular Lining**
Tabular lining figures have the same height as capital letters. Like proportional lining figures, they are uniform in height, but all have the same width. Tabular lining figures are preferably used when numerals will be read in columns.

**Standard Ligatures**
A ligature replaces a sequence of characters with a single ligature glyph, where characters may overlap or could be better positioned. The most common are *f*-ligatures, where *f* is combined with its following letter to adjust spacing and reach a more pleasing appearance.

**Discretionary Ligatures**
Special ligatures, oftentimes solely aesthetic combinations, which can be applied at the user's discretion to offer variation.

**Historical Ligatures**
These are ligatures like long *s* combinations, which are obsolete in today's writing but can be applied at the user's discretion.

**All Caps**
All letters of a word or text are set in capital or uppercase letters.

**Small Caps**
Lowercase characters are replaced by glyphs that look like uppercase letters but reduced in height and weight, close to the surrounding lowercase glyphs.

**Capitals to Small Caps**
Capital letters are replaced by small caps, which are glyphs that look like uppercase letters but reduced in height and weight, close to the surrounding lowercase glyphs.

**Petite Caps**
Small Caps are 30% larger than the x-height of the font's letters, and 70% of the height of full capital letters. To differentiate between these two character types, the x-height form is called Petite Caps, preserving the name *Small Caps* for the larger variant.

**Capitals to Petite Caps**
Capital letters are replaced by Petite Caps.

**Superscript**
Characters that are set above the baseline of the typeface, oftentimes to indicate a foot-called superscript. They are usually smaller than the lowercase letters.

**Subscript**
Characters that are set at or below the baseline of the typeface, often seen in chemical equations or the like. Usually subscript is smaller than the lowercase letters.

**Ordinals**
Ordinal numbers indicate a progression and are often times written with numerals followed by letter suffixes. In English, for example, you would write 1st, 2nd, 3rd, etc., with the suffix acting as an ordinal indicator.

**Titling Alternates**
Characters with special forms created for Display use, which are meant to be used in large sizes.

**Swashes**
Swashes are energetic terminals on a glyph. You can also call them tails or entry strokes. Often times they can be found on the Italics of a serif font.

**Contextual Swashes**
Contextual Swashes are swashes added to letters based on the characters around them.

**All Alternates**
Presents all alternate forms of the chosen character in a list.

**Contextual Alternates**
Applies a second substitution feature based on a match of a character pattern within a context of surrounding patterns.

**Fractions**
A single mathematical glyph, which combines two or more numbers separated by a slash.

**Alternative Fractions**
An alternative single mathematical glyph, which combines two or more numbers separated by a slash.

**Numerator**
A number, which is usually smaller than the lowercase letters of a typeface and meant to be used above the slash in a fraction glyph.

**Denominator**
A number which is usually smaller than the lowercase letters of a typeface and meant to be used below the slash in a fraction glyph.

**Ornaments**
Decorative symbols, which are sometimes included in a typeface character set and match its temper and style.

**Arrows**
Symbols showing direction, which are included in a typeface character set to match with its temper.

**Stylistic Alternates**
This OpenType feature offers various alternatives to different letters and letter combinations, giving the user more options. Some change only the appearance of a single character, others the look of a whole word or phrase.

**Stylistic Sets**
Stylistic Sets group different sets of Stylistic Alternates together based on appearance, so that choosing between several Stylistic Alternate options becomes simpler for the user.

**Historical Forms**
Obsolete forms of characters, which can be applied at the user's discretion.

**Slashed Zero**
The Slashed Zero is an alternative to the number *0* (zero), with a slash through it. The glyph is often used to differentiate the number zero *(0)* from the capital letter *O*.

**Justification Alternates**
Used mainly in cursive languages like Arabic, where the justification is usually achieved not by extending the space between the characters but by extending the width of some characters.

**Alternate Annotation**
Provides special characters like circled digits, inverse letters etc.

**Localized Forms**
Offers a range of distinct forms of one character appropriately adapting different script languages and their particularities.

**Case Sensitive Forms**
Shifts various punctuation marks up to a position that works better with all-capital sequences or sets of lining figures and changes oldstyle figures to lining figures.

**Unicase**
Lowercase and uppercase letters are replaced with a set of single case glyphs like for example in the Arabic, Hebrew, and Georgian alphabets. These are unicase alphabets.

**Mark Positioning**
Fine positioning of a mark glyph like *?* to its preceding character.

**Initial Form**
The Initial Form is a special form of a letter occurring at the beginning of a word. This can be seen in Arabic script a lot.

**Medial Form**
The Medial Form is a special form of a letter that only occurs between certain letters within a word. This can often be seen in Arabic script.

**Terminal Form**
The Terminal Form is a special form of a letter occurring at the end of a word. This can often be seen in Arabic script.

**Isolated Form**
The Isolated Form is the special form a letter takes, when it occurs on its own, outside of the word. This can often be seen in Arabic script.

**Randomize**
Creates a randomness in the composition while using, for example, script typefaces, making them seem more handwritten.

**Optical size**
Offers two or more versions of a typeface designed for use at different sizes. They are intended for viewing at a particular size and often they are named accordingly, like *Small Text*, *Body Text*, or *Display*.

**Font Variations**
Incorporates multiple font faces within a font family into a single font file. A variable font allows variation along a set design axis, changing only fixed parameters, such as weight and width.

Microsoft Corporation, OpenType Layout tag registry, registered features—definitions and implementations, www.microsoft.com/typography/otspec/features_ae.htm, (l.o. January 10th, 2018)

Friedrich Forssman, Ralf de Jong, Detailtypografie, Verlag Hermann Schmidt, fifth edition (June 15th, 2004)

**Yearbook of Type #6 2022/23**

**Publisher**
Slanted Publishers UG
(haftungsbeschränkt)
Nördliche Uferstraße 4–6
76189 Karlsruhe, Germany
T +49 (0) 721 85148268
info@slanted.de
*slanted.de*
@slanted_publishers


ISBN: 978-3-948440-41-1
2nd edition, 2022



Bibliographic information published by the Deutsche Nationalbibliothek. The Deutsche Nationalbibliothek lists this publication in the Deutsche Nationalbibliographie, detailed bibliographic data is available online at *dnb.d-nb.de*

**Publishing Direction**
Lars Harmsen, Julia Kahl

**Creative Direction**
Lars Harmsen

**Art Direction & Managing Editor**
Juliane Nöst

**Graphic Design Assistance**
Saehyeen Shin, Clara Weinreich

**Proofreading**
Vicky Blake, Julia Kahl, Lies Wolf

**Website *yearbookoftype.com***
Kolja Buscher

**Fonts**
Suisse Neue + Suisse Int'l,
Swiss Typefaces, *swisstypefaces.com*

**Cover Fonts**
Aerobik, p. 46/47
Asgard, p. 66/67
Bakewell, p. 86/87
Ereganto Serif, p. 162/163
Futura Now, p. 186/187
MD Nichrome, p. 302/303
Povetarac Display, p. 348/349
Quartier, p. 360/360

**Printing**
Stober Medien GmbH, *stober-medien.de*

**Book Binding**
Buchbinderei Klotz GmbH,
*buchbinderei-klotz.de*

**Cover Material**
PEYDUR neuleinen, 135 g/sm
peyer graphic gmbh, *peyergraphic.ch*

**Paper**
Inside: Holmen TRND 2.0, 80 g/sm,
*holmenpaper.com*
Endpaper: SURBALIN seda, 115 g/sm,
Pastellblau 8099, peyer graphic gmbh,
*peyergraphic.ch*

**Spot Colors**
HKS Warenzeichenverband e.V.
*hks-farben.de*
HKS 6 N, HKS 8 N, HKS 12 N, HKS 17 N, HKS 34 N, HKS 243 N, HKS 43 N, HKS 38 N, HKS 50 N, HKS 97 N

**With Thanks to**
So-Hyun Bae, Tom Barbereau, Karen Ann Donnachie, Diana Girrbach, Sofia Orfanidou, Matthieu Salvaggio, Rainer Erich Scheichelbauer, Andy Simionato, Jeremy Tankard, Martin Tiefenthaler, Lies Wolf

**Specimen Fact Sources**
We do not take any responsibility for the substance of facts on the type specimen pages.

**About Slanted Publishers**
Slanted Publishers was founded in 2014 by Lars Harmsen and Julia Kahl. They edit and publish the award-winning blog and print magazine Slanted, giving an inside view into the international design and creative scenes. In addition to the blog and magazine, Slanted initiates and creates design-related projects and publications.